T

*The Bel[...]*
against [...]
part of [...]
a differ[...]
interest[...]
looks a[...]
modest [...]
relation[...]
of mora[...]
which l[...]
and mo[...]
action. [...]
an argui[...]
versions[...]

**Alison** [...]
of St Jol[...]

# The Beloved Self

*Morality and the Challenge from Egoism*

Alison Hills

OXFORD
UNIVERSITY PRESS

# OXFORD

UNIVERSITY PRESS

Great Clarendon Street, Oxford OX2 6DP
United Kingdom

Oxford University Press is a department of the University of Oxford.
It furthers the University's objective of excellence in research, scholarship,
and education by publishing worldwide. Oxford is a registered trade mark of
Oxford University Press in the UK and in certain other countries

© Alison Hills 2010

The moral rights of the author have been asserted

First published 2010
First published in paperback 2012

British Library Cataloguing in Publication Data
Data available

Library of Congress Cataloging in Publication Data
Library of Congress Control Number 2009942571

ISBN 978–0–19–921330–6 (Hbk)
ISBN 978–0–19–965516–8 (Pbk)

Printed in the United Kingdom by
Lightning Source UK Ltd., Milton Keynes

To Philip and Eleanor

# Contents

# Acknowledgements

This book began as my PhD thesis. I would like to give particular thanks to my PhD supervisors Jimmy Altham and Onora O' Neill for their guidance, advice, and patience. The book would have contained many more mistakes without the helpful comments of many other people, including: Alexander Bird, John Broome, Jessica Brown, Roger Crisp, Rowan Cruft, Dorothea Debus, Jimmy Doyle, John Hawthorne, Brad Hooker, Rob Hopkins, Matt Kramer, Hallvard Lillehammer, Elijah Millgram, Greg Scherkoske, Oliver Sensen, Bart Streumer, Ralph Wedgwood, Tim Williamson, and audiences at Birmingham, Bristol, Oxford, Cambridge, Sheffield, and San Diego.

I am particularly grateful to Jimmy Lenman, Eric Wiland, Alison Denham, and an anonymous reader for the Oxford University Press for their comments on the entire manuscript, and for the support and patience of Peter Momtchiloff. I would also like to thank Alexander Erler, who helped with proofreading and with compiling the index.

I could not have written this book without periods of research leave, funded by Clare College, Cambridge, Bristol University, and the Arts and Humanities Research Council (AHRC). I am very grateful for their support.

Some of the material in this book has already been published. Much of Chapter 3 appeared as 'Kant on Happiness and Reason' in *History of Philosophy Quarterly* (July 2006). Chapter 4 contains material from three articles: 'Duties and Duties to the Self', *American Philosophical Quarterly* (2003); 'Rational Nature as the Source of Value', *Kantian Review* (2005); and 'Kantian Value Realism', *Ratio* (2008). Parts of the paper 'The Significance of the Dualism of Practical Reason', *Utilitas*, 15 (2003) appear in Chapters 2 and 7. Some material from Chapter 7 is reprinted from 'Is Ethics Rationally Required?' *Inquiry* (2004). And, finally, Part Three contains material from 'Moral Testimony and Moral Epistemology', *Ethics* (2009). I am grateful to the publishers of these journals for permission to reprint this material.

# Abbreviations

*Anthropology*      Immanuel Kant, *Anthropology from a Pragmatic Point of View*, trans. M. J. Gregor (The Hague: Martinus Nijhoff, 1974). References cite the volume and page number of *Kants gesammelte Schriften* (Berlin: Preussische Akademie der Wissenschaften/W. de Gruyter, 1902– ).

*CJ*      Immanuel Kant, *Critique of the Power of Judgment*, trans. P. Guyer and E. Matthews (Cambridge: Cambridge University Press, 2000). References cite the volume and page number of *Kants gesammelte Schriften* (Berlin: Preussische Akademie der Wissenschaften/W. de Gruyter, 1902– ).

*CPrR*      Immanuel Kant, *Critique of Practical Reason*, trans. M. J. Gregor (Cambridge: Cambridge University Press, 1997). References cite the volume and page number of *Kants gesammelte Schriften* (Berlin: Preussische Akademie der Wissenschaften/W. de Gruyter, 1902– ).

*G*      Immanuel Kant, *Groundwork of a Metaphysic of Morals*, trans. H. J. Paton (London: Routledge, 1991). References cite the volume and page number of *Kants gesammelte Schriften* (Berlin: Preussische Akademie der Wissenschaften/W. de Gruyter, 1902– ).

*Lectures*      Immanuel Kant, *Lectures on Ethics*, trans. P. Heath; ed. P. Heath and J. B. Schneewind (Cambridge: Cambridge University Press, 1997). References cite the volume and page number of *Kants gesammelte Schriften* (Berlin: Preussische Akademie der Wissenschaften/W. de Gruyter, 1902– ).

*MM*            Immanuel Kant, *Metaphysics of Morals*, trans.
                M. Gregor (Cambridge: Cambridge University Press,
                1991). References cite the volume and page number
                of *Kants gesammelte Schriften* (Berlin: Preussische
                Akademie der Wissenschaften/W. de Gruyter,
                1902– ).

*NE*            Aristotle, *Nicomachean Ethics*, trans. S. Broadie and
                C. Rowe (Oxford: Oxford University Press, 2002)

*Religion*      Immanuel Kant, *Religion within the Boundaries of Mere
                Reason*, trans. A. Wood and G. di Giovanni
                (Cambridge: Cambridge University Press, 1998).
                References cite the volume and page number of *Kants
                gesammelte Schriften* (Berlin: Preussische Akademie der
                Wissenschaften/W. de Gruyter, 1902– ).

# 1

# The Holy Grail of Moral Philosophy

Yet according to the imperfect way in which human affairs are conducted, a sensible knave, in particular incidents, may think that an act of iniquity or infidelity will make a considerable addition to his fortune, without causing any considerable breach in the social union and confederacy. That honesty is the best policy, may be a good general rule, but is liable to many exceptions; and he, it may perhaps be thought, conducts himself with most wisdom, who observes the general rule, and takes advantage of all the exceptions. I must confess that, if a man think that this reasoning much requires an answer, it would be a little difficult to find any which will to him appear satisfactory and convincing.

Hume, *An Enquiry Concerning the Principles of Morals*, sect. IX.

At the start of book two of the *Republic*, Glaucon tells a story. A shepherd, Gyges, is watching over his flock when a storm breaks and an earthquake opens the ground next to him. Looking around, he finds a giant corpse wearing a gold ring, which he promptly removes. Twisting the ring this way and that, Gyges finds that he can make himself invisible and appear again. He immediately works out how to use this to his advantage. He seeks out the king's wife and seduces her. With her help he murders her husband, Candaules, and takes the crown for himself.

Gyges has done wrong. But which of us, Glaucon asks, would do anything else if we had this kind of power? He finds the story very disturbing, because he thinks that we all *ought* to be just even in the unusual circumstances described when it would be in our interests to do otherwise. And he asks Socrates to prove that he is right.

Socrates spends the rest of the *Republic* trying to explain why Gyges really ought not to steal, kill, and commit adultery. He tries to show that someone who is unjust is always psychologically damaged, and so, despite appearances, it is not in Gyges' interests to use the ring for nefarious purposes. Readers of the *Republic* tend to find Glaucon's question more compelling than Socrates' reply, however, and moral philosophers ever since have struggled to improve on it. Henry Sidgwick, for example, tries to defend morality in his monumental work *The Methods of Ethics* but it ends, literally, with the word 'failure'. As Hume reports with characteristically elegant understatement: it is difficult to give an argument that a 'sensible knave' has reason to do what is morally right that is at all convincing.

Should we take Glaucon's problem seriously, though? The story of Gyges might be entertaining but it makes no claims to realism. We know that in real life wrongdoing has consequences; no one could expect to emulate Gyges and get away with it. People who care about their own interests should for the most part do what is morally right. And, indeed, they do. Even the sensible knave admits that honesty is usually a good policy.

Glaucon thinks the story is important, however, and he is right. What Gyges should do once he has put on the ring shows something very significant about morality: it shows whether there are *reasons* to do what is morally right even when it is in your interests to do otherwise. We all know that justice and morality often have good consequences for you and injustice and immorality bad ones. The ring of Gyges story separates out the acts from their normal consequences. If you should still do what is morally right nevertheless, clearly you have a reason to do what is right which is not based on your self-interest.

According to Glaucon—and to most of us—morality makes demands on us and its demands do not cease simply because it is in our interests to do otherwise: Gyges has reason not to kill, for example, even if it would be advantageous to him. We may call this a part of *common-sense morality*. According to common-sense morality, morality has *practical authority*—we have reasons to do what is morally right and not to do what is morally wrong, and not merely because it is usually in our interests to do so.

Moreover, according to common-sense morality, responding to these moral reasons for action is very important. Genuine moral action is not just a matter of doing the right action; to act well, you need to do the right action for the right reasons. So, when the sensible knave does what is honest because it is in his interests to do so, he is not acting well. Of course, we often have no idea of another person's reasons for action. As morality and self-interest frequently coincide, the sensible knave will often act outwardly just like someone who acts for moral reasons. This is another reason why the story of Gyges is intriguing. Up until he finds the ring, Gyges may have lived a morally irreproachable life—as far as anyone else can tell. But once he can turn himself invisible and get away with any kind of immorality, he follows self-interest. This gives us a good reason to suspect that, all along, he was not acting well. He might have been doing the right thing, but not for the right reasons. We can see that this could be true of anyone.

Of course, the sensible knave disagrees with all of this. He cannot find any reason to be honest when dishonesty will benefit him. He claims that he has reason to do what is in his interests and no other reasons for action. He is an *egoist*. Though many of us do not agree with the knave, we do feel the temptation of acting from self-interest. What can we say to an egoist, or even to ourselves, to prove that we have reason to resist the temptation to do wrong? Can we find an argument that will persuade him that he has reason to be moral? A compelling argument against egoism has been described as *the Holy Grail of moral philosophy*. Many moral philosophers feel themselves obliged to search, but the goal, like the grail, has proved strangely elusive.

How can you argue against egoism? You might try a similar tactic to Socrates, and attempt to show that doing wrong cannot really be in your interests after all. It might look as if Gyges profited from his crimes but if being moral is an essential component of a good life, then his life could hardly have gone worse. Aristotle thought that in order to lead a good life one had to have the virtues, including justice and honesty, and modern virtue theorists who follow him tend to agree. But the sensible knave has an obvious riposte: their notion of the good life is bizarre. It is simply crazy to deny that Gyges had a good life: he married a queen! He ruled a kingdom! The knave can develop his own account of a good life and a corresponding theory of virtue, where the virtues are the traits of character that are most likely to allow you to end up with an attractive partner together with plenty of money and power. Now our question becomes: which of these conceptions of the good life and the virtues should we accept? Which do we have reason to try to achieve? We are more or less back where we started.

Kant took the challenge from egoism very seriously. He saw the appeal of self-interest, and indeed was worried that most of us succumbed to it most of the time. We might usually do the right thing, but only because it is in our interests to do so:

I am willing to admit—out of sheer generosity!—that most of our actions are in accord with duty; but if we look more closely at our thoughts and aspirations we keep encountering the beloved *self* as what our plans rely on, rather than the stern command of duty with its frequent calls for *self*-denial.[1]

Kant thinks that morality has an especially great authority: when morality commands us, we *must* obey. So, if we do act wrongly, our choice is not simply morally at fault. It is a choice we have an overriding reason not to make. Kant takes up the challenge of defending common-sense morality by trying to show that a fully rational person would never act immorally.

Kant's response to the knave is hard to understand, however, partly because it involves perhaps the deepest and most difficult part of his philosophy, his theory of freedom; partly because his target is not very plain. When the knave puts his beloved self in place of stern duty, Kant seems to think that he is putting his happiness first. But since Kant is not very clear about what happiness or the pursuit of happiness is, it is difficult to be certain exactly what his objections to it are and hard to assess whether they succeed.

Moreover, just as the knave can answer the virtue theorist by producing his own account of the good life and the virtues, he can answer Kant by doing the same, devising a parallel to Kant's moral law. We can call this *Kantian egoism*. Once again, the challenge becomes to defend morality against the knave's rival account of reasons for action.

This book is about the quest for the Holy Grail of moral philosophy: the challenge from egoism and how we can respond to it. The first part of the book clarifies the challenge by looking in more detail at the opponent, the sensible knave, setting out a small but important selection from the wide variety of theories of egoism. It begins with the most familiar, standard egoism, the theory that each person has reason only to maximize his or her

---

[1] Kant, G 4: 407. This translation is by Jonathan Bennett from his website <http://www.early moderntexts.com>.

own happiness. In Chapter 2, I compare standard egoism to utilitarianism, pointing out the obvious similarities between the two. Next, the focus turns to Kant, and what it might mean for one's plans to rely on the 'beloved self ': first, Kant's own idiosyncratic account of the pursuit of happiness is discussed and second, the theory that parallels the moral law is laid out. In Chapter 4, the knave's version of virtue theory is explored.

The point of this part of the book is not to defend any particular egoist theory, or indeed to defend egoism generally—in fact the plan, later in the book, is to vindicate morality, not self-interest. Consequently, I make no attempt to assess each version, to determine which is the most plausible or whether any is acceptable. I do think, however, that reflection on different moral theories can help us to develop novel and interesting conceptions of self-interest and of self-interested reasons for action, and this in turn can illuminate aspects of the original moral theory. For example, in Chapter 3, I discuss in some detail what it means for rational nature to be a source of value, and give a new account of this key Kantian idea. Chapter 4 critically examines the idea that having the moral virtues is in your interests. My purpose in Part I, however, is to prove that egoism is both more interesting and more various than it is sometimes regarded, for standard egoism is often the only version ever discussed. Whilst it may be the most popular and most traditional form of egoism, there are many others and it is much harder to argue against egoism if you have to take on all versions of the theory, not just one.

The remainder of the book takes up egoism's challenge to morality and tries to answer it. Parts II and III of the book can to some extent be read independently of Part I, but not completely: some of the arguments against egoism apply to all egoist theories, but some apply to only one or more versions of the theory and fail against others.

In Chapter 5, I distinguish some more or less ambitious ways in which we might try to respond to an egoist. The ideal, the Holy Grail, is bold: an argument that even an egoist should accept that egoism is false. Some philosophers, including Parfit, Korsgaard, and Nagel have tried to formulate arguments along these lines, casting doubt on whether the knave's idea of reasons for action or his conception of personal identity is satisfactory. It is widely accepted that these arguments do not work. I show that they do indeed fail, and give some reasons why others are not likely to succeed either. Egoism is not internally inconsistent, nor has any argument against it, based on premises that an egoist should accept, been successful. The prospects for an ambitious vindication of morality are bleak.

Does this matter? It is not unusual in philosophy to be unable to answer an opponent in her own terms. Consider a sceptic who thinks that we have no knowledge of the external world. It is difficult, and perhaps even impossible, to prove to such a sceptic that we do have such knowledge. It is easier—though hardly straightforward—to show to our own satisfaction that we do. This vindication of our knowledge of the external world may be modest, but it is none the less important. It looks as if the best response to the egoist might be similar. We might just insist that we do have moral reason to help others, not to lie, not to kill, and so on—and since egoism denies this it must be false. Of course, no sensible knave is going to be very impressed by this argument. But now we have given up trying to answer him in his own terms, and we are searching for something less demanding: an argument that we at least find compelling.

A modest reply to an egoist is an argument based on premises that the egoist denies, but that we accept. This kind of argument looks like it should be easier to provide than a more ambitious argument trying to defeat the egoist in her own terms. But modest replies to egoism encounter significant problems. I consider two of them. First, in Chapter 6, I defend these arguments against the charge that they are not 'cogent', that is, they cannot resolve doubt about their conclusions or convince anyone of their truth. I argue that this problem is not insurmountable: modest arguments against egoism can be cogent. Unfortunately, they encounter a more serious difficulty, the subject of Chapter 7: the problem of disagreement. The very fact that there is considerable disagreement in ethics, between moral agents as well as with egoists, means that it is exceptionally difficult to establish a justification for the claim that we have moral reasons to act. As Part II closes, it looks as if we may not even be able to give a modest defence of morality.

The arguments of Part II of the book are overwhelmingly negative, suggesting that attempts to defend egoism, either ambitious or modest, fail. But in the most important part of the book, Part III, I defend morality. I show that it is reasonable for us to accept that we have moral reasons for action. So *we can modestly vindicate morality* after all. And at the same time I develop an extremely unusual objection to egoism: an *epistemic problem for egoism*. The argument of this part of the book is complicated and in the course of it I will defend several extremely controversial claims about the relationship between knowledge and action, the difference between moral knowledge and moral understanding, the nature and importance of morally worthy action, and finally the rational response to moral disagreement.

I argue that there is a significant difference between the standards of epistemic rationality for beliefs about explicitly moral matters (including moral reasons for action) and the standards for beliefs about ordinary non-moral matters. In Chapter 8, I suggest that the standards of epistemic rationality are connected to the function that those beliefs will play, including their role in contributing to action. In the following two chapters, I argue that moral beliefs (including beliefs about moral reasons for action) play a different role in action than beliefs about non-moral matters, and show that that indicates that different standards of epistemic rationality apply to each. The standards of epistemic rationality for non-moral beliefs are related to knowledge (or if not knowledge, truth), whereas the standards for moral beliefs depend on something different: *moral understanding*. In Chapter 9, I argue that moral knowledge and moral understanding are distinct and that moral understanding, not moral knowledge, is the more significant: moral understanding plays a crucial role in moral virtue and in morally worthy action. In doing so, I give a new account of morally worthy action, of doing the right act for the right reasons.

In Chapter 10, I explain which responses to moral testimony and moral disagreement are appropriate if you are aiming to acquire and use moral understanding rather than moral knowledge. In Chapter 11, I draw out the implications of all of this for disagreements between supporters of common-sense morality and egoists, and draw conclusions about the epistemic standing of common-sense morality and egoism.

I show that there is a striking *epistemological asymmetry* between the most plausible forms of egoism and morality. In their own terms, it is not epistemically rational for those egoists to believe their own theory, but it is epistemically rational for moral agents to believe that morality has authority. It turns out that we can defend morality—at least to our own satisfaction—and it is egoists who are left struggling for a view that is both plausible and epistemically respectable. We can modestly vindicate morality, and most egoists cannot reply in kind. We may not have vanquished egoism entirely, but it is common-sense morality that ends up in by far the stronger position.

# I
# Egoism

# 2

# Standard Egoism

## 1. The Authority of Morality

According to Ray Monk's biography, at eight or nine years of age, Ludwig Wittgenstein was struck by a philosophical question for the first time. Why should one tell the truth if it is to one's advantage to tell a lie? Having thought about the matter and having found no satisfactory reason, he concluded that there was, after all, nothing wrong with it.[1]

Wittgenstein's question can be understood in several different ways. First, it could be a question about moral right and wrong: is lying really morally wrong when it is in your interests? Your victim might be upset if he became aware that he had been deceived, but if he never found out, surely you would not have harmed him at all; so perhaps there is nothing wrong with lying in your own interests, as long as you are not discovered.

These are questions about the *content* of morality. Moral theories are developed to give systematic answers to them. According to utilitarianism, it is morally right to maximize the general happiness and morally wrong to do otherwise: lying is usually wrong, because it usually fails to maximize happiness. According to Kant's ethical theory, it is morally wrong to act on maxims that you cannot at the same time will to be universal laws: lying is always wrong because you cannot will a universal law of lying (if there were such a law, there would be no trust and lying would be ineffective).

But Wittgenstein could be asking a different question. He might acknowledge that lying is morally wrong, but wonder whether, given the advantages of lying, he has *reason* to tell the truth.

[1] Monk 1991: 3.

Practical reasons are considerations that favour or count against an action. According to some theories of practical reason, each of us has reason only to promote her own interests; Wittgenstein does have a reason to lie when it would be to his advantage. According to others we have reason to do what is morally right even when doing so is costly to ourselves. Some reasons count in favour of an action without requiring you to perform it. It is a consideration in favour of going to the cinema that you would enjoy yourself, but of course you are not required to attend. You might, by contrast, be required not to lie, no matter how much you might benefit from doing so.

What is the connection between moral right and wrong and reasons for action? According to common-sense morality, we do have reasons to be moral.

*Moral reasons.* Everyone always has reason to do what is morally right and reason not to do what is morally wrong.

What is the ground of those reasons? Perhaps we always have reason to be moral because it is always in our interests to be moral. If you regularly had dealings with the same group of people, it is more than likely that you would get on much better with them if they think you will tell the truth, keep your promises, and help them when they are in trouble. They will be much more willing to cooperate in return. So you have good reasons of self-interest to do what is morally right, under many circumstances.

But common-sense morality makes a further claim. Morality has *practical authority*: everyone has reason to do what is morally right (and to refrain from doing what is morally wrong) *precisely because* it is morally right (or because of the reasons that make it right).[2] I will call this claim the Moral Authority thesis.[3]

---

[2] This formulation is intended to include theories that claim that it is moral rightness itself that grounds reasons for action, or theories similar to Scanlon's (1998) 'buck-passing' view of value that claim that the features that ground moral rightness also ground reasons for action.

[3] We can distinguish two different questions about the practical authority of morality. The first is a question of scope. Do you always have reason to do what is morally right and reason not to do what is morally wrong? The second question concerns the strength of reasons to do what is morally right and avoid what is morally wrong. Must those reasons be balanced against the benefits you might obtain? Do they override opposing reasons, no matter how much you would profit? Do they silence your other reasons, so that any benefits you might gain simply do not count in favour of action? Or can moral reasons be outweighed by other kinds of reason, such as reasons of self-interest? It is sometimes thought that morality has a uniquely powerful practical authority: moral reasons override other kinds of reasons for action. We can distinguish a stronger thesis, *Moral Supreme Authority*: everyone has an overriding reason to do what is morally right and an overriding reason not to do what is morally wrong.

*Moral authority*. Everyone has reason to do what is morally right and reason not to do what is morally wrong. The grounds of these reasons are either the action's moral rightness (or wrongness) or the features that ground the action's moral rightness (or wrongness).[4]

Why accept that morality has practical authority? Recall the story of Gyges, who used the magic ring to get away with murder. Like Glaucon, many of us think that what he did was morally wrong and that he had reason not to do so; not because he would get found out and punished or because he would be racked by guilt (he might not), but precisely because murder is morally wrong.

In this book, I will consider whether common-sense morality can be defended against the challenge of egoism, and it is specifically the practical authority of morality that I shall try to defend. In the next section I set out the main threat, egoism (Section 2), distinguishing it from a different but well-known challenge to the authority of morality (Section 3). The remainder of the chapter (Sections 4–6) sets out the most common and popular version of egoism and outlines Sidgwick's doomed efforts to show that it is rational to reject that theory and act as a utilitarian instead.

## 2. The Challenge from Egoism

Suppose that Wittgenstein did after all have reason to lie whenever doing so would benefit him; in fact, he always had reason to do what was in

---

The grounds of these reasons are either the action's moral rightness (or wrongness) or the features that ground the action's moral rightness (or wrongness). And there is an even stronger claim that one might make: that moral reasons are the only kind of reasons for action that there are (*Moral Sole Authority*): everyone has a reason to do what is morally right and a reason not to do what is morally wrong. The grounds of these reasons are either the action's moral rightness (or wrongness) or the features that ground the action's moral rightness (or wrongness). There are no other reasons for action. It is questionable, I think, whether common-sense morality is committed to the supreme or sole authority of morality. But it is clearly committed to morality having practical authority, in the sense expressed by the Moral Authority Thesis.

[4] Sometimes the thesis that I call 'Moral Authority' is discussed in terms of whether it is irrational or unreasonable to be immoral. But the terms 'irrational' and 'unreasonable' are often reserved for people who make no attempt to reason at all, or who use blatantly invalid arguments or, in the practical realm, who fail to act for reasons that they themselves acknowledge (Scanlon 1998: 25–30). Of course, you can deny the practical authority of morality without being irrational in that sense. An egoist who believes that she has reason only to promote her own interests may be very ingenious in doing so. It seems odd to call such an agent irrational. But if Moral Authority is true, she has reason to do what is morally right, though she does not realize it.

his interests, and never had reason to do anything else. Then a theory of practical reason that I will call *egoism* is true.

Two different theses have been known by the term 'egoism'. The first is psychological egoism, the claim that each person always does act in her own interests. The second thesis is rational egoism, the claim that each person has *reason* to act in her own interests. Rational egoism is a totally distinct theory from psychological egoism, and it may be true even if psychological egoism is false. Each person may have reason to act only in her own interests, though in fact she does not always do so. In this book, I am concerned only with rational egoism as a challenge to the practical authority of morality, so references in this book to 'egoism' are always references to 'rational egoism'.

*Rational egoism.* Everyone has reason to do what is in her own interests, and no other reasons for action. The grounds of this reason are the interests of the agent.

As the stories of Gyges and of Wittgenstein's lie show, doing what is morally wrong can be in your interests. So if rational egoism is true, you do not always have reason to do what is morally right—the Moral Reasons thesis is false. And even when you do have reason to do what is morally right, it is not because doing so is morally right that you have reason to do it, but because doing so is in your interests. So if rational egoism is true, the Moral Authority thesis is false: morality does not have practical authority.[5]

Rational egoism is sometimes confused with another popular theory of practical reason, instrumentalism. According to instrumentalism, each agent has reason to take the necessary means to her goals, but she has no reason to choose any goals over any others. Of course, achieving your goals will often contribute to promoting your interests. So, according to egoism, it is often true that you have reason to take the necessary means to your ends. But, suppose that you have chosen a goal whose satisfaction will not contribute to your interests, you have, for example, chosen to help someone else at a cost to yourself. According to instrumentalism you have reason to take the means to that end. According to egoism you do not; you have reason to pursue your own interests instead.

It is also important to distinguish rational egoism from the following theory.

---

[5] I discuss further whether self-interest and morality are really in conflict in sect. 6 of this chapter and in Chapter 4.

*Moorean egoism.* Each agent has reason to maximize my own interests; and no other reasons for action. The ground for this reason is my interests (or that my interests are good).[6]

Suppose that eating chocolate ice cream benefits the person who eats it. According to rational egoism, everyone has a reason to eat it as often as possible. According to Moorean egoism, everyone has a reason to encourage me to eat chocolate ice cream, but has no reason to do so themselves.

Moorean egoism is a puzzling theory because it claims that there are significant differences between different people's interests. Mine are practically important, grounding reasons for action that apply to everyone. Everyone else's interests are not practically important, grounding no reasons for action at all. Moorean egoism is faced with the difficult task of explaining the difference between my interests and those of everyone else. It is very unlikely that this explanatory requirement could be met. I shall assume that Moorean egoism is not defensible, and I will focus on rational egoism in the remainder of the book. According to rational egoism, each person's interests generate the same kind of reasons: each person has reasons to act based on her own interests. There is no difference between my interests and those of everyone else.

Rational egoism challenges the authority of morality. I will look more closely at this challenge in later sections of this chapter. But first I want to distinguish it from another well-known problem for the authority of morality: an argument from Bernard Williams.[7] I will argue that this is not a genuine challenge to morality, however, since whether Williams is right or not does not settle the question of the practical authority of morality.

## 3. The Challenge to Morality from Internal Reasons

Do we always have reason to do what is morally right? Bernard Williams has challenged not just the practical authority of morality but also the weaker

[6] This version of egoism is named after G. E. Moore (Moore 1903: 96ff.). Moore rejects egoism, but only considers a version similar to the less-plausible theory that I call 'Moorean egoism', not the version that I here call 'rational egoism'.

[7] See 'Internal and External Reasons' in Williams 1981 and 'Internal Reasons and the Obscurity of Blame' in Williams 1995.

Moral Reasons thesis, arguing that we may not always have reasons to do what is morally right. He begins by distinguishing two kinds of reasons for action. *Internal reasons* are based on an agent's subjective motivational set (S)—that is, her desires, values, and commitments; an agent has an internal reason to do X if she would be motivated to do X if she underwent a process of sound deliberation, based on elements of her S. *External reasons* are not relative to an agent's motivations. Williams argues that there are no external reasons, because they do not have the features essential to a genuine reason for action.

Reasons for action need to be able to feature in explanations of why an agent acted as she did. A proper explanation of an action must explain why it was that the agent was appropriately motivated. But an external reason has no connection with an agent's motivational set: someone can have an external reason to act without having any motivation to do so. So, by itself, an external reason cannot explain action. Moreover, reasons are supposed to 'rationalize' as well as to explain action: it should be possible to give an explanation of why an agent acted that shows that she acted for good reason. But an external reason cannot rationalize the action if the agent has come to accept it by some accident; it must be because she has been thinking about the matter in the right way. In other words, if a reason is both to explain and to rationalize action, the agent must have acquired a motivation to act after having deliberated correctly. But, in that case, she must have an *internal* reason not to act. Williams concludes that only internal reasons are genuine, only they can both explain and rationalize action. Of course we make external reasons claims all the time. But this is just 'bluff'. In reality, we have only internal reasons to act.

Let us assume for the moment that there are no external reasons for action. It follows that the reasons each person has depends on her motivational set. But it does not follow that we have no reason to do what is morally right. Even if all reasons were internal, everyone would have reasons to be moral, provided that we all desired to be moral, or we could reach such a desire via a sound deliberative route from our current motivations. But of course some people do not seem to be interested in what is morally right or wrong; they just do not care about it and some people seem positively to like doing what is morally wrong.

Williams thinks that there are no particular concerns that an agent must have to qualify as rational. Someone who had absolutely no concern for her own future well-being, or who was completely indifferent to the well-being of others, might be fully rational. But this may not be correct. Perhaps it is actually part of being rational that you care about morality.[8] In that case, agents would have internal reasons to be prudent and moral, because any rational agent could become motivated to act from them through a sound deliberative route. We would all have reasons to be moral, and further, morality could have practical authority.[9]

Even if Williams is right that there are no external reasons, we need not give up on the Moral Authority thesis. But is he right? Williams argues that an agent's believing that she has an external reason cannot explain her action. Adopting a 'Humean' model of action-explanation, he thinks that any adequate explanation of action must consist in both a belief and a desire (or some element of S). So your belief that you have a reason to provide for your old age will only explain your action in combination with a desire, such as a desire to provide for your own future. One might dispute this Humean model, arguing that some acceptable explanations of action do not cite a belief plus a desire.[10] But suppose that we accept it. Your belief

---

[8] Call this conception of rationality, *substantive rationality*. By contrast, we will call the conception of rationality wherein an agent's reasons depend entirely on his current S, once he has merely eliminated false belief and has fully imagined each element, a version of *procedural rationality* (Parfit 1997; Hooker and Streumer 2004; see also Korsgaard 1996a: 311–34; Wallace 1990). Wallace, for example, suggests that to every desire or motivation there is a corresponding evaluative belief with which it is associated: your desire that you have a pleasant future is associated with the evaluative belief that it is desirable that you have a pleasant future. Borrowing Nagel's (1978) terminology, Wallace calls the kind of desire that admits of a rationalizing explanation a 'motivated desire'. It is a mistake to think that the requirements of procedural rationality are uncontroversial, or that they need no defence. In fact, one might question why an agent's reasons depend on her correcting false beliefs. Why should an agent be concerned about what she would desire if she had only true beliefs? Perhaps an agent must be concerned about this to qualify as rational. But then even Williams may have to acknowledge that at least some of an agent's reasons do not depend on her current motivational set—that is, that there are at least some external reasons (Lillehammer 2000).

[9] I have suggested that morality has practical authority in the sense that it is morality itself (or the reasons that ground moral rightness and wrongness) that ground our reasons for doing what is morally right. It might seem that we could always have an internal reason for doing what is morally right without morality having practical authority in the requisite sense. For the grounds of those internal reasons would be our desires, not morality itself. This is certainly possible. But if it is part of being a substantively rational agent that you care about doing what is morally right, because it is morally right, there is a good sense in which the ground of those internal reasons would ultimately be morality. Hence it would be reasonable to claim that morality would have practical authority.

[10] Cohon 1986: 548–50; Dancy 2000. If a belief on its own could explain action, Williams's argument against external reasons would not go through. But the idea that a belief on its own could explain action is not very appealing. Beliefs can be distinguished from other mental states because they are states whose contents are supposed to represent accurately the way things are in the world. But to act is to attempt to affect the way the world is. The sources of action cannot simply be states whose contents

that you have a reason to provide for your old age will not explain what you do; you need a desire or some other motivation too. If you reached this motivation through a sound deliberative route, it would be an internal reason. Perhaps you might reach it, not through a sound deliberative route, however, but through some other means, a 'conversion'.[11] If there was a route to a motivation that did not qualify as a sound deliberative route but which could rationalize action, there could be external reasons. Williams thinks there is no such thing. But since he deliberately leaves the concept of a sound deliberative route both open-ended and vague, it is impossible to tell whether or not he is right. It follows that there might, after all, be external reasons to be moral.[12]

Despite the huge literature on Williams's argument against external reasons, there is no clear consensus on whether he has proved that there are no external reasons. But what is most important for our purposes is that the debate does not, after all, settle the question in which we are interested. Every rational agent might nevertheless have reason to do what is morally right precisely because it is morally right, even if all reasons for action are internal, as a desire to do what is morally right might be part of being a rational agent. On the other hand, if Williams is wrong and external reasons are legitimate, it does *not* follow that morality has practical authority. There may be reasons that are not based on the agent's desires, which are *not* reasons to do what is morally right. Notably, egoism may be true: we may all have reason to do what is in our own interests (whether or not we could be motivated to do so via a sound deliberative route).

The debate over external reasons is therefore a distraction from the question in which we are interested. Whichever way the issue is decided, morality might have practical authority—or it might not. In the remainder of the book, therefore, I assume that Williams's argument does not settle the question of the authority of morality; there might be external reasons

---

represent the world. They must include 'goal-directed' states, whose contents are such that the world is to be made to match them. When one is motivated to act, one cannot be moved solely by beliefs; one also needs goal-directed states—that is, desires or motivations (Wallace 1990: 359–60; Smith 1994; Smith 1995).

[11] McDowell 1995.

[12] Since you would have external reasons to do what is morally right precisely because it is morally right (or for the reasons that make it morally right), it follows that morality would have practical authority.

to be moral, or it might be part of being a substantively rational agent that you are motivated to be moral. Instead, I return to the challenge to morality from egoism.

## 4. Standard Egoism

Since egoists think all reasons for action depend on self-interest, two obvious questions follow: what is self-interest? And what kind of reasons does self-interest ground?

The most common answer to these questions is: it is in your interests to be happy.[13] And you have reason to promote your happiness as much as possible. We can call this standard egoism.

*Standard egoism.* Each agent has reason to maximize her own happiness; and no other reasons for action. The grounds for this reason are the agent's own happiness (or that the agent's own happiness is good for her).[14]

When we think of an egoist, it is usually someone who tries to make herself as happy as possible: a standard egoist.

Standard egoism and common-sense morality conflict, for doing what is morally right does not always make you as happy as doing what is morally wrong. To defend common-sense morality, we have to show that standard egoism is false.[15] But many find standard egoism plausible and appealing. It will not be easy to defend morality against it.

Not everyone believes that we need to take seriously the challenge from egoism, however. In his book *Morality*, Bernard Williams suggests that the life of a genuine egoist is wholly unappealing:

---

[13] There are many different theories of happiness, the most prominent being 'mental state' accounts, according to which happiness is pleasure, 'desire-satisfaction accounts', according to which happiness is getting what you want, and 'objective goods' theories, whereby happiness is having certain kinds of valuable goods (see Parfit 1984: Append. I for more discussion). There is much more to say about the different versions of standard egoism that each of these theories of happiness generates, but the differences between these types of egoism are not my focus in this chapter.

[14] This formulation is intended to include theories that claim that the agent's own happiness itself grounds reasons for action, and those that claim that the value of the agent's happiness grounds reasons for action (though the egoist should not claim that the agent's happiness is valuable in the sense of grounding reasons for everyone to promote or pursue it).

[15] Some supporters of egoism claim that egoism is not really a rival to morality, because an adequate theory of morality can in fact be derived from egoism. This is discussed specifically in relation to virtue ethics in Chapter 4, and in a general way in Chapter 5.

Is there anybody whose sufferings or distress would affect him? If we say 'no' to this, it looks as though we have produced a psychopath. If he is a psychopath, the idea of arguing him into morality is surely idiotic, but the fact that it is idiotic has equally no tendency to undermine the basis of morality or of rationality . . . The psychopath is, in a certain way, important to moral thought; but his importance lies in the fact that he appals us, and we must seek some deeper understanding of how and why he appals us.[16]

According to Williams, the importance of such characters to moral philosophy is to understand the ways in which they are repellent, rather than in trying to prove that they are mistaken about the authority of morality.[17]

But Williams is wrong. Egoists are not necessarily very different from us, nor are they necessarily appalling. One of the most entertaining presentations of such a character is in George MacDonald Fraser's *Flashman* books. Flashman, a bully expelled from school for drunkenness, ends up in the British army and finds himself at almost every important event of the Victorian era. His character is best described in his own words:

When a man is as old as I am, and knows himself thoroughly for what he was and is, he doesn't care much. I'm not ashamed, you see; never was—and I have enough on what Society would consider the credit side of the ledger—a knighthood, a Victoria Cross, high rank and some popular fame. So I can look at the picture above my desk, of the young officer in Cardigan's Hussars; tall, masterful and roughly handsome I was in those days . . . and say that it is the portrait of a scoundrel, a liar, a cheat, a thief, a coward—and, oh yes, a toady.[18]

Flashman has managed to acquire the highest reputation for bravery, modesty, and loyalty, despite having none of those virtues. In fact, he has practically no virtues at all: he is profoundly selfish and untrustworthy. He is as near as humanly possible to a true egoist. Is he a psychopath? Possibly, but his motivations and thought processes are not at all alien to us. Finding himself in the most difficult and dangerous situations, he will do absolutely anything to save his own life and he can see no reason for doing

[16] Williams 1972: 23–4.

[17] Williams concedes that an amoralist can have more appeal if he does have affections for others, and he does act for others when he feels like it. There is no 'bottomless gulf' between this kind of agent and someone who is genuinely moral, according to Williams, who suggests that the appropriate response to this more attractive amoralist is to try to extend his imagination and understanding and so enlarge his sympathies (ibid. 24–5). Though surely it is often as difficult to see how one might enlarge an egoist's sympathies, as it is to envisage arguing him into morality.

[18] Fraser 2005: 13.

otherwise. We may hope to do better whilst secretly suspecting that we might not. Moreover, far from being universally despised, Flashman has his own appreciation society.[19] Some people at least find that thoroughgoing egoism has its charms. All of us have felt the appeal of acting in our own interests at the expense of others, and it is not at all strange to wonder whether we really have reason to do otherwise.

Egoists do not have to pursue a cramped, narrow, short-term conception of their own interests, wholly oblivious to the effects on anyone else. You are unlikely to live a good, happy life if you do that and it will probably be better in egoist terms if you do not actually directly pursue happiness for much of the time. Standard egoism can be *self-effacing*: it can require you for much of the time to choose actions as if common-sense morality were true and you did have reason to be moral, as if you had genuine friendships and relationships of trust and loyalty, all for the sake of your long-term self-interest. It can even be *completely self-effacing*: it can require you to believe that egoism is false and common-sense morality is true (if that is the best way for you to further your self-interest). As soon as we recognize that standard egoism can be self-effacing, we can see that Williams was quite wrong to characterize egoists as psychopaths. In fact, in most circumstances, standard egoists will act *exactly* like the rest of us, outwardly at least, for it is in their long-term interests to do so.[20] Just as Flashman is regarded as a man of honour and tremendous courage, it may be almost impossible for us to distinguish egoists in real life from people who are genuinely moral. We can appreciate the force of Kant's worry that:

if we look more closely at our thoughts and aspirations we keep encountering the beloved *self* as what our plans rely on, rather than the stern command of duty with its frequent calls for *self*-denial.[21]

Many people you come across may well accept and act on standard egoism, either directly or indirectly. This threat to morality is not merely theoretical. We would be foolish not to take the challenge of egoism seriously.

---

[19] See <http://www.harryflashman.org/>.

[20] Williams might be correct that some egoists—those who pursue their own interests in a very narrow way, refusing to acknowledge reasons to help others even when they might help in return—are indeed psychopaths. But some egoists will appear quite normal.

[21] Kant, G 4: 407.

## 5. The Parallels between Egoism and Morality

Why is egoism a particularly serious challenge to the authority of morality? Egoism is intriguing because, despite not acknowledging any moral reasons for action, egoist theories can be remarkably similar to moral theories. For example, according to standard egoism, each person has reason to maximize her own happiness, and no other reasons for action. This theory has obvious affinities with a well-known moral theory: utilitarianism. The close connection between egoist and moral theories is the major theme of this part of the book. In the remaining chapters, I will set out egoist theories that are counterparts to other major moral theories, including Kant's moral theory and virtue ethics. These egoist theories are, I think, interesting in their own right and they can illuminate the moral theories that they parallel, but I have another more important reason for introducing them. It is only by paying attention to the many various forms that egoism can take that we recognize the force of egoism's challenge to the authority of morality.

Suppose that you accept the authority of morality and you want to argue against standard egoism. You may accept a moral theory that has some affinities with standard egoism, like utilitarianism, or you may accept some quite different moral theory, such as Kant's theory or virtue ethics. Attacking standard egoism from the perspective of utilitarianism will turn out to be rather difficult, as we shall see in this chapter and in Chapter 6, since the two theories have so much in common. Attacking standard egoism from the perspective of a different moral theory may seem to be rather easier. But suppose that you argue that reasons for action are not reasons to maximize anything, or they are not based on happiness and your arguments convince the egoist. He may reject standard egoism. But he need not embrace morality instead. He may continue to insist that he has only reasons of self-interest, of whichever kind that you have defended, relating to the source of reasons that you suggested to him. He is still an egoist, and he has neutralized your arguments against egoism by changing the form of egoism he accepts.

I will have more to say about this challenge later in this part of the book and the next part too, but first I want to look more closely at the comparison between standard egoism and utilitarianism.

Utilitarianism has many different forms, but in its simplest version it claims:

*Utilitarianism.* It is morally right for each agent to maximize the general happiness (and morally wrong to do anything else).

By 'the general happiness' I mean the happiness of anyone, or anything, that is capable of happiness and suffering. According to this simple version of utilitarianism, what is morally right and wrong depends entirely on how much happiness is produced, no matter whose it is.[22]

If utilitarianism is true, and morality has practical authority, then a theory of practical reason I call 'rational utilitarianism' is true.

*Rational utilitarianism.* Each agent has reason to maximize the general happiness. The ground for this reason is the general happiness (or that the general happiness is good).[23]

According to rational utilitarianism, someone who always tells lies even when doing so does not maximize happiness is not just morally wrong: she is also failing to do what she has reason to do (though it may not be the strongest reason that she has). Rational utilitarianism therefore conflicts with standard egoism, which denies that such reasons exist.

Some utilitarians adopt a stronger version of the Moral Authority thesis. Sidgwick, for example, may accept the following.[24]

*Rational utilitarianism\*.* Each agent has reason to maximize the general happiness; and no other reasons for action. The ground for this reason is the general happiness (or that the general happiness is good).

According to this theory, the *only* reasons that anyone has are reasons to maximize everyone's happiness. This is a much stronger claim than

---

[22] There are many different forms of utilitarianism, corresponding to different theories of happiness, claiming that each agent morally ought to maximize pleasure, desire-satisfaction, and so on. These differences will not matter in the rest of this chapter. According to some versions of utilitarianism, the distribution of happiness matters as well as its quantity: it is bad if some people are much happier than others, even if under a more even distribution the total amount of happiness enjoyed by everyone would be less. For simplicity, I will consider only one version of the theory, according to which it is right to maximize happiness, and the distribution of happiness does not matter; but the argument should apply to all versions.

[23] This formulation is intended to include both utilitarian theories that claim that the general happiness itself grounds reasons for action and those that claim that the value of the general happiness grounds reasons for action.

[24] Sidgwick does not explicitly endorse this thesis, but it fits with his other claims about the theory he calls 'utilitarianism'.

that made by rational utilitarianism, which allows that there may be other, non-moral reasons for action as well as moral reasons.

Rational utilitarianism⋆ very closely parallels standard egoism. Both theories claim, first, that happiness alone is the source of reasons for action, and second, that each agent has reason to maximize happiness.[25] Of course, they differ because according to standard egoism it is one's own happiness, not everyone's happiness, that one has reason to maximize.

Rational utilitarianism⋆ might seem far too strong because it does not give sufficient weight to the 'personal point of view', from which your own happiness seems particularly important. Many of us think that we have reason to promote other people's happiness, but that we are entitled to give special weight to our own, rather than treating it as no more significant than that of other people.

There are circumstances, however, in which even rational utilitarianism⋆ will license a particular concern for your own happiness and perhaps that of your friends and family too. You are more likely to be successful at making yourself, your friends, and family happy than strangers. Their likes and dislikes are already familiar to you, and you can more easily affect their lives. When it is more efficient to use your time and energy making yourself, your friends, and your family happier, rational utilitarianism⋆ will allow you (and may even require you) to focus on their needs rather than on the needs of strangers. Indeed, in some circumstances, you might maximize the general happiness if you acted as if you had special responsibilities to care for yourself and your family (because you can make a greater difference to their happiness than to that of strangers). Moreover, since you are more likely to do so if you think you have special responsibility for them, according to rational utilitarianism⋆, you would have reason to believe that you had these special responsibilities (even though you do not actually have any). Like standard egoism, rational utilitarianism⋆ can be self-effacing, even completely self-effacing, requiring you not to choose actions by using it as a decision procedure, but to choose on the basis, for example, of common-sense morality instead.

---

[25] According to rational utilitarianism, happiness is one of the sources of practical reason, but it may not be the only one.

## 6. Are Morality and Egoism Really in Conflict?

Recognizing that rational utilitarianism★ and standard egoism can both be self-effacing in the way described earlier, it is clear that often followers of each will act in the same way. An 'enlightened' standard egoist will follow the rules of common-sense morality in many circumstances; and so will the rational utilitarian★. So it is reasonable to ask whether morality and self-interest really are in conflict.

The happy tendency of enlightened egoists to comply with morality can be strengthened with extra measures. Sanctions give an agent reason to conform to a rule that she might not otherwise accept—for example, by arranging that the consequences of an agent's failing to do so include a high chance of a loss to her. There can be legal sanctions: arrest, trial, and imprisonment; social sanctions: disgrace and banishment. There can be 'personal' sanctions too, from your own conscience. A desire to avoid feelings of guilt can be a powerful motive not to do wrong.

One obvious problem with reconciling egoism and morality through sanctions is that they are not always effective. A resourceful egoist in a position of power or wealth may simply avoid or absorb the social costs of doing wrong and find that he can learn to live with residual feelings of guilt. He will not always have self-interested reasons to do what is morally right.

When Sidgwick tried to resolve the conflict between egoism and utilitarianism he thought that a sympathetic egoist who suffered when others were unhappy would have at least some reason to take account of the happiness of others. But, concerned that sympathy alone would not do the trick he also considered a more radical possibility. God could ensure that any egoist has an overriding reason to act as a utilitarian, by threatening a significant loss of happiness if he does anything else: 'a rational egoist can want no further inducement to frame his life on utilitarian principles.'[26] Since God is omniscient, an egoist can never get away undetected with a violation of morality. And, since he is omnipotent, he will always be able to impose the appropriate sanction. God can guarantee that every egoist has sufficient egoist reasons to act as a utilitarian.

---

[26] Sidgwick 1907: 504.

This argument from self-interest is supposed to show that egoists have reason to do what is morally right. But, whilst it is very plausible that egoists have reason to act as morality requires in some circumstances, it is extremely hard to believe that they do in all realistic circumstances, let alone all possible ones.

Sidgwick was reduced to positing the existence of a God to guarantee sanctions against egoists who do what is morally wrong. Of course, no egoist will conform to morality in order to avoid an imaginary threat from a fictional deity. So this is, at most, a way of showing that egoism and morality can *in principle* be reconciled.[27] In the absence of Sidgwick's God, we have to rely on legal and social sanctions, which will almost certainly allow a certain amount of wrongdoing to go undetected or unpunished. Sympathy and feelings of guilt cannot be relied upon to make up the difference. In situations where she can escape detection, even an enlightened egoist will choose an option that increases his happiness at the expense of everyone else. Of course, if egoism is completely self-effacing, the agent will accept common-sense morality (for example) rather than egoism, and so will not take advantage of situations in which she could benefit herself through wrongdoing. But, for precisely this reason, it is likely to be best for standard egoism to be partly but not completely self-effacing. The agent would follow common-sense morality rather than egoism for the most part, but at the same time would be on the lookout for opportunities to promote her own happiness at the expense of others when she could get away with it. Standard egoists do not always have reasons of self-interest to do what is morally right.

But, more importantly, even if we were able to show that all egoists do have reasons of self-interest to do what is morally right, this is not a genuine defence of common-sense morality. According to common-sense morality, morality itself has authority (or the properties that ground morality do). If rational utilitarianism* is true, your reasons to do what is morally right depend on the general happiness, not on your own happiness (as standard egoism implies).

---

[27] Sidgwick recognized that the two theories were only reconciled if the deity actually existed: 'If then the reconciliation of duty and self-interest is to be regarded as a hypothesis logically necessary to avoid a fundamental contradiction in one chief department of our thought, it remains to ask how far this necessity constitutes a sufficient reason for accepting this hypothesis' (Sidgwick 1907: 508).

Moreoever, it is part of genuinely moral action—acting well—that you do not merely do the right thing, but that you do it for the right reasons. If rational utilitarianism★ required that an agent maximize everyone's happiness for the right reasons, that is, because everyone has reason to maximize everyone's happiness, then a standard egoist who responded to sanctions would not properly be following rational utilitarianism★ after all. Egoism and rational utilitarianism★ could not, after all, be reconciled. However, we have seen that both standard egoism and rational utilitarianism★ can be *completely self-effacing*: they can determine what an agent has most reason to do without requiring the agent to use the theory directly to decide what to do. Rational utilitarianism★ can require someone to use common-sense morality, or even egoism, to decide what to do, if by following those theories she will thereby maximize happiness. So, according to this conception of utilitarianism, it does not matter if an agent chooses her actions for egoist reasons provided that she actually maximizes everyone's happiness.[28] But, precisely in this respect, this type of utilitarianism is not a good fit with common-sense morality.[29]

Could we avoid all these problems, however, by a very simple means: by stipulating that the correct moral theory is a version of enlightened egoism? Sophisticated standard egoists will often help other people and keep their promises: why not call them moral agents? If egoism were true, but reasons

[28] Since Sidgwick thought that egoism and utilitarianism could be reconciled if the divine sanctions held, he must have accepted a version of utilitarianism according to which an agent acted rightly if he maximized everyone's happiness, no matter why he chose the action. And there is other evidence that he held such a view. He thought that it might be best in utilitarian terms for the majority of people not to believe in that theory at all, a view Williams (1993: 108) called 'Government House Utilitarianism': 'it may be right to do and privately recommend, under certain circumstances, what it would not be right to advocate openly, it may be right to teach openly to one set of persons what it would be wrong to teach to others' (Sidgwick 1907: 489).

[29] Suppose that we accept the importance of doing the right action for the right reasons. And, further, suppose that some version of egoism were completely self-effacing, requiring the egoist to accept and act on the basis of common-sense morality. Surely someone who believed and acted on common-sense morality would be acting for the right reasons, with the right motivation—even if she started off believing egoism and adopted common-sense morality for reasons of self-interest. Perhaps this is true (though even, in this case, her ultimate grounds for accepting common-sense morality might matter). But in any case it is extremely unlikely that any version of egoism will be completely self-effacing. Whilst pursuing goals other than your own interests can be in your interests, pursuing them in the wrong way—becoming too obsessed with them, pursuing some at the expense of others—is bad for you. And if you were to believe and act on common-sense morality it is likely that you would pass up many opportunities to further your own interests at the expense of others when you were unlikely to be discovered or face serious sanctions. So, even if your own interests are not your sole aim nor always at the forefront of your mind, it is likely to be better if they are somewhere in the background, able to play a role if necessary in regulating the pursuit of your other goals.

of self-interest were at the same time moral reasons, morality would have practical authority.

To some extent, this is merely a question of terminology. In so far as it is, defenders of enlightened egoism can call their theory anything they want; anyone can call their favourite theory 'morality' if they choose. What is more, if every candidate theory of practical reason were labelled a moral theory, all practical reasons would be moral reasons. The Moral Authority thesis could not fail to hold. Who would have thought that the Holy Grail of moral philosophy would turn out to be a trivial truth?

Obviously this simply avoids the original problem, which was to defend common-sense morality. We could, if we wanted, recast the story of Gyges as a challenge to common-sense morality from a rival *moral* theory, not a rival egoist theory. We could get moral authority 'on the cheap'. But, changing the name of its opponent obviously gets us no closer to vindicating common-sense morality.

In my view, it is helpful to distinguish theories according to which an agent has what we recognize as moral reasons to act: reasons based on the interests of others or reasons to do what is morally right, not simply reasons to act for her own sake. It makes sense to restrict the term 'moral' for theories that fit with common-sense morality and not to use it for those that we would consider opposed to morality. So I will continue to use the term 'egoism' for theories that all reasons for action are based on the agent's own interests, and 'morality' for theories that moral factors, such as the interests of others or the rightness of an act, ground reasons for action. It follows that the Moral Authority thesis is substantive and controversial, not trivially true.

Sidgwick realized that a proper defence of morality must show that there are reasons for action that are not ultimately based on self-interest. He must prove that egoism is false. To his disappointment, he finds that he cannot:

It would be contrary to Common sense to deny that the distinction between any one individual and any other is real and fundamental, and that consequently 'I' am concerned with the quality of my existence as an individual in a sense, fundamentally important, in which I am not concerned with the quality of existence of other individuals: and this being so, I do not see how it can be proved that this distinction is not to be taken as fundamental in determining the ultimate end of rational action.[30]

---

[30] Sidgwick 1907: 498.

He believed that there was a *dualism of practical reason* between morality and egoism, or, more precisely, between rational utilitarianism★ and standard egoism.[31] There is a dualism of practical reason when there are two different candidate theories of practical reason and it is impossible to show which is correct.[32] Sidgwick did not think we have to give up on morality as a consequence, but he did think we have to abandon 'rationalizing' it. In other words, we may continue to regard some actions as morally right and some as morally wrong, but we cannot defend the view that this has any practical importance. We cannot show that morality has practical authority: we are left with only 'universal scepticism'.

## 7. Morality Strikes Back?

Sidgwick ended the *Methods of Ethics* in despair, but some have found his conclusion unwarrantedly negative. We do not really find practical reason in contradiction with itself, they think. Rather, we have discovered that neither standard egoism nor rational utilitarianism★ is the correct theory of practical reason.

There are times at which it seems right to consider one's own interests: when I am dealing with people I do not know well, for example. If someone invited me to invest my life savings in her company, I would naturally ask how I might at least get the money back again, and perhaps even make a profit: I want to know what is in it for me. By contrast, at other times it is quite obvious that I have reason to make a small sacrifice

[31]  Ibid. 496–509.
[32]  Sidgwick's argument has been interpreted as pointing out a conflict between a moral theory (utilitarianism) and a theory of reasons for action (egoism), and as a conflict between two moral theories: one incorporating a utilitarian and one incorporating an egoist conception of morality (Brink 1988; Frankena 1974). I interpret the dualism in a third way. I regard both rational utilitarianism★ and standard egoism as candidate theories of practical reason—that is, each is a potential answer to the question: 'what have I reason to do?' If the conflict is between an ethical theory and a theory of reasons for action, then the problem is to show that someone who accepts the theory of practical reason and denies that she has a reason to do what is morally right and avoid what is morally wrong is making a mistake. If the conflict is between a candidate ethical theory (utilitarianism) and a rival self-regarding ('egoist') ethical theory, then the problem is to show someone who accepted the rival self-regarding ethical theory that she has reason to do what is morally right according to the *candidate* moral theory (e.g., utilitarianism). Although theories that include only self-regarding reasons are called 'egoist' theories here, this should not be understood as implying that they could not in principle be called moral theories, though I think it is better not to use the term 'moral' for a theory so unlike common-sense morality as standard egoism.

to give a great benefit to some other people, even if I will never be compensated for this loss. In other words, our common sense judgements about reasons seem to acknowledge *both* reasons to promote everyone's happiness, *and* self-regarding reasons to promote one's own happiness. Some have thought that the appropriate response to Sidgwick's argument is to find a compromise between rational utilitarianism★ and standard egoism, acknowledging that my own happiness and everyone's happiness are both sources of reasons.

There are a number of different ways in which a theory could allow both self-interest and morality as sources of reasons. One possibility is rational utilitarianism★ with an egoist bias.

*Rational Utilitarianism★ with an egoist bias*: each agent has reason to maximize a weighted combination of everyone's happiness and her own happiness; and no other reasons for action. The grounds of these reasons are the general happiness (or that the general happiness is good) *and* the agent's own happiness (or that the agent's own happiness is good for her).

Rational Utilitarianism★ with an egoist bias is a 'hybrid' theory that acknowledges both 'impartial' reasons for action, reasons to promote everyone's happiness, and self-regarding reasons to promote your own happiness, but no others.[33] The ground of these reasons, according to this theory is a weighted combination of the agent's own happiness and the general happiness. Different versions of the theory will give different weights to one's own and to others' happiness: your own happiness might be twice as important as anyone else's happiness, or it might be ten times

---

[33] A similar theory is defended by Scheffler (1994). Scheffler thinks that the best ethical theory is a form of utilitarianism that includes 'agent-centred prerogatives'—that is, permissions to give extra weight to one's own concerns. Scheffler's theory requires an agent to take account of the effect of her action on everyone's happiness (the impartial perspective) but allows an agent to give extra consideration to her own concerns (the personal perspective). Unlike rational utilitarianism★ with an egoist bias, however, Scheffler's theory does not require an agent to give extra weight to her own concerns (Scheffler 1994: 22–3), and he suggests that your own concerns may or may not be restricted to your own happiness (you might be concerned that your friends are happy, for example; Scheffler 1994: 69–70). According to Scheffler, it is rational either to maximize everyone's happiness or to maximize a weighted combination of one's own concerns and the general happiness. If your own concerns are restricted to your happiness, this is equivalent to the claim that it is rational to act either as a rational utilitarian★ or as a rational utilitarian★ with an egoist bias. Roger Crisp's (1996) 'dual source' theory of practical reason is also quite similar to rational utilitarianism★ with an egoist bias.

as important. The theory can require an agent to act differently from what either standard egoism or rational utilitarianism★ demands.[34]

On the other hand, this kind of theory does not really represent the conflict between self-interest and morality that Sidgwick identified as 'practical reason divided against itself'. Though it may be difficult to assess how we should weigh our own happiness against the general happiness, once we have worked that out it is always perfectly clear what we have reason to do. The conflict may be more serious than this. For example, we might say that practical reason is genuinely divided between two sources: morality and self-interest. Only when the two sources coincide is it determinate what you have reason to do.

*Dual source theory*. Each agent has moral reason to maximize everyone's happiness and self-interested reason to maximize her own happiness, and no other reasons for action. When these two sources of practical reason both support an option, she has reason to take that option. When the two sources support different options, it is indeterminate what she has reason to do. The grounds of these reasons are the general happiness (or that the general happiness is good) *and* the agent's own happiness (or that the agent's own happiness is good for her).

If anything, the dual source theory takes the conflict between egoism and morality too seriously: if I can make a huge benefit to others at minimal cost to myself; or can benefit others only a little at a great cost, surely it is obvious what I have reason to do? Not according to the dual source theory: it is indeterminate.

Another problem is that the theories considered so far include only moral reasons and reasons of self-interest. Perhaps there are other sources of reasons too.

*Multiple-source theory*. Each agent has moral reason to maximize everyone's happiness and self-interested reason to maximize her own happiness, and other reasons for

---

[34] For example, suppose I have to choose between three options, in the first of which the general happiness would be at one hundred units and my happiness at 1 unit, in the second the general happiness would be at 95 units and my happiness at 4 units, and in the third the general happiness would be at 80 units and my happiness at 6 units. If the rational utilitarian★ theory were correct, I would have to choose the first option; if standard egoism were correct, I would have to choose the third option. According to utilitarianism with an egoist bias, which option I must choose depends on how reasons from the two sources (my own happiness and the general happiness) are weighted. Suppose that my own happiness counts for double anyone else's, I should choose the second option.

action based on other grounds. The grounds of these reasons are the general happiness (or that the general happiness is good) *and* the agent's own happiness (or that the agent's own happiness is good for her), *and* other sources.

Multiple-source theories endorse the practical authority of morality, accept that reasons of self-interest have a separate weight, but also acknowledge other kinds of reason for action: these might be aesthetic reasons to act gracefully, for example, or reasons based on relationships that fall outside the scope of moral reasons. Different versions of the multiple-source theory might make different claims about the way these reasons should be weighed against each other, if indeed they can be.

No doubt many other theories of practical reason could be devised that combine moral reasons and reasons of self-interest in different and perhaps more satisfactory ways. But what would be the point?

A theory of morality that fully captures our common-sense moral judgements, a theory of practical reason that best matches our common-sense judgements about practical reason: both of these are well worth having. One of the hybrid theories combining moral and self-interested reasons may be better than rational utilitarianism* in either respect. But standard egoism conflicts not just with the moral theory it most closely parallels, rational utilitarianism*, but also with all of these hybrid theories that incorporate elements of each. Since all the hybrid theories accept that, at least sometimes, we have reason to do what is morally right (though we may not always have reason to do so, and even when we do, those reasons may be outweighed), they all to a greater or lesser extent accept the practical authority of morality. But we were intending not just to *capture* this aspect of common-sense morality in our theory of practical reason, but also to *defend* it. Even if we find that our common-sense judgements about reason do not support standard egoism or rational utilitarianism but instead favour one of the alternatives, all that this tells us is that *we do not think standard egoism is true*. This is hardly a revelation, nor will it trouble an egoist who does not share our intuitions. Sidgwick, Hume, and Glaucon didn't think that egoism was true either, but this didn't help them find a good argument that it was false.

## 8. Conclusion

When most people think of a sensible knave, they think of someone who only accepts reasons to act that are based on making herself as happy as possible. In other words, they are thinking of a standard egoist.

Standard egoism is the most common form of egoism and it has very close connections to rational utilitarianism★. Both theories pick out the same source of reasons (happiness), the same kind of reasons (maximizing), but differ as to whether these reasons are entirely self-regarding or entirely impartial. In other words, we can regard each theory as a combination of three claims.

Rational utilitarianism★ can be expressed as:

(1) Source of reasons: happiness.
(2) Kind of reasons: maximizing.
(3) The relation between the source and the reasons: impartial. Each agent has reason to maximize the general happiness.

Whereas standard egoism can be regarded as:

(1) Source of reasons: happiness.
(2) Kind of reasons: maximizing.
(3) The relation between the source and the reasons: self-regarding. Each agent has reason to maximize her own happiness.

There are many other theories of practical reason that accept (1) and (2) and that incorporate both impartial and self-regarding reasons in various combinations. Sidgwick was wrong that there is a 'dualism' of practical reason. There are not just two rival theories of practical reason, there are innumerable others as well, even if we restrict our attention to theories based on happiness as a source of reasons.

In order to defend the practical authority of morality in this context, we need to show that practical reasons are not all self-regarding: at least some (and, if we are defending rational utilitarianism★, all) are impartial. In other words, we have to attack the egoist's third claim. This is no easy task (as we will see in Chapter 5) and so we may find it unsurprising that Sidgwick found himself at a loss.

There is an easier way to attack egoism, we might think, though, via claims (1) and (2). Suppose that we do not think that happiness is a source of reasons at all, or we do not think that practical reasons are maximizing. Then we can reject standard egoism straight away, without worrying how to argue that practical reasons are impartial. Of course, we may find it difficult to defend our alternative conception of practical reason, especially if we aim to do so without begging the question against standard egoism. But we may be tempted to think that the conflict between morality and self-interest is particularly problematic for a rational utilitarian, who concedes far too much to the egoist by agreeing that moral reasons for action are reasons to maximize happiness. Defending the authority of morality is more difficult if we start with the wrong moral theory.

This is Kant's strategy to establish the priority of morality over self-interest. Kant's conception of a sensible knave is someone who thinks that all his reasons for action are based on his own happiness, but they are not reasons to maximize his happiness; an interesting variant on standard versions of prudential reason. But Kant thinks that moral reasons are completely different. They are not based in happiness. They are unconditional rational requirements that apply to all rational agents. There is no interesting conflict or dualism between morality and self-interest: morality, with its supreme practical authority, is the uncompromising victor. In the following chapter, I assess whether his arguments in defence of morality succeed, beginning with a careful look at his conception of happiness.

# 3

# Kantian Egoism

## 1. Introduction

According to standard egoism, each of us has reason to maximize our own happiness.

*Standard egoism.* Each agent has reason to maximize her own happiness; and no other reasons for action. The grounds for this reason are the agent's own happiness (or that the agent's own happiness is good for her).

Standard egoism is probably the most common and the most appealing form of egoism. It is therefore sometimes assumed that it is the only real alternative to common-sense morality; if you can dispose of standard egoism, then common-sense morality is the only viable option left, and everyone will accept it by default, including its claims about the practical authority of morality. But this is completely wrong.

Suppose that you do not think that reasons for action are reasons to maximize some end. You therefore reject standard egoism. Does it follow that you must accept the authority of morality? Of course not. You could accept some slightly different egoist theory, according to which all of your reasons for action are based on your own happiness but they are not reasons to maximize your happiness. In this chapter (in Sections 2 and 3), I set out a couple of versions of this kind of egoist theory, inspired by Kant: these are the Kantian variations on standard egoism.

Kant himself is committed to a particularly strong version of the Moral Authority thesis, Moral Supreme Authority: if an action is morally right, everyone is *required* to perform it. Moral reasons for action are categorical imperatives, unconditional requirements that bind all rational agents and override all other reasons for action, including reasons based on happiness. Kant's views on happiness (and why, unlike morality, it cannot ground categorical imperatives) repay close attention. As well as allowing us to develop some interesting variations on standard egoism, we can see why Kant thought that egoism could not be a genuine rival to the moral law (Section 4).

In the second half of the chapter (Sections 5–8), I take a different approach, however. I use ideas from Kantian ethics to develop an entirely new, distinctively Kantian version of egoism that is quite different from standard egoism. Unlike that theory in any of its variations, it is not based on happiness. Instead, new Kantian egoism parallels the moral law. It is a theory of self-regarding categorical imperatives, a self-regarding shadow of the moral law. In discussing this theory, I address some fundamental issues in Kant's practical philosophy; in particular, in Section 7, I give a new 'realist' account of the importance of rational nature, and the way in which it is the source of other kinds of value, which is, I think, a considerable improvement on the more familiar constructivist interpretations of Kant.

The purpose of this chapter is to introduce a new egoist theory. But, in doing so, I hope to uncover much of interest in Kant's moral theory, not only in what he would consider the most fundamental question—the value of humanity—but also something that is not his central concern but about which he nevertheless made many intriguing remarks: the nature and importance of happiness.

## 2. The Pursuit of Happiness

Kant does not talk in detail or at length about happiness, and it is difficult to be certain exactly what he thinks it is, but at various points he identifies it with the satisfaction of the sum of your desires.[1] He also thinks that desires

---

[1] G 4: 399; *Lectures*, 27: 276; *Religion*, 6: 58. One of the striking features of understanding happiness in this way is that these inclinations can be directed at anything, not merely at things that are connected with one's own life. Of course, you can desire that you gain money and power, but you can also have inclinations that others do so too, or that they do not. In contemporary discussions, many philosophers accept the desire-satisfaction account of happiness, but only with certain restrictions, on the grounds that the satisfaction of only some of your desires contributes to your happiness: those that are in some

play a somewhat unusual role in action: that we do not act directly on the basis of our desires; rather, we choose to set ourselves ends and incorporate those ends into maxims on which we act. If you want to become very rich, you may choose to set as your end that you become wealthy, and incorporate that end into a maxim of action; for example, 'I will get a well-paid job in order that I become wealthy'. Since we each have different desires—you want to be rich, I want to be powerful—we set ourselves different ends. Kant thinks, however, that happiness has a special status: we *necessarily* have happiness as our end:

> There is however *one* end that can be presupposed as actual in all rational beings (so far as they are dependent beings to whom imperatives apply); and thus there is one purpose which they not only *can* have, but which we can assume with certainty that they all *do* have by a natural necessity—the purpose, namely, of *happiness*.[2]

Commentators have found Kant's view of prudential reason, particularly his claim that happiness is necessarily our end, very puzzling. Korsgaard describes it as 'perplexing'. Wood finds it unclear. Johnson argues that his theory is internally inconsistent. Paton attributes to Kant 'waverings and even confusions'.[3] No one is sure what Kant was trying to say here.[4] I will try to explain. What Kant meant, I think, is that there is a sense in which creatures like us are bound to have happiness as an end.[5]

According to Kant, having a desire is having an incentive to adopt the object of the desire as an end. To have a desire that you become very wealthy, for example, is for your becoming wealthy to seem appealing to

---

ways 'connected' to your life (e.g., Griffin 1986: 13–23). Kant's conception of happiness is not so restricted. Happiness is not merely a matter of things going well for you personally: you are happy when the world is the way that you want it to be. But, given the connection that he believes to hold between pleasure and the formation of inclinations, he does think that you can be completely happy with all your desires satisfied, only if you are contented.

[2] G 4: 415.    [3] Korsgaard 1998: 59; Wood 1999: 67; Johnson 2002; Paton 1963: 127.

[4] Wood and Korsgaard have recently discussed Kant's account of prudential reason in some detail, but Korsgaard denies that it makes sense, and Wood offers an interpretation that conflicts with other important claims that Kant makes about practical reason (Wood 1999: 65–70; Korsgaard 1999a; see also Korsgaard 1998).

[5] I extensively draw on and extend Korsgaard's account of the importance for agency of self-unification here. Korsgaard's interpretation of Kant's theory of action emphasizes unifying yourself as an agent at a particular time (Korsgaard 1998; Korsgaard 1999a; Korsgaard 1999b). Though in earlier work she acknowledged that this has implications for self-unification through time (Korsgaard 1996a: 363–97), she does not make any reference to it in her discussion of Kant's prudential principle. In her most recent book, she emphasizes the importance of constituting yourself through a practical identity (e.g., Korsgaard 2009: 18–26). This is not part of my conception of self-constitution.

you. This incentive does not compel you to act, and on reflection you can choose not to fulfil it, if you judge that it is not good after all or you have some reason not to satisfy it. Setting an end is always free, because nothing forced you to choose that end. But that does not mean that nothing influences your choice of ends. According to Kant's view of action, when there are no competing considerations, typically you will adopt the object of your desire as your end and pursue it.[6]

All of us, however, have many incompatible desires that cannot all be satisfied at once (and sometimes, that cannot be satisfied together at all). When you are in this position, you cannot straightforwardly pursue everything that you want. If you consider yourself as part of the natural world, you may see yourself as simply being caused to act by your strongest desire. But when you see yourself as an agent, you must reflect on your desires: whether they are attainable, how best to achieve them, and whether you should pursue them at all.[7] You can *choose* whether or not to pursue any of them. Agency is not a matter of being pulled in different directions by your competing desires. To be an agent, you have to make a decision, and choose which object you will pursue right now. This is a process of *unifying yourself*. This self-unification makes you into an agent, rather than something that is merely pushed around by the forces within you; it is necessary if you are to *act* at all.[8]

This idea can be extended to include self-unification through time as well. Suppose that you want to do some work and you also want to meet with your friends for a drink. You sit down at your desk and look over a few papers, but before you have made any progress, you begin to get bored and you ring up a friend to see if you can meet up. Whilst you are talking to her, you start to feel bad about not doing your work, so you hang up and go back to your files. Very quickly you get restless again, and call a different friend and you decide to meet in a bar. As soon as you arrive, however, you think about what will happen the next day when you turn up without your report. You cannot enjoy your drink, and so you go back home, but by

---

[6] For a more detailed account of Kant's theory of action, see Grenberg 2001.

[7] At one time Kant believed that reason could be an invaluable tool in achieving happiness through the process of eliminating unattainable desires, though later he was much more sceptical because he acknowledged that sometimes the desire will persist despite the fact we have decided not to satisfy it, making us frustrated and dissatisfied. As Guyer points out (2000: 108), at first Kant seemed to believe that freedom and reason were valuable because they provided a more secure basis for happiness.

[8] Korsgaard 1999b: 13–29.

this time you are too tired to work.⁹ If you let yourself be guided by what you want most strongly at each moment, it is easy to achieve absolutely nothing, not even the satisfaction of your own desires. If you choose to pursue one of your desires at a time, making a decision solely for the moment—right now, I am going to work—then a few minutes later you make another decision—right now, I am going to phone a friend—this is not satisfactory, because whenever you have incompatible desires, you cannot pursue them all at once, and you are making no provision for those that you have decided not to pursue immediately. You can choose to act for one of them only, and reject the rest.

This is not a hard problem to overcome: your desire to work and your desire to meet your friends are compatible, provided that you conceive of yourself as an agent who can act both now and in the future. You can make a plan to fulfil those desires that cannot all be satisfied at the same time. Now, you need also to take into account the desires that you predict you will have in the future when you will carry out the later parts of your plan. You can regard your current and future desires as a complex whole or sum, and use this to regulate what you do. Sometimes you will have to modify your desires; sometimes you will have to reject a desire that you cannot satisfy, given what else you want. For example, suppose you decide to see your friends straightaway and meet them in a bar. Because you are taking into account your other desire to get your work done you make sure that you do not take too long or drink too much. You regulate the way that you satisfy one desire with regard to the sum of your inclinations.¹⁰

⁹ Korsgaard tells a very similar story in Korsgaard 1997: 247 and Korsgaard 1999b: 19 to illustrate the necessity of self-government for genuine agency, rather than merely being pushed around by one's desires.

¹⁰ The satisfaction of this sum is clearly similar to what Kant called happiness, but seems to differ from it in a key respect. The sum that you construct will include the present inclinations whose objects you will pursue now and in the future, and the inclinations you expect to have whilst you are carrying out this plan that will provide incentives to act in the future. It will therefore include only your inclinations in the present and the immediate future, the satisfaction of which may seem to fall short of what Kant called happiness, which was the satisfaction of the sum of your inclinations throughout your life. But there will normally be no clear limit to the future inclinations that you need to take into account when you form your conception of the sum of your desires. It depends how far into the future your plans reach. Some of your projects may take a long time to achieve, and you may not be certain exactly how long; for example, it may take you a lifetime to accumulate political power. Sometimes you now have inclinations for the further future; for example, that you die wealthy. Often you will have projects that will naturally extend into larger and more complex ones; for example, when you have acquired the money that you wanted, you form the desire for even more. At any time in your life, you may only have considered some of your future inclinations; you may have incorporated only

When we think of happiness as an end, it is natural to assume that it is a first-order end: an end we pursue directly in the same way that we might pursue money, power, or anything else. But this is not, I think, the best way of thinking of how we should pursue happiness, according to Kant.[11]

Suppose that you want money and you are considering whether to set that as an end. You may reflect on whether pursuing it will prevent you from fulfilling your other desires. If pursuing money could prevent you from having good friends, for example, you may choose to limit your pursuit of it. Happiness can function as a *second-order end* that blocks the pursuit of a first-order end when that conflicts with the fulfilment of your other strong desires. On this view, happiness itself is not normally directly pursued. Instead, it has a regulatory role, ensuring that we do not pursue one object, money for example, at the expense of everything else that we want. It is a limiting condition on first-order ends. These first-order ends

a few of them into the sum of your inclinations. But what should be included in this sum is always indeterminate; it depends on how far into the future your plans extend which is usually unclear: the only determinate limit to your plans is your death. This sum of your inclinations is therefore of an indeterminate size but in principle may be extended to include all of your future inclinations. Bearing in mind that Kant repeatedly insisted that happiness was indeterminate, and no one could be sure what elements were included in it (G 4: 399; 4: 418), it makes sense to identify the satisfaction of this sum of inclinations with Kant's conception of happiness. I assume that, since the aim of constructing the sum of one's inclinations is to develop a plan of action for the present and future, it is only one's inclinations in the present and future rather than one's past desires that are included. Parfit (1984: 149–58) discusses this complex issue.

[11] If happiness were just a first-order end like any other, it would have no particular authority; it would be one end among many. The pursuit of happiness would have to be weighed against the pursuit of other first-order ends, and there would be nothing at all odd or unreasonable about pursuing money, power, or anything else at the expense of happiness. Though some people do in fact choose specific ends above happiness, doing so is normally considered to be unreasonable. And Kant agrees, describing those who succumb to such passions as mad, sick, and deformed (*Anthropology*, 7: 252–4). This suggests that happiness is not a first-order end, after all. In order to explain its authority, we might appeal to the contrast between final and instrumental values. A final end is something that is valued for its own sake, whereas an instrumental value is valued as a means to something else. For example, suppose that I want to be rich, but I think wealth is valuable only as a means to gaining the respect of other people, which is worth having for its own sake: I regard money as instrumentally valuable, and the respect of others as finally valuable. We could explain the authority of happiness, if it were a *supreme end*; that is, if it were the only final end that we set for ourselves, with all other ends chosen in virtue of their contribution to our happiness. If happiness were a supreme end, it would be clearly unreasonable to choose to pursue money or honour at the expense of happiness, for we ourselves would regard these ends as valuable only when they contribute to happiness. But this is so only because no other ends would be worth pursuing for their own sake—and this is clearly false. We do not regard ends like friendship or power as merely instrumentally valuable. Happiness cannot therefore be a supreme end. But there is a third possibility: happiness as a second-order end.

are not valued merely as a means to happiness; but, at the same time, happiness has a special authority over them.[12]

You are now unifying yourself as an agent in two ways. First, you are unifying yourself right now, by carrying out one end, rather than being pulled this way and that by conflicting desires. But, secondly, by regulating the end that you have set and your mode of pursuing it with regard to all of your desires, you are unifying yourself through time too. You refuse to allow yourself to be pushed around at the mercy of your own future desires.

Kant said that all rational dependent beings have happiness as their end by necessity. On my interpretation, happiness is not a naturally necessary end for us, as we are free to adopt it or to reject it at any time by refraining from setting the objects of our desires as our ends. But if we do choose to set the objects of our desires as our ends, we are required to have happiness as a (second-order) end too: rational, dependent beings who have a number of inclinations, some of whose objects they choose to adopt as ends, must regulate the pursuit of those ends by a conception of the sum of their present and future inclinations, if they are to unify themselves as agents through time. Since we do tend to set the objects of our desires as our ends, we are bound to have happiness as our end.

## 3. Kantian Variations on Standard Egoism

Kant did not set out a version of egoism, but from his conception of happiness and its pursuit we can construct an egoist theory: we can take

---

[12] This is very similar to the way that the motive of duty functions in Kant's ethics, according to some prominent recent interpretations (Herman, 1993: 14–22; Baron 1995: 129–32). On these views, duty is not normally a first-order motive; rather it functions as a secondary end that regulates the first-order ends on which we decide to act. For example, suppose that you have set as an end for yourself getting some money, and you are considering robbing a little old lady to do this. Your motive of duty rules this out as an acceptable means of achieving your end, as you would impermissibly be treating the old lady as a mere means, not as an end in herself. Your conception of happiness, regulating the pursuit of your ends in a different way, may also rule this out as an acceptable means of pursuing this end, because, as an unpractised and incompetent mugger, you are likely to be caught and sent to prison, which will severely interfere with your fulfilling your other inclinations. Recall in our discussion of standard egoism in the previous chapter that standard egoists need not directly pursue happiness and choose each action on the basis of its contribution to happiness (indeed that doing so was likely to be self-defeating). This conception of happiness as a second-order end is a way in which happiness can play a crucial and authoritative role in your decisions without being something that you pursue directly.

Kant's view of one's reasons for action relating to one's own happiness, and devise a couple of theories of practical reason according to which those are the only practical reasons that there are.

These theories are interesting alternatives to standard egoism. In particular, standard egoism is committed to all of our reasons for action being reasons to maximize happiness. But why should all reasons for action be reasons to maximize some end? According to Kant's conception of happiness, our reasons for action relating to happiness are not reasons to maximize anything at all. One way of formulating this variation on standard egoism would be the following.

*First Kantian variant on standard egoism.* Each agent has reason to modify the pursuit of her first-order ends with respect to her happiness, and no other reasons for action. The ground of this reason is the importance of her happiness to self-unification.

On this view, a sensible knave will not directly pursue his happiness. And this is indeed sensible, since we know that it is likely to be counterproductive. Rather, happiness, that is, the sum of his present and future desires, has a regulatory role. It affects how he goes about trying to achieve his other ends, whatever they are.

This new egoist theory obviously has some similarities with traditional standard egoism, the theory that each of us has reason to maximize her happiness (particularly versions which, like Kant, take happiness to be desire-satisfaction). But, according to my interpretation, you can unify yourself without satisfying your desires maximally, and this Kantian variant on standard egoism does not require you to maximize your happiness.

Nevertheless, this first variant on standard egoism is plainly not the view that Kant takes of happiness. For it is quite clear that happiness has a function as a second-order end for us *only if* we set the objects of our desires as our ends. Kant clearly thinks that we *will* all choose to pursue our desires—that is why he thinks that happiness is an end for each of us—but, at the same time, he does not think that we *have* to do so. It is certainly not a requirement of reason that we should. You could set and pursue ends that have nothing to do with your desires, and provided that you pursued them with reasonable consistency through time you would be unified as an agent.[13]

---

[13] Presumably this is what Kant thinks a divine will (which has no inclinations) does.

So Kant's views on happiness are better represented by a different variant on standard egoism.

*Second Kantian variant on standard egoism.* Each agent has reason to modify the pursuit of her first-order ends with respect to her happiness, if she chooses to set the objects of her desires as her ends, and no other reasons for action. The ground of this reason is the importance of her happiness to self-unification.

According to this theory, reasons for action apply only to those agents who choose to pursue their desires. They have reason to modify how they pursue this end with regard to their other desires, present and future, in order to unify themselves as agents through time.

These Kantian variations are interesting because although, according to them, reasons for action are still entirely based on happiness, they are very different from the standard egoist account of reasons maximally to promote one's happiness. Even happiness-based theories of egoism can be quite different from one another.

Kant, however, was fundamentally opposed to egoism, giving a number of reasons why the sensible knave is not really a threat to the authority of morality.

## 4.  Kant against Egoism

Kant claims that there are two kinds of practical reason: unconditional rational requirements (or categorical imperatives) and hypothetical imperatives (reasons to take the means to ends that you have set for yourself). Kant classifies prudential reasons as hypothetical imperatives, implying that you have reason to take the means to your happiness only because you have set happiness as your end; if you had not set it as your end you would have no reason to do so. He notes, however, that prudential reasons are unlike ordinary hypothetical imperatives, which specify ends that some of us have adopted and others have not, because in fact we have all set happiness as our end. He calls these *assertoric* imperatives.[14] Moral reasons by contrast are categorical imperatives. It follows that reasons based on the pursuit of happiness are always subordinate to moral reasons for action: a

---

[14]  G 4: 414–15.

conflict between a hypothetical imperative and a categorical imperative must be resolved by your dropping the end specified in the hypothetical imperative and doing what is required by the categorical imperative. If prudential reasons are a kind of hypothetical imperative, therefore, they will be overridden or limited by moral categorical imperatives whenever the two conflict.

According to Kant, therefore, egoism cannot be correct. It must be an inadequate conception of practical reason because there are practical reasons that are unconditional rational requirements and they are not prudential. But, of course, this objection to egoism succeeds only if first, there actually are categorical imperatives at all, and second, that reasons to promote happiness are not categorical imperatives. Kant makes a number of arguments for this second claim, that categorical imperatives cannot be based on the pursuit of happiness, many of which are not very good.[15]

---

[15] For example, he repeatedly insists that we (always) want happiness and, as a consequence, we cannot be required to pursue it (*MM* 6: 386; 6: 387; *CPrR* 5: 25). If our reason to pursue happiness were based solely on that inclination, there could be no categorical imperative to pursue happiness, for we would not be required to pursue our happiness independently of our inclination for it. But Kant admits that we can be overcome by particularly strong desires, such as passions for money or power, which we know will prevent us from satisfying our other desires and leave us unhappy. To avoid succumbing, we need to form a conception of our own happiness and use it to regulate our actions. Kant is simply wrong, therefore, that our reasons for setting happiness as our end solely depend on our desire for happiness. Secondly, Kant points out that what will make you happy is not knowable a priori, whereas he thinks that we can know a priori what is unconditionally required of us (*CPrR* 5: 25–6; *MM* 6: 215–16). We can know a priori, by reflection on what is required of us as agents who can act now and in the future, that we must limit the pursuit of the objects of any of our inclinations with regard to the sum of all of our inclinations. It is what we want, now and in the future, and therefore what in particular we are required to do that we cannot know a priori, for the components of happiness, our present and future inclinations, are what Kant calls 'empirical' or 'sensuous'; they are not based in reason (*G* 4: 418; 4: 442; *CPrR* 5: 23; 5: 26; 5: 61; *Lectures*, 27: 257; *MM* 6: 215–16). But, similarly, we can know a priori that we must help other finite rational agents without knowing a priori exactly what we ought to do in order to help them. Since we are categorically required to help others, this does not seem to be a good reason for denying that we could be categorically required to pursue our own happiness. Kant also makes a stronger claim: it is impossible for us to know at all, even by induction, what will make us happy. He describes happiness as 'an ideal of the imagination' (*G* 4: 418–19, 399; *CJ* 5: 430; see also *MM* 6: 215–16; *Anthropology*, 7: 230–9). As you reflect on your own happiness, you will acquire new desires that you need to satisfy. Even if you do manage to make a consistent set of your current inclinations, they will change through time, and even if you do gain the pleasure you expected from satisfying your desires, eventually you will become bored and dissatisfied and will begin to want a change. Complete happiness will still be out of your reach. Even if we do manage to form a clear idea of the sum of all of our inclinations, there is no guarantee that we will be able to achieve happiness. Many of our inclinations are for things that are not fully under our control: we want money or the admiration of others; but, however hard we try, we may not be able to satisfy these desires; and so we may never be able to achieve happiness. But, similarly, we may rarely succeed in genuinely benefiting others, but that does not preclude our being under a categorical duty to try to do so. Of course, we know the kinds of thing that tend to make people happy. We can

He seems to have been more certain that there were no such categorical imperatives than he was sure why. The strongest arguments seem to me to be two.

First, when you regulate your choice of ends with reference to your happiness, you choose a principle only for your own life. You might choose to place health over the pleasures of taste; others might reasonably do the opposite. Kant also thinks that we have natural inclinations to do better than others, and these are typically incorporated into our conception of happiness. We do not just want power, money, and honour, but we want more power and money and honour than our neighbours. If he is correct, it is not hard to see that people who pursue their own happiness will endlessly compete with one another, and most of them will end up unhappy, since most will have less power, money, and honour than the lucky or skilful few.[16] Presumably, it is only a contingent fact that we do have these desires to do better than others and we might have had inclinations that could all be satisfied together, but Kant does not regard the mere chance of harmony as sufficient.[17] Categorical imperatives are the laws governing the 'kingdom of ends', and it is part of Kant's conception of the ideal community of rational agents that they will not live by laws that prescribe the war of all against all.[18]

Of course, it is questionable whether it really is part of the concept of a practically necessary law, as Kant claims, that rational agents who follow that law will live in harmony.[19] Certainly, defenders of standard egoism or the Kantian variations on it will deny this. But, in any case, there is a more compelling reason why reasons for action based on the pursuit of happiness cannot be categorical.

Recall that there were two Kantian variations on standard egoism. According to the first, anyone, whatever ends she set for herself, was required to modify pursuit of those ends with regard to happiness. But this theory was not warranted by the argument considered here, that the requirement to pursue happiness is connected to unifying yourself as an

---

formulate 'counsels of prudence' that advise us to seek these goods. But we cannot devise exceptionless laws that, if we follow them, will certainly lead us to happiness. It is part of Kant's conception of categorical imperatives that they are exceptionless, as well as universal, necessary requirements; so the happiness-based principles cannot be categorical imperatives.

[16] *CJ* 5: 430.    [17] *CPrR* 5: 26.    [18] *G* 4: 433–4; *CPrR* 5: 28.
[19] O'Neill 1989: 17–27.

agent. You can unify yourself as an agent through time in lots of different ways; you do not need to do so by means of a conception of your happiness. It is only if you choose to satisfy your desires that you must modify pursuit of any one of them with respect to the others. The second variation on standard egoism took this into account.

*Second Kantian variant on standard egoism.* Each agent has reason to modify the pursuit of her first-order ends with respect to her happiness, if she chooses to set the objects of her desires as her ends, and no other reasons for action. The ground of this reason is the importance of her happiness to self-unification.

This theory directs a rational agent only if she chooses to satisfy her desires; otherwise it gives no guidance whatsoever. But no one is required by reason to do what she wants. Of course, all of us do anyway, so in practice we all have to set happiness as our end. We are not wrong to choose to pursue our desires, but we are not rationally required to either. It follows that reasons based on happiness cannot be categorical, because they are not genuinely unconditional requirements on any rational agent.[20]

Kant of course believes that there are unconditional requirements of this sort. Indeed, he thinks that you can formulate a universally valid principle just by considering what you could will to be a universal law; and that this universal law generates unconditional duties to others, including the duty not to keep false promises and the duty to help others—duties that apply to all rational agents, no matter what they desire. The formula of universal law therefore is an unconditional law of reason.

If Kant is right, the Kantian variations on standard egoism *cannot* be genuine rivals to the moral law. If fulfilling your desire conflicts with the moral law, you must choose, at least at that particular moment, not to satisfy it, in which case you quite obviously are not required to regulate its pursuit

---

[20] Korsgaard believes that both of Kant's principles of reason, the categorical imperative and the hypothetical imperative, can be derived from the very idea of an agent's exercising self-determination. But she is extremely sceptical that an 'egoistic principle', a principle of promoting your own happiness, could be justified thus: 'it is not plausible to think that you only succeed in exercising self-determination if you aim to maximize the satisfaction of your desires; or that you are not really willing unless what you will is maximum satisfaction . . . the egoistic principle simply seems to be *the wrong sort of thing* to be a principle of practical reason' (Korsgaard 1999a: 17). She emphasizes that it is possible to be a self-determined agent who does not seek to maximize the satisfaction of her desires; in fact, the key point is that it is possible for a rational, self-determined agent to choose not to act on her desires at all. Any rational agent who chooses to set the objects of her inclinations as her ends will be rationally bound by the prudential principle, as it is interpreted here, however, though she will not be required to maximize desire-satisfaction.

with regard to happiness. It is only when you choose between options that are morally permissible that you are entitled to adopt the objects of your inclinations as your ends, and thereby to commit yourself to happiness too. Prudential reasons are relevant to the options left open by the moral law. But the pursuit of happiness can never challenge the authority of morality: morality will always win.

The parallels that could be drawn between rational utilitarianism* and standard egoism are simply absent here. It may be tempting to think that the conflict between morality and self-interest is particularly problematic for a rational utilitarian, who concedes far too much to the egoist by agreeing about the importance of maximizing happiness. Kant seems to have avoided this problem by arguing that moral and prudential reasons are completely different kinds of reason, and morality, unlike self-interest, can ground laws of reason with overriding practical authority.

How will a sensible knave respond to Kant's argument? He may of course deny that there are any categorical imperatives. Kant cannot expect the knave simply to admit that there is a kind of reason that always overrides reasons based on happiness: he must give an argument for this, and there is no guarantee that he will be successful.

But let us for the sake of argument suppose that the egoist accepts that reasons for action based on happiness do not have the authority of laws of reason, and yet that there are such laws: there are categorical imperatives that apply to all rational agents and express reasons for them all, independently of their desires.

Has the egoist given up the game and conceded everything? Not necessarily. Egoism based on happiness is only one form of the theory, though admittedly it is the most common kind. The egoist may propose a new egoist theory of practical reason according to which there are categorical imperatives but *they are not moral reasons*. They are *self-regarding* categorical imperatives, based on a highly unusual conception of self-interest. This new kind of egoist theory is likely to come under attack from two sides. People unsympathetic to Kant's project are likely to be suspicious of categorical imperatives quite generally, but particularly self-regarding ones, or 'duties to the self'. On the other hand, Kant and his followers will be puzzled too. How can an egoist possibly accept that there are categorical imperatives and refuse to acknowledge the authority of morality? Categorical imperatives precisely express that authority. But I will show that it is possible to develop a coherent egoist theory, according to which there are categorical imperatives that are not moral reasons for action: this is Kantian egoism, the self-regarding shadow of the moral law.

## 5. Duties to the Self

Kant's own moral theory draws a clear distinction between self-interested reasons based on happiness and moral categorical imperatives. But it is not impossible for a sensible knave to accept an egoist theory that includes categorical imperatives. The raw material that will provide the foundation of this theory is a part of Kant's ethics that is often neglected: duties to the self.

Kant thinks that we have duties to the self as well as duties to others and he sees self-regarding duties, especially the duty not to commit suicide, as fundamental to his ethics.[21] But many people regard duties to the self as absurd or incoherent. How can I both be under an obligation and owe that very obligation to myself?[22]

---

[21] *MM* 6: 417–24.

[22] A person can have a number of roles in relation to a duty: as the subject of the duty, who is required to act to fulfil the duty; as the object, to whom the subject owes her duty; or as the beneficiary, who benefits by the subject's fulfilling her duty. For example, suppose Anna promises Ben to look after Charles. Then Anna is the subject of the duty, since it is she who must fulfil the duty; Ben is the object of the duty, as Anna owes her duty to him; and Charles is the beneficiary, since he gains by Anna meeting her obligation. A duty is a duty to oneself when it is *owed* to oneself; it is a duty in which the subject and the object of the duty are the same person. These different roles are distinguished by Reath (1998: 113). In the *Metaphysic of Morals*, Kant worries about the legitimacy of self-regarding duties. He claims that the solution lies in recognizing two attributes of a man, as a sensible being, of the phenomenal world, and as an intelligible being, of the noumenal world (*MM* 6: 418. Kant makes the same claim in his *Lectures* (*Lectures* 27: 510, 579, 592–3)). Obviously, we would expect him to claim that the two attributes of man correspond to the two relations to an obligation, as subject and as object. For example, we might expect that the noumenal agent is the object of the duty, imposing the obligation, and the phenomenal agent is the subject of the duty, under an obligation to act in a certain way (Wick 1960: 162–3; see also Denis 1997: 334–5). But it is difficult to understand how the noumenal agent can impose an obligation on the phenomenal agent, because *qua* phenomenal agent there can only be a causal explanation of an action, not an explanation in terms of reasons; from the phenomenal point of view, an agent can be caused to act in a certain way, but cannot be under an obligation. As Kant himself says, from the phenomenal perspective, 'the concept of obligation does not come into consideration'. But if it is only as a noumenal being that one can create obligations and be obligated, then in the case of a duty to the self, the same noumenal agent is both the object and the subject of the obligation. It may be that we need the noumenal/phenomenal distinction in order to understand some features of duties to the self, but it does not help explain how duties to the self can be binding.

In fact, duties to the self are perfectly coherent; moreover, the very duties to the self that Kant endorsed are defensible, given some assumptions about the value of rational nature. These duties to the self are categorical imperatives, and a theory of practical reason consisting only in them can be devised which is an egoist theory of categorical imperatives. I discuss this at some length since, unlike standard egoism, the resulting Kantian egoist theory is not at all familiar. I hope to show both that Kantian egoism is coherent and that it should have some appeal, at least to anyone who has some sympathy with the Kantian conception of the importance of rational nature.

The phrase 'I promised myself' is probably as common as 'I owed it to myself', and promising to oneself may seem to be a source of duties to the self which we could use as a model to explain how duties to the self can be legitimate. It may seem that just as when you make a promise to someone else you have a duty to that person to do what you promised, when you make a promise to yourself you have a duty to yourself. But the analogy between promising to others and promising to the self is misleading, because promising to the self does not in fact generate any self-regarding duties.

If you make a promise to someone else, typically the person to whom you have made the promise can release you from the promise: the duty is waivable.[23] So, if you make a promise to yourself you should be able to release yourself from that promise at any time. But a duty from which you can release yourself at any time is not a genuine duty at all.[24] It is hard to see how a waivable duty to the self could be a normative requirement.[25]

If you can release yourself from a duty, then whether or not you have the duty depends on whether you choose to release yourself. Suppose that you can release yourself from a duty to $\varphi$ whenever you prefer not to $\varphi$. You have a duty to $\varphi$ only when you want to $\varphi$. But a normative requirement

[23] Though it is perhaps not always permissible for the promisee to release the promiser—for example, if others are relying on the promise to be fulfilled.

[24] It might be argued that the obligation to keep a promise is based on the more fundamental obligation not to deceive other agents. This explains why the promisee can usually release the agent from his promise. If the promiser obtained the consent of the promisee (that is, he was released from the promise), he would no longer be deceiving the promisee, using her in a way to which she did not consent. The duty not to deceive other agents is not waivable; the subject cannot be released from this duty by the object of the duty. But even if the unwaivable duty not to deceive grounds the duty to keep promises it does not ground a duty to keep promises to oneself, since one cannot generate false expectations in oneself in the same way that one can in others.

[25] This argument against duties to the self is put forward by M. G. Singer (1959; 1963) and discussed by Hill (1991: 138–50) and Hills (2003).

to $\varphi$ should be valid whether or not you want to $\varphi$, for a normative requirement is a reason to act which holds whatever you desire.[26] If you could release yourself at any time from a duty to the self, that duty would not be a genuine normative requirement; it would not be a genuine duty at all.

Promises to the self cannot be analogous to most promises to others, because if promises to the self are waivable (as are most promises to others) they cannot ground genuine duties.[27] Promising to the self is not a good model of a duty to oneself, and cannot be used to show that duties to the self are coherent. Does it follow that we cannot make sense of duties to the self? Fortunately not.

The argument that duties to the self are impossible relies on the premise that duties are always waivable. It is true that the concept of a waivable duty to the self does not really make sense. But duties are not always waivable. No one can release me from my duty not to deceive him: if I

---

[26] Suppose that you can release yourself from a duty to yourself, but not simply on the basis of a desire. Could this duty be a genuine requirement? For example, you might be able to waive the duty if there were strong reasons in favour of so doing. But then you do not have a genuine choice about whether or not to waive the duty. You have the duty if there are no strong reasons against it. If there are sufficiently strong reasons against performing the duty, then the duty may be overridden, or may no longer apply to you. In neither case can you *choose* to waive the duty.

[27] Could promises to the self be analogous to those special promises to others that are unwaivable? Suppose that you are divided into two temporal parts, 'your early self' (E) and 'your later self' (L). At some point in time, E goes out of existence, and is replaced by L. A promise to the self might be interpreted as an obligation owed by L to E to fulfil the expectations created in E that L will act in a certain way. E cannot release L from this duty, because E no longer exists (just as you cannot be released from a promise made to someone who has since died). L seems to have a genuine duty to the self (more precisely, to your early self) from which she cannot be released. But now it is not at all clear how L acquired this duty in the first place. Your later self did not make a promise to your early self. E made a promise to herself, and generated expectations which can only be fulfilled by L. But why does the requirement to fulfil these expectations transmit from E (who made the promise) to L (who did not)? You are not normally required to keep a promise made by someone else when you did not even exist. On the other hand, suppose that L is sufficiently closely connected to E to take on the obligations incurred by E in making the promise. Why doesn't L also acquire the rights that E had, including the rights to waive duties? Either your later self has no duty to keep the promise (because E not L made the promise) or she can waive the duty (because if she incurs the duties of the earlier self, she also acquires the right to waive duties). In either case, she has no unwaivable duty. So promising to oneself cannot be explained by means of temporal parts of a person. Could we explain it by means of parts of the person that are around at the same time? But then the part of the person to which the promise had been made would be present, and capable of releasing the promiser part of the person from the promise. This kind of promise to the self would be waivable unless you can generate expectations (in one compartment of your mind) and also plan not to fulfil them (in some other part). It is quite hard to make sense of such self-deception. The two parts of you would have to be quite separate and not able to interact and influence one another, since otherwise the part which had made the promise could influence the other part to release it from the duty. This does not seem possible in a normal person (though it might be true of someone with a 'split personality').

obtained his consent in the deceit, I would not really be deceiving him at all. No one can release me from my duty to help him; rather, I have a duty to find a way to help that he can accept.[28] I have duties to others from which I cannot be released. So I may also have duties owed to myself from which I cannot release myself. If the object of an obligation cannot release the subject of the obligation, it does not make any difference whether the object and subject of the duty are the same person. Unwaivable duties to the self are perfectly coherent, and duties to the self are just as legitimate as unwaivable duties to others.

## 6. The Rational Nature Principle

Kant's duties to the self are based on the principle that an agent cannot rationally will to undermine his functioning as a rational agent (what I will call his rational nature). I call this the 'Rational Nature' principle.

*The Rational Nature principle.* You cannot rationally will to undermine your rational nature for the sake of anything other than rational nature.

According to the principle, an agent is rationally required to choose to protect her functioning as a rational agent. This requirement is a duty to herself; it is her own rational nature she must protect. The agent *qua* subject is obliged to choose to protect her rational nature. The agent *qua* object of the duty cannot release herself from the duty to protect her rational nature, since she cannot rationally choose to undermine her rational nature (except for the sake of rational nature itself). The Rational Nature principle therefore grounds duties to the self.

Indeed, it grounds those duties to the self that Kant identifies in the *Groundwork*, the duty not to commit suicide and the duty to promote your talents. According to Kant, you have a duty not to kill yourself 'from self-love', an example of which is killing yourself to avoid pain, in other words choosing to undermine completely your capacity to function as a rational agent for the sake of avoiding pain. If the Rational Nature principle is correct, it is never rational to will to undermine your rational nature

---

[28] Wick 1960; Paton 1990.

for the sake of something else.[29] So, you could not rationally choose to kill yourself to avoid pain, therefore, you have a duty to yourself not to commit suicide to avoid pain.[30]

The Rational Nature principle also supports the duty to promote your talents: you undermine your rational nature when you neglect certain skills. Whatever other ends you set for yourself, you will always need to be able to acquire food; in different circumstances, you will have to develop different skills to do this. The specific talents that you must cultivate may be relative to the society in which you live. But if the Rational Nature principle is correct, you have a duty to yourself to develop at least some of your talents, to enable you to survive and thrive as a rational agent.[31]

The principle also plays an important role in other parts of Kant's theory. In discussing the formula of humanity, Kant argues that there is an imperative to treat oneself as well as others as ends not as mere means. It is not obvious what it means to treat yourself, or rather 'humanity in your own person' as an end not as a mere means. But the examples Kant discusses imply that it includes the requirement not to undermine your rational nature for the sake of anything else. Since Kant thinks that the moral law, including the formula of humanity, is the law of practical reason, he therefore also must accept that you cannot rationally will to undermine your rational nature for the sake of anything else. So the formula of humanity, understood as a law of practical reason, entails the Rational Nature principle.[32]

---

[29] As a consequence, it is never rational to will that it should be a universal law to undermine one's rational nature for the sake of something else. Clearly, I cannot rationally will a universal law of suicide if I cannot rationally will that I should commit suicide. So, according to the formula of universal law, I have a duty not to commit suicide for the sake of avoiding pain. This could replace Kant's unconvincing universal law argument against suicide in the *Groundwork*, which is based on his natural teleology.

[30] Is suicide always forbidden? Kant suggests (*MM* 6: 423–4) that self-killing may be permitted in certain circumstances; for example, it may be permitted to risk death for the sake of protecting one's future rational nature (as when one is vaccinated against a disease). But risking death in order to protect your rational nature is not contrary to the Rational Nature principle, which requires you not to undermine your rational nature for the sake of something else. Kant also suggests that suicide may be permitted when there are moral reasons in its favour—that is, it can be reasonable to undermine your own rational nature for the sake of other people's rational nature (but not for the sake of something other than their—or your own—rational nature).

[31] Since you cannot rationally choose to neglect your talents, you cannot will that there be a universal law of neglecting talents. So, the duty to protect your talents also follows from the formula of universal law.

[32] This interpretation of the formula of humanity is endorsed by Korsgaard (1996a: 124). The Rational Nature principle may also have other uses within Kant's ethical theory. For example, it is used by Herman (1993: 55) in her derivation of the duty of beneficence.

## 7. Rational Nature as the Source of Value

If the Rational Nature principle is correct, duties to the self are possible. Kant clearly accepted the principle; in fact he seems to regard it as undeniable: 'This is the way in which a man necessarily conceives of his own existence' (G 4: 429). But some people do contemplate committing suicide to avoid pain and some do not develop their talents: they do not respect their own rational nature as Kant requires. According to the Rational Nature principle, it is not rational to undermine your rational nature for the sake of anything else: no other goal can be normatively more important than protecting rational nature. Why might rational nature have this special status?

One possible answer, suggested by Korsgaard and Wood, is that rational nature is the source of the value of all our goals; as a consequence, it can never be rational to undermine rational nature for the sake of some other goal, for that goal cannot be more valuable than rational nature.[33] This kind of argument depends on what it means for rational nature to be a source of value; unfortunately, neither Korsgaard nor Wood explains this very clearly. And the very idea that rational nature might be the source of value has recently come under vigorous attack.[34]

There are at least two different ways in which rational nature might be the source of the value of our goals; I call these the *conferral* model of value, and the *constitutive* model.

If rational nature is the source of value, it might be that each end is valuable only because some rational agent has chosen to adopt it as a goal and to pursue it.[35] For example, the goal of understanding Kant's ethical theory is valuable because I, as well as other rational agents, have chosen to adopt it as a goal. This picture of value as *conferred* by rational choice is puzzling for two reasons. First, the explanation of the source of value of our goals was supposed to explain why the Rational Nature principle holds, that is, why it cannot be rational to undermine my rational nature for the sake of one of my goals. But suppose that I care a lot about avoiding pain; I would prefer to kill myself than to suffer a painful illness. Why

---

[33] Korsgaard 1996a: 194–7; Korsgaard 1996b: lecture 3; and Wood 1999: 124–32.
[34] Regan, for example, argues (2002: 267) that 'rational nature cannot be valuable in a Kantian world'.    [35] Korsgaard 1996a: 194–7; Wood 1999: 127.

can't I confer more value on avoiding the illness than on staying alive and suffering? The conferral model fails to explain why I can't confer sufficient value on one of my goals to make it rational to pursue that goal even at the expense of my rational nature.[36]

Secondly, if all value is conferred by rational choice, then nothing can have value before it is chosen (rational choice 'brings value into the world'). All the options open to you before you have made your choice are equally worthless; there is nothing to be said for any of them. But if nothing has any value antecedent to a rational choice, there could be no possible reason for choosing any option rather than another. So how can it be rational to choose any of them over any other? Moreover, how can a capacity to select one worthless option over another equally worthless option be valuable? Surely such a capacity must itself be worthless. In trying to explain how rational nature is more valuable than anything else, we have in fact shown that it cannot be valuable at all![37]

Some have taken the problems with the conferral model as a decisive reason to abandon Kantian ethics entirely (Regan 2002) or at least to reject the claim that rational nature is the source of value (Sussman 2003). But we need to distinguish the view that rational *choice* is the source of value from the different claim that rational *nature* is the source of value. Provided we reject the former, we can still maintain the latter, by accepting an account that I call the *constitutive model* of rational nature as the source of value.[38]

Suppose that all rational wills, that is, all persons, are valuable. In order to function as a rational agent, you need to adopt and pursue some ends. In some respects, it does not matter which ends, because in setting and pursuing many different ends, you can be acting rationally. Non-moral

---

[36] Korsgaard and Wood both claim that it could not be true that my goals are valuable only because I have rationally chosen them, and at the same time true that my rational nature is not worthwhile. But they are not very clear about why this is impossible. One possible explanation is that value might 'flow' from our will to our goals, as water flows from the source of a river to the ocean, or energy flows from battery to light bulb (Korsgaard 1996a: 259). We might conclude that, just as the battery must provide at least as much energy as the light bulb uses, so the will must be as valuable as the goals on which it confers value. If value were constantly transferred from our will to our goals in this literal sense, we could see why the will must be at least as valuable as any of our goals. But, clearly, it would be absurd to think that value was literally transferred in this way. So Korsgaard and Wood still need to explain why a capacity to confer value cannot be less valuable than the ends on which it has conferred value.
[37] Regan (2002) forcefully presses this issue.
[38] I do not intend to endorse the constitutive model as the correct theory of value here; rather I want to argue that it is coherent, consistent, and the best reconstruction of Kant's ethics available to us.

ends are valuable not because they are *chosen* by the rational will. Instead, their value depends on *their contribution to the functioning* of a rational will.[39]

Suppose that you have been told by your doctor to take up some kind of sport for the sake of your health. As far as you are concerned, the value of sports like tennis and squash depends on the fact that if you take them up as a hobby, you will exercise and benefit your health. Of course, there are important differences between different sports: tennis will contribute more in this regard than darts, so tennis is more valuable to you than darts, and you have more reason to take up tennis.

According to the constitutive model, ends that we set acquire value in the same way that tennis and darts acquire value from their contribution to your health. Tennis is a *way* of exercising: it is a *constitutive means* of physical exercise. Similarly, setting a particular object as your end and pursuing it is not an instrumental means to be a rational agent, it is a way of being a rational agent. For example, you may choose to read the *Critique of Pure Reason*. According to the constitutive model, this project is valuable as a constitutive means of exercising your rational nature. It, or some similar project, is worth setting as an end, because it is worthwhile exercising your rational nature.

Many objects are suitable to be set as ends. But some would contribute more than others to your exercising your rational agency. Some projects are more complex than others, and require you to set more than one end; it may be difficult to identify a suitable means to achieve the end, or the means may be very difficult to carry out, and so on.[40]

---

[39] The view presented here as the constitutive model of value implies that our rational nature is valuable independently of whether we have chosen to confer value on it, that anyone who did not choose to treat her rational nature as valuable would violate duties to herself and would not be acting reasonably. Some commentators on Kant have attributed a similar view to him—for example, Herman (1993: esp. 202–40), who emphasizes Kant's claims about the value of rational agency, though she interprets the value of our rational nature as *limiting* the ends that we may legitimately pursue (Herman 1993: 39–40), rather than as *grounding the value* of those ends, as the constitutive model claims. In several places, Guyer has pointed out (1996: 420–3; 1998: 33–5; 2000: 129–31, 148–55) Kant's claim that freedom—that is, the freedom to set and pursue ends, is valuable, though he distinguishes this from the claim that it is our reason that is of value. Guyer also suggests (1996: 413) that the formula of humanity might require us to pursue projects that protect and enhance our rational agency, but he does not claim, as does the constitutive model, that the value of projects *depends* on their contribution to exercising, protecting, and enhancing rational nature.

[40] This picture of the relationship between value and the rational will has some similarities to Thomas Hurka's Aristotelian conception of the importance of our rational nature (Hurka 1993). According to Hurka, we have reason to exercise our rational capacities, and to achieve as much as we can. But this is because our rationality is essential to our nature, and we have reason to perfect our own nature. The Kantian conception of the importance of rational nature is similar, but does not rest on a claim about what is essential to our nature.

Since the value of the ends that we set for ourselves depends on their contribution to our exercising our rational nature, then simply by choosing an object you cannot make it any more valuable than it was before.[41] So the constitutive model is not a version of constructivism, but rather a distinctively *Kantian value realism*. We do not construct value through our choices; rational nature is valuable whether or not we recognize that it is and choose to treat it as valuable. Our non-moral ends are valuable in virtue of their contribution to our functioning as rational agents: we do not 'confer' value on them through our choices. According to the constitutive model, the value of all our non-moral ends depends on their contribution to the exercise of rational nature, so there *could be no reason* for any of us to pursue some end at the expense of rational nature.

When we decide which of the non-moral ends we might choose are worth pursuing, it is very plausible that one of the ways in which we evaluate them is in terms of their contribution to the exercise of rational nature. Other things being equal, an end is more valuable if satisfying that end would be an *achievement*. When we assess whether satisfying some potential end would be an achievement, we do so on the basis of the *effort* that is needed to satisfy that end and the *level of skill* that is required. For example, it is a greater achievement to prove Fermat's Last Theorem than that there is no highest prime number, because it takes an immensely greater amount of time, concentration, and skill for someone to prove the former than the latter.[42]

At least one of our everyday ways of assessing the value of our ends is in terms of their contribution to the exercise of our rational nature, and in this regard the constitutive model fits with our ordinary practice. But in other ways it does not. Even if we do assess possible ends in terms of achievement, we do not normally think of them as merely instrumentally valuable, valuable in terms of their contribution to rational nature.

---

[41] The value of objects depends on their contribution to rational nature, but once you have chosen one option over another, you have some reason to pursue that project, since carrying out the goals you have set yourself is an important aspect of rational action. Others have reason to respect your choice, rather than trying to force you to do what they would prefer. In this limited sense, your choice can confer some reason to pursue what you have set as an end.

[42] Does this mean that we should all be trying to prove Fermat's Last Theorem? Clearly that would be absurd, since most of us could make no progress at all towards doing so. We would have no idea what to do, and would most likely end up doing nothing. Instead, we should set and pursue ends that we can at least make some progress towards achieving, so that we do actually exercise our rational nature.

But, according to the constitutive model, our potential ends are valuable in a very special way. Most instrumental means are separate from the ends to which they contribute. For example, having money is an instrumental means to buying nice things, so it is worthwhile as a mere means, for the sake of an entirely separate further end. A constitutive means is not separable in the same way from the end to which it contributes.[43] For example, playing tennis is not an instrumental means to exercising: it is itself a form of exercise. The two types of activity are not identical, for you can exercise without playing tennis; but the token activities are identical: when you play tennis, you are exercising. So, if exercise is valuable, your playing tennis is not valuable for the sake of some further end that is separate from it. There is a sense, therefore, in which it is true (though perhaps somewhat misleading) to say that you are playing tennis for its own sake, since your playing tennis is valuable for the sake of something that is token-identical with it.

Similarly, pursuing our ends is not an instrumental means to the end of exercising rational nature. For example, your reading a poem may be valuable for the sake of exercising your rational nature, but when you read a poem you are exercising your rational nature: the two activities are token-identical (though of course not type-identical, for one can exercise rational nature without reading a poem). So reading a poem is valuable, not for the sake of some further end that is separate from it, but for the sake of something token-identical with it. In this sense, it is true to say that reading a poem is worth doing for its own sake.

Constitutive means are importantly different from other kinds of instrumental means. Whereas it would be a considerable confusion—though no doubt one that many people make—to think that a mere instrumental means, like having money, was worthwhile for its own sake, a constitutive means is in fact valuable for its own sake, at least in the sense that it is valuable for the sake of something token-identical with it. So it is understandable that we talk about our non-moral ends and think of many of them as valuable for their own sake. This need not conflict with the claim that they are valuable as ways of exercising our rational nature, when that claim is properly understood.

The constitutive model can acknowledge the point of assessing ends in terms of enjoyment. Since we have set happiness as our end, it is rational

---

[43] For a discussion of constitutive and instrumental means, see Marras 2003.

for us to choose a project that we would enjoy as a means to that end. We can choose a project on the basis of the enjoyment it would give to ourselves or others; or on the grounds that we will be able to carry it out with our friends; or because it is exciting or frivolous or fun. We are completely right that a project that will make us happy is worth pursuing. But there is an important difference between the status of enjoyment and the status of rational nature, because the value of projects that contribute to enjoyment depends on our having set that as our end (or, more precisely, on our having chosen to satisfy our desires, thereby committing ourselves to setting happiness as our end), whereas the value of projects that contribute to our exercising our rational nature does not depend on our setting that as our end, for rational nature alone is unconditionally valuable.[44]

The constitutive model of rational nature as the source of value is coherent and it fits reasonably well with our common-sense assessment of the value of our goals.[45] But, if the constitutive model is correct,

---

[44] Suppose that you are wondering what to do. You could count some blades of grass for no particular reason, which would neither be a substantive exercise of your rational nature, nor particularly enjoyable. You could lie on a beach all day, which would be more enjoyable, but would not be a substantial exercise of your rational nature. Or you could set yourself some demanding task, like reading the *Critique of Pure Reason*, the satisfaction of which would be an achievement and which you would enjoy, or learning some mathematics, which would also be an achievement, but which you would hate. According to the constitutive model, the demanding tasks are valuable as potential contributors to the exercise of your rational nature and consequently it would be reasonable for you to choose either. Assuming that you have set happiness as one of your ends, however, you have a reason to choose the *Critique* over the mathematics, as the former but not the latter will contribute to making you happy. There is clearly no reason at all for you to count blades of grass, a worthless, boring activity. Choosing to waste your life on such a project could not make it any more valuable. What about lying on the beach? This would be pleasant, but is no achievement, and so a life devoted to such a pastime would not be worthwhile (compare Kant's discussion of the South Sea Islanders (G 4: 423)). On the other hand, you are not required to *maximize* the exercise of your rational nature, but merely to respect your rational nature. As Kant says, we have only a wide, imperfect duty to develop our talents and skills: we do not have to do so on every occasion to the maximum degree (G 4: 430). It might be compatible with respect for your rational nature that you could spend an afternoon on the beach, provided that your other projects involved a more substantial exercise of your rational nature. The constitutive model requires us to be able to recognize more or less substantial exercises of rational nature independently of the value of the ends that are pursued. This fits well with an assessment of our projects in terms of whether their success would qualify as an achievement, and how great an achievement it would be. According to the constitutive model, this is the key measure of non-moral value. Projects whose successful completion would count as an achievement are valuable because the exercise of rational nature is valuable, and the more substantial the exercise of rational nature, the better. But the constitutive model is compatible with value pluralism in the following sense: we are entitled to use other modes of assessment of our projects too.

[45] A full assessment of the constitutive model is beyond the scope of this chapter, though I do think that it is the best reconstruction of Kant's conception of the value of humanity. But it is perhaps worth pointing out a few of its strengths and limitations. It is plausible that our rational nature is valuable, and

rational nature does have a special status. It is not rational to undermine your rational nature for the sake of anything else. You therefore have duties to yourself not to do so. Now we can use this idea of duties to the self to formulate a Kantian theory of egoism that parallels the moral law.

## 8. Kantian Egoism

Kant's formula of humanity requires an agent to treat humanity whether in his own person or the person of another, always as an end, never merely as a means (G 4: 429). This generates duties to others, including duties not to deceive and duties of beneficence; as well as duties to the self, including the duty to develop your own talents and the duty not to commit suicide.

Consider now the theory of practical reason that consists only in the following formula.

*The Formula of Kantian Egoism*

Always treat humanity in *your own* person as an end, never as a mere means.

This theory of practical reason generates self-regarding imperatives, including the duty to develop your own talents and the duty not to commit suicide, but no duties to others; for according to this theory you are required to treat yourself as an end, but you are not required to treat anyone else as an end.

Kant describes the duties to the self that are derived from the moral law as moral duties, because they are categorical imperatives that are based on respect for humanity. They must be distinguished from the reasons for action based on desired ends that are hypothetical imperatives. In Kant's theory, these duties are derived from a moral principle, a requirement to treat *everyone* as an end.

But consider the self-regarding imperatives derived from the formula introduced above. They are based on the requirement to respect your own

that assessments of our goals in terms of achievement are related to the exercise of rational nature. It is less plausible that all value can be explained in this way. For example, can the value of non-rational animals, of the environment, of art, of emotion, of human relationships be explained in terms of the value of rational nature or of the choices of rational agents? (Hills 2008).

humanity, to treat yourself as an end.[46] But they are not derived from a *moral* principle that you should treat everyone as an end, but from a *self-regarding* requirement that you should treat only yourself as an end. It is reasonable to classify imperatives derived from this formula as *prudential*. The formula is a *prudential principle*, because it generates reasons for action based on your own interests: these reasons are not concerned with your interest in satisfying your desires or in being happy, but with your interests in exercising your rational nature. This Kantian version of egoism, consisting in your interests as a rational agent, I shall call *Kantian Egoism*.

Kantian egoism is based on the requirement to respect *your own* humanity. These duties are derived from a principle that has some similarities with the Rational Nature principle, but is importantly different from it.

*The Egoist Rational Nature principle.* You cannot rationally will to undermine your rational nature for the sake of anything other than your own rational nature.

The Egoist Rational Nature principle grounds duties to the self, including a duty to develop your talents, and a duty not to kill yourself to avoid pain, but no duties to others at all. It is based on each agent's interest in exercising her rational nature. But it does not require an agent to maximize the exercise of her rational nature; instead she is required to respect it, to treat it as an end, not as a mere means, and to refrain from undermining it for the sake of anything else.

According to the constitutive model of value, all of our ends are valuable in virtue of their contribution to rational nature, and so it is not rational to pursue any goal at the expense of rational nature. But the model can be understood in two different ways. The first version supports the Rational Nature principle:

(1) Ends are valuable in virtue of their contribution to anyone's rational nature, and it is not rational to will to undermine your rational nature for the sake of anything except rational nature—your own or that of another.

The second version supports the Egoist Rational Nature principle and, therefore, Kantian Egoism:

---

[46] This conception of 'categorical prudence' is anticipated in Brink (1997a), who notes that there may be categorical prudential imperatives of this kind, and that there may be a dualism between prudential and moral categorical imperatives, but does not show that the moral law is no better justified than the prudential theory.

(2) Ends are valuable in virtue of their contribution to your rational nature, and it is not rational to will to undermine your rational nature for the sake of anything except your own rational nature.

The explanation of the constitutive model in the last section was compatible with both these claims, and nothing that I have said so far settles whether a Kantian should support the Rational Nature principle (and therefore the moral law) or the Egoist Rational Nature principle (and so Kantian egoism).

Kantian egoist imperatives are self-regarding, prudential categorical imperatives. According to Kant, genuine unconditional rational requirements must meet a number of conditions. First, they cannot be based on what an agent desires. Categorical imperatives apply to any rational agent and bind her no matter what she wants. Kantian egoist imperatives have nothing to do with desires. They are based on a rational requirement to treat yourself as an end, not as a mere means, which itself depends—as does the formula of humanity—on the special value of rational nature.[47] The major difficulty in regarding happiness-based reasons as categorical imperatives was that we are only conditionally required to pursue happiness. We must do so if we choose to set the objects of our desires as our ends, but we are not required by reason to do that. So, happiness-based reasons must be conditional—or hypothetical—imperatives. But we are not merely conditionally required to treat ourselves as ends, depending on what we choose. We are rationally required to do so, according to Kantian egoism. Kantian egoist imperatives are quite plainly not hypothetical.

---

[47] One of the problems with regarding the Kantian variations on standard egoism as known a priori is that the components of happiness, inclinations, are what Kant calls 'empirical' or 'sensuous'; they are not based in reason. We cannot know empirical or sensuous matters a priori; Kant claims that we can know a priori what is unconditionally required of us. But clearly this is not a problem afflicting Kantian egoist imperatives, which concern rational nature, an end set by reason that is neither empirical nor sensuous. If Kant is prepared to accept that we can know that the formula of humanity is a law of reason, perhaps by knowing that rational nature is the source of all value, then he cannot consistently deny that one could in principle know Kantian egoism a priori by knowing about the value of rational nature. Both regard rational nature as the source of all value; according to the formula of humanity, it follows that you must not undermine any rational nature for the sake of anything else, whereas according to the formula of Kantian egoism you must not undermine your own rational nature for the sake of anything else. It is reasonable for a Kantian egoist to claim that you can work out that Kantian egoism is correct about that and the moral law mistaken a priori (especially since Kant presumably would have to endorse a similar claim: that you can determine that the moral law is true and Kantian egoism false a priori).

The final issue is more serious. It is part of Kant's conception of an unconditional law of reason that rational agents who follow that law will live harmoniously in the kingdom of ends. This is clearly a problem for Kantian variants on standard egoism since (on Kant's view) if we each pursue our own happiness we will tend to come into conflict with one another. But it is also potentially a problem for Kantian egoism. If we each treat ourselves as an end, not as a mere means, but do not do the same for others, we might well end up in conflict, attempting to cheat or lie to each other or otherwise pursuing our own goals at the expense of others. We might not be required to do this, but we would be permitted to do so.

But a Kantian egoist might reasonably object to this characterization of categorical imperatives. Of course, we might expect that a community who followed a moral law to live harmoniously with each other, and Kant identifies the moral law with the law of reason. But the Kantian egoist does not, and she might protest that there is no good reason to think that a community of rational agents, who all do what is rationally required of them, will live without conflict. Why should they? Perhaps we would not expect conflicts between them to be inevitable, and we might question a supposed law of reason that would lead inexorably in every circumstance to the war of all against all. But conflict is not an inevitable result of following Kantian egoism, though it can be, depending on the circumstances. Kantian egoism unsurprisingly cannot be a *moral* law, but it is a perfectly good candidate to be an unconditional law of reason.

Kant accepts the supreme authority of morality. To defend that against egoism, it is not simply enough to defend it against standard egoism or some variant of it. He must also attack Kantian egoism.

The moral law and Kantian egoism cannot both be correct. They each pick out a different property as the ground of reasons for action. The two also have different practical implications. The moral law requires you to treat others as an end, whereas Kantian egoism does not. For example, according to Kantian egoism, Wittgenstein would have no reason not to tell a lie; according to the moral law, this would be forbidden.

Even if you need never decide between totally different courses of action, however, the moral law and Kantian egoism still do not coincide in practical terms. In a number of famous examples, Kant makes it clear that there is a significant moral distinction between actions done *from duty* and actions done *in accordance with duty*.[48] A shopkeeper who only gave customers the right change to preserve his reputation for honesty and to protect his profits is not really honest. His actions are not morally worthy, even though he performs the same actions that a genuinely honest shopkeeper would perform. The honest shopkeeper acts from duty, the self-interested shopkeeper in accordance with duty, and only the action performed from duty has true moral worth. What does it mean for an action to be performed from duty? Kant does not make it entirely clear, but it may mean that the action must be chosen because it conforms to the moral law, or at the least that it would not have been chosen if it had not conformed to the moral law. An action which is chosen for any other reason, for instance, because it conforms to Kantian egoism (or that would not have been chosen had it not conformed to Kantian egoism) cannot, therefore, have been done *from duty* even when the action performed is the same, such as in situations in which only duties to the self are relevant.[49] It is only an accident when the Kantian egoist does what is morally required; for Kant, this shows that his action has no moral worth.

## 9. Conclusion

Initially it seemed that Kant, unlike the rational utilitarian★, was in a good position to combat egoism. He refused to accept that happiness could ground laws of reason, and so could never have overriding practical authority. But even if an egoist concedes to Kant there are categorical imperatives and that they are not based on happiness, the battle is far from over. It is only one version of egoism (if a particularly common and attractive version) that has been vanquished. The egoist can regroup and return in another more resilient form.

Kantian egoism stands to the moral law just as standard egoism parallels rational utilitarianism★. It includes categorical imperatives: duties to the self, based on the value of your own rational nature. These are not moral duties because they derive from an entirely self-regarding principle, which

---

[48] G 4: 397–9.
[49] A Kantian egoist may choose maxims because they conform to Kantian egoism but I do not think that she must do so (see Chapter 11 for further discussion).

grounds no duties to others whatsoever. Kantian egoism is a perfectly coherent egoist rival to the moral law, and any defender of morality who wants to show that we all have reason to do what is morally right must show that it is false. Arguments about the status of happiness are irrelevant to a Kantian egoist, and if Kant and his followers are to defend morality, they will have to develop an entirely new strategy. In Part II, I assess their best efforts, but first I turn to the third major ethical theory, 'virtue ethics'.

Some versions of virtue ethics seem to be uniquely well-placed to defend morality by avoiding a conflict with egoism altogether. According to these theories, anyone who has the virtues will act morally but will also have a good life: it is, after all, in your interests to be moral. Can this version of virtue ethics avoid the challenge from egoism altogether?

# 4

# Virtue Egoism

## 1. Virtue Ethics

In the *Republic*, when Glaucon pointed out that Gyges led a very good life after committing acts of spectacular injustice, Socrates responded that he might have had wealth and power; but without justice, Gyges's soul was in turmoil, battling against itself. An egoist who knew what was good for him would be just after all, even if it meant giving up the chance to marry a queen and take the throne.

Aristotle basically agrees. He begins the *Nicomachean Ethics* by asking what is the highest good for man. He rejects wealth, on the grounds that it is only worth having as a means to other goods; and also pleasure, as a life of pleasure is also open to other animals and so is not distinctively human. He proposes that the highest good for man is *eudaimonia*, or 'flourishing'. Eudaimonia, as Aristotle understands it, is the activity of reason in accordance with excellence in a complete life.[1] The excellences, or virtues, are dispositions to act and feel in the right way and to take pleasure and pain in the right objects. For example, the courageous person faces danger to the right extent and at the right time; the rash person does so too much; the coward too little.[2] Aristotle sets out the virtues—courage, temperance, liberality, justice, and several others—and their corresponding vices; just as for Socrates, it turns out that the best human life is the life

---

[1] *NE* 1098a7–18

[2] *NE* 1106a15–30; *NE* 1115b25–35. Each virtue is a 'mean' between two vices, of acting and feeling too much, or too little. Aristotle applies this idea of the virtue as the mean to different areas of human life—facing danger, physical pleasure; the getting and spending of money, the distribution of benefits in society, and so on, to derive the traditional virtues of courage, moderation, liberality, justice, and so on.

of moral virtue.[3] Gyges might have had wealth and pleasure, but he has missed out on the best goods of all.

If this is right, there is no genuine conflict between pursuing self-interest and doing what is morally right. Unsurprisingly, some contemporary moral philosophers have found this appealing and have followed Aristotle in arguing that the best life for us is a distinctively human life of virtue.[4] The two most prominent examples, whose theories I will discuss in this chapter, are Philippa Foot, especially in *Natural Goodness*, and Rosalind Hursthouse, in her book *On Virtue Ethics*. These theories are known as *neo-Aristotelian virtue ethics*.

The distinctive feature of these theories is the link they claim exists between the virtues and the good life. Foot suggests that virtues play a necessary role in a human life. Hursthouse explicitly defines virtues by their connection to self-interest.

*Virtue.* A virtue is a character trait a human being needs for eudemonia, to flourish or to live well.[5]

There was a clear problem of conflict between rational utilitarianism* and standard egoism, because it was plainly possible that the action that best promoted your own happiness might not be the action that best promoted the happiness of all. Similarly, you might treat yourself as an end, without treating all other people as ends, so there is a conflict between Kantian egoism and the moral law. But if you need the virtues in order to live well, there is no point pursuing self-interest at the expense of doing what is virtuous, because you are condemned to fail. This type of virtue ethics seems to be in a very good position, then, to defend morality; for, in fact, there is no conflict between virtue and self-interest.

In this chapter, like the last, I will introduce another new egoist theory that is quite different from standard egoism. This time, though, it reflects virtue ethics (specifically, neo-Aristotelian virtue ethics); it is a form of

---

[3] Aristotle's views are in fact more complicated, however. Later in the *Nicomachean Ethics* he appears to rank a life of contemplation higher than a life of moral virtue. I will ignore these complications here, since it is the link between the good life and the life of moral virtue which appears to give us the opportunity of avoiding a challenge to morality from egoism.

[4] There are other versions of virtue ethics that are not Aristotelian in that they do not link flourishing and having the virtues, and some versions of Aristotelian virtue theory do not put as much weight on the link as others. In this chapter, I focus particularly on those versions of virtue ethics that defend the link strongly, since those are the ones that seem to have the best resources to answer the egoist.

[5] Hursthouse 1999: 29.

*virtue egoism*. I will elaborate some egoist virtues, including egoist versions of justice and benevolence (section 4). Once again, the main purpose of the chapter is to set out a new non-standard version of egoism, but I hope that it will also illuminate the moral theory which it mirrors. In this case, I will focus on the two key claims of virtue ethics that the virtues are characteristic of humans (Section 3) and, most importantly, that the virtues benefit their possessor (Section 2).

## 2.  The Virtues Benefit their Possessor

One of the main points of virtue ethics is that the focus of ethical theory should be the agent herself, and what kind of person she is, not what she does. Virtue theory tends to emphasize traits of character rather than right action, and may therefore appear to remain silent about whether we have reason to do what is morally right. But, in fact, many versions of virtue theory do make claims specifically about right action. For example, Hursthouse explains morally right action in terms of virtue: 'An action is morally right if and only if "it is what a virtuous agent would characteristically (i.e. acting in character) do in the circumstances".'[6]

By accepting a definition of right action in terms of virtue, virtue theorists can endorse a version of the original Moral Authority thesis.

*Rational virtue ethics.* Everyone has reason to do what the virtuous agent would characteristically do in the circumstances, and avoid doing what the virtuous agent would characteristically refrain from doing in the circumstances, precisely because this is what the virtuous agent would do (or for the reasons why this is what the virtuous agent would do).[7]

---

[6]  Ibid. 28. Hursthouse's account of right action really needs to be modified, perhaps to the following claim: right action is what an informed virtuous agent would want the agent to do in the circumstances. This formulation allows that there may be circumstances where a less than fully virtuous person should act differently from the fully virtuous; for example, a less than virtuous person should avoid temptation, whereas a fully virtuous person who is confident that she will not succumb to temptation has no need to avoid it (Copp and Sobel 2004: 546). Even this conception of right action may not be wholly adequate. But I will continue to discuss Hursthouse's simpler account of right action, not considering these more complicated formulations, as this will not make a difference to the argument.

[7]  There are important questions for virtue ethics about the order of explanation of the link between virtue and right action (is the action right because it is what the virtuous do, or is it what the virtuous do because it is right?) But this issue is not important here, so I will not discuss it. It is sufficient that virtue ethicists like Hursthouse are committed to an account of right action of one kind or another.

But, according to neo-Aristotelian virtue ethics, being virtuous and doing what the virtuous agent would characteristically do is in your interests. Consider the rational egoist theory that all reasons for action are based on the agent's own interests.

*Rational egoism.* Everyone has reason to do what is in her own interests, and no other reasons for action. The grounds of this reason are the interests of the agent.

Rational egoism is consistent with rational virtue ethics, in the sense that the rational egoist has reason to do what the virtuous agent would characteristically do, for doing so is in her interests.[8] There is no such thing as a *sensible* knave after all.

Can it really be in your interests to be honest and courageous and just? We clearly need to look more carefully at the proposed connection between self-interest and virtue. The link can be understood as a claim about virtuous actions or about having a virtuous character:

(1) Every virtuous act benefits the agent.
(2) Having the virtues benefits the agent.

To measure whether an individual act is in your interests, you compare the consequences of that act with the consequences of the other acts open to you. To measure whether having a character trait is in your interests, you need to compare the whole lives of individuals with the character trait and without it. You may do extremely well out of a single act of betrayal, where you empty the joint bank account, run off, and change your name. But it is likely that your life as a whole will go better if you are loyal than if you are treacherous, because you can have true friends and genuine relationships only if you are loyal. It may be in your interests to have the virtue of loyalty, even though some individual loyal acts may harm your interests. (1) is therefore a stronger claim than (2); it is implausibly strong: it is extremely likely that some loyal and courageous actions will not be in your interests; so we will reject (1) and turn to (2).

---

[8] Rational virtue ethics is not committed to rational egoism, however, because rational virtue ethics leaves open the possibility that there are reasons for action that are not based on what the virtuous agent would do, and therefore which are not in that agent's own interests, whilst rational egoism implies that there are no reasons for action that are not based in self-interest.

(2) can be understood in a stronger or weaker sense:

(2a) Having the virtues benefits the agent more than having any other character traits.

(2b) Having the virtues for the most part benefits the agent more than having any other character traits.

There is an obvious objection to the claim that the virtues benefit their possessor. First, you may be unlucky and be unhappy even though you are virtuous. Your house may catch fire in the night, and though you risk your life to save your children, you can only save one, not the other, and none of your possessions. Even though you are virtuous, your life is hardly flourishing. But all this example shows is that you can be so unlucky that no matter what dispositions you had and what you did you would still be unhappy. It follows that the virtues are not sufficient for flourishing. But it does not follow that any other disposition—self-centredness or self-indulgence—is any better. Virtue may nevertheless be necessary for flourishing.

On the other hand, it is quite clear that sometimes being virtuous will be very costly to you. It might be courageous to risk your life for someone else, or to tell the truth when you are threatened with imprisonment for doing so. Because the threat to your self-interest is so great, it is very plausible that you would have been better off, considering your life as a whole, if you were cowardly and dishonest, or at least less than fully courageous and honest.

Foot agrees that happiness requires favourable external circumstances: it can be out of the reach of the best kind of person through no fault of their own.[9] Hursthouse concedes that there may be circumstances in which the virtuous do not flourish because they are unlucky, or because in their situation it is costly or even dangerous to be virtuous, but she claims that no other set of character traits is reliably better than the virtues.[10] She makes a comparison with prescriptions for health: you can die young even if you do not smoke, either through luck or because not smoking is dangerous in your special situation. Bertrand Russell claimed to have once survived a plane crash along with all the others in the smoking compartment, whereas

---

[9] Foot 2001: 96–7.     [10] Hursthouse 1999: 172–4.

all those in the non-smoking compartment died.[11] But we are right to take seriously the fact that not smoking is still a better bet than smoking, and a doctor would be right to advise everyone not to smoke.

Even so, an agent with low cunning will do very well in many, perhaps most, societies, and certainly better than someone without that trait of character. Is low cunning a virtue then? This depends on the relevant conception of self-interest. What is a virtue must depend on what is in your self-interest (understood in a non-moralized way).

*Substantive (non-moralized) egoism.* Which character traits are the virtues depends on which traits promote your self-interest, where this is understood independently of what is a virtue.

Or what is in your self-interest must depend on what is virtuous.

*Formal (moralized) egoism.* Whatever the virtues (independently understood) promote is in your self-interest.

Formal egoism, as the name suggests, is merely formally concerned with self-interest. The conception of self-interest it employs is fully 'moralized': whatever is a consequence of acting virtuously is good for you. The theory relies on our having some independent conception of what the virtues are, rather than using the link with self-interest to develop an account of which character traits are the virtues.[12]

What would a sensible knave think of this moralized conception of self-interest? Suppose that courage is a virtue. Courage leads you to face danger in the pursuit of a good cause. Suppose that you die or suffer terrible injuries as a consequence. Formal egoism implies that your death and excruciating pain are good for you, because you sustained them through virtuous action. This is very difficult to believe. Any sensible knave will pointedly suggest that a life of suffering and premature death is not going very well. Formal egoism can sustain the link between virtue and self-interest only by

---

[11] Russell 1969: 21.

[12] Foot distinguishes different senses of happiness, but thinks that happiness can be seen as conceptually inseparable from virtue, in such a way that you cannot truly be happy if you are wicked. She may have in mind formal egoism, but she might instead endorse reciprocally moralized egoism (2001: 94, 96).

employing a conception of self-interest that is very far removed from the common understanding of the term.[13]

Suppose instead we take a non-moralized conception of self-interest, a conception with which the sensible knave agrees. A good life is a long life of enjoyment. We can identify the virtues as the traits of character that promote self-interest in this sense. Which traits of character will turn out to be virtues? Courage is certainly not an obvious candidate, for it can easily lead to suffering and death. Low cunning, on the other hand, that leads you to cheat others without their finding out, might well count as a virtue.[14] If we use a fully non-moralized conception of self-interest from which to derive the virtues, it is quite possible that 'traditional' virtues of justice, courage, and so on will no longer be classed as such, and some traits of character that we normally think of as vices will count as virtues.

Formal egoism threatens to do violence to our understanding of self-interest; substantive egoism threatens to pick out the wrong traits of character as the virtues. The best way of understanding the connection between virtue and self-interest may be a third option. Neither self-interest nor the virtues can be understood independently of the other; instead we form a conception of them both together, as reciprocal concepts. I will call this third view: reciprocally moralized egoism.

*Reciprocally moralized egoism.* What is a virtue is constrained by which character traits for the most part promote self-interest, and at the same time what is in your self-interest is constrained by the virtues.

We have some idea initially of which character traits should count as virtues: justice, beneficence, courage, temperance, and so on. We have

---

[13] Hursthouse agrees with this criticism of formal egoism, and rejects that theory on the basis that the virtuous and vicious can both agree that death and suffering are bad for us. She emphasizes that an important component of the flourishing life is the 'smile factor', a non-moralized conception of enjoyment, which can be understood as worth having by a vicious person and an egoist as well as by the virtuous.

[14] In addition, there are many different attitudes towards risk that one can take: one can be averse to risk, or enjoy risk-taking. If different attitudes to risk are reasonable, different sets of character traits will count as the virtues. For example, making money through con tricks is a high-risk strategy with potential high returns, but if such risky behaviour can be reasonable, it could count as a virtue. (Lawrence 1995).

some idea of what counts as flourishing, including continued survival, pleasure, freedom from pain, and so on. The idea of reciprocally moralized egoism is that we modify our account both of the virtues and of self-interest, so that we finally end up with a conception of each so that the virtues contribute to self-interest.

Hursthouse seems to accept this kind of theory, with her reference to a 'Neurathian' procedure: instead of having an independently understood foundation of self-interest or of virtue, we have to build up our understanding of each at the same time.[15] She also says that morality cannot be judged 'from the outside' on the basis of neutral facts open to both the vicious and the virtuous. The virtuous and the vicious may disagree not just about evaluative facts (e.g., what counts as your interests) but also about human nature. It is not in fact a neutral fact what is a matter of 'bad luck' and what is 'only to be expected': the virtuous will think being betrayed a matter of luck, the vicious that it is to be expected.[16] Similarly, Foot writes:

Presumably the happy unjust man is supposed, as in Book II of the *Republic*, to be a very cunning liar and actor, combining complete injustice with the appearance of justice: he is prepared to treat others ruthlessly, but pretends that nothing is further from his mind. Philosophers often speak as if a man could thus hide himself even from those around him, but the supposition is doubtful, and in any case the price in vigilance would be colossal.[17]

Whereas the moral agent might agree that the price of injustice in vigilance outweighs the benefits, the egoist might well disagree, and it is not clear that there is a neutral means of settling this dispute.

This reciprocally moralized egoism is better than formal egoism or substantive egoism at securing the link between self-interest and the moral virtues. But it is worth emphasizing that the link between self-interest and the traditional moral virtues is indefensible without a considerably moralized conception of self-interest.[18]

---

[15] Hursthouse 1999: 165–6.     [16] Ibid. 184–5.     [17] Foot 1978: 129.

[18] It is perhaps also worth repeating that this is not the only version of virtue ethics and other kinds of theory do not endorse the same link between virtue and happiness. But those theories do not seem to be as well-placed as neo-Aristotelian virtue ethics to counter the threat to morality from egoism.

## 3.  The Virtues and Human Nature

A second distinctive feature of neo-Aristotelian virtue ethics is that the virtues are linked not only to flourishing but also to human nature.[19] Foot, for example, defends a theory, according to which virtue in humans is supposed to be one part of an account of goodness in nature generally.[20]

Foot emphasizes the similarities between assessment of humans and of animals and plants. She points out that we frequently assess plants and animals based on our view of the characteristics of their species.[21] These characteristics are expressed, according to Foot, by a distinctive logical form, the *Aristotelian categorical*.[22] For example, *oak trees are strong and resilient*. This does not, of course, mean that *all* oak trees are strong, nor need it mean that *most* of them are. Instead, it implies that *it is characteristic of oak trees to be strong*. The strength of oak trees is part of the function of the species, the way in which oak trees distinctively carry out their life and reproduction. So we can say that an oak tree that is not strong is thereby *defective*. It is not a good oak.

Foot believes that we can use the same types of consideration to assess human lives too. She argues that the virtues are essential to the characteristic goods of human life:

> the teaching and observing of rules of justice is as necessary a part of the life of human beings as hunting together in packs with a leader is a necessary part of the life of wolves, or dancing part of the life of the dancing bee. As Elizabeth Anscombe has said about one aspect of justice—the keeping of promises—a great deal of human good hangs on the possibility that one man can bind the will of another by getting him to promise to do something.[23]

Hursthouse too thinks that ethical evaluation is not different in kind to assessing plants and animals. We evaluate plants, she claims, in terms of their parts (leaves, stalk, roots, flowers, etc.) and their operations (growing, taking in water, photosynthesis, etc.) with regard to their characteristic purposes: notably survival (through the characteristic life-span of the species) and reproduction. The evaluation of animals is more complex, for its actions,

---

[19] Hursthouse 1999: 193.     [20] Foot 2001.

[21] '*Goodness* in plants and animals nests in an interlocking set of general concepts such as *species, life, death, reproduction* and *nourishment*' (Foot 2001: 36; see also 31–3).

[22] Foot 2001, who is following Thompson 1995.

[23] Foot 2002: 168; see also Foot 2001: 45–51.

emotions, and desires are also evaluated in terms of the survival and reproduction, but also with respect to the characteristic pleasure and pain of the species and the good functioning of the social group. For example, a dog that does not feel pain when it is injured is defective, as is a wolf that does not join in the hunt with other wolves. According to Hursthouse, it is an objective matter what the characteristic features of particular species of plants and animals are; it is determined by their biology, though, as with Foot, it is not straightforwardly a matter of statistical normality.[24]

Hursthouse thinks that we can use the same strategy to find the human good. In fact, she thinks that humans should be evaluated with respect to the same four ends as social animals:

(1) the survival of the individual animal through the characteristic life-span of the species;
(2) the continuance of the species, including the characteristic nurturing and teaching of the young;
(3) the characteristic pleasure and pain of the species; and
(4) the good functioning of the social group.

The virtues are dispositions for action and feeling that contribute to these ends. For example, courage is a disposition that leads one to defend oneself, one's offspring, members of one's social group, and worthwhile activities within the social group. Honesty, generosity, and loyalty help foster relationships that contribute to the good functioning of the social group, and to the characteristic enjoyment of individuals. Charity helps the continuance of species and the survival of other individuals, and also supports cohesion in the social group.[25]

One immediate difficulty is that it may be a matter of controversy what is the characteristic way in which humans function, either individually or

---

[24] There are a number of questions about this model in the assessment of animals. Different scientists, engaged in different kinds of assessment, may use different ends to make their evaluation. For example, scientists engaged in descriptive biology, evolutionary biology, or veterinary science may assess animals in different ways. Nor is it clear why we must evaluate animals as a member of a species, in terms of the characteristic features of that species, rather than evaluating them as a member of some other kind (Copp and Sobel 2004: 534).

[25] Hursthouse (1999: 209). Once again, it is hard to see why, even if goodness for us has something to do with our nature, it must have something to do with our being a member of a particular species. For example, a concern for all life, or all sentient life, is likely to contribute to the flourishing of other animals and plant species, rather than that of our own species. But it is hard to see why on those grounds it should not count as a virtue (Copp and Sobel 2004).

in a social group. Consider Foot's claim that it is characteristic of humans to keep their promises as a matter of justice. This is not obviously true. Many humans are not completely just; some hardly at all. It might be difficult to live a characteristically human life if no one ever kept any promises, but of course diligent promise-breaking is not the only alternative to justice. Perhaps keeping promises when it is in your interests to do so is characteristic of humans. It certainly might be more common than keeping them as a matter of justice.

Foot might reply that the truth of her claims does not depend on whether most or even many humans really are just. This is not a statistical claim about humans, it is another Aristotelian categorical.[26] It follows that we cannot tell whether justice is characteristic of humans by 'counting heads'. Nor can we appeal to evolutionary biology, and the functions that we have evolved to have.[27] But then how do we decide whether keeping promises from self-interest or keeping them from justice is characteristically human, and therefore a virtue? Foot does not explain, and it is not at all clear that there is a neutral method of settling this question, or that there could be one. The egoist can reasonably contend that to insist that justice is characteristic of humans is begging the question against him.

There is a deeper problem as well, which is that the significant differences between humans and other animals casts doubt on whether we can be evaluated in the same way. It is unclear that humans have species-characteristics in the way that other species do. Are there characteristic human pleasures? Even if animals have a 'characteristic way of going on' that can be spelled out in biological detail, do we? Hursthouse acknowledges this difference by claiming that, unlike other animals, we have just one characteristic way of going on: a rational way, any way that we can rightly see that we have reason to do.[28] If this is right, there must be a great difference between the evaluation of animals, which appeals to biological facts; and the evaluation of humans, which appeals to what we see ourselves as having reason to do. It is difficult to see why Hursthouse privileges the four ends that she picks out as important to the assessment of animals in

---

[26] Thompson 1995: 247–96; Foot 2001: 31–2.     [27] Foot 2001: 32.

[28] Hursthouse 1999: 228. In addition, initially it seemed that Rational Virtue Ethics would explain (moral) reasons for action in terms of what the virtuous person would characteristically do, but now it seems that what the virtuous person would characteristically do is to respond appropriately to reasons. So instead of explaining reasons in terms of the virtues, Hursthouse will have to give a separate account of reasons for action in order to give a full account of the virtues.

the evaluation of humans. It not at all clear why we should pay these ends any attention at all in evaluating human life.

In addition, recall that Hursthouse was hoping to show a connection between the virtues contributing to flourishing and their making the virtuous a good human. Presumably, the link is that it benefits us to achieve those four ends or, rather, the character traits that tend to be conducive to achieving the four ends also tend to be conducive to our flourishing. For example, it is in part because trust is important in our social life that the virtuous agent thinks that honesty is a component of a flourishing life. The connection is not, however, obvious. Suppose that the social group may function particularly well if I distribute my wealth to the poorest members of the group: there is a perfectly good sense in which it could be better for me to be uncharitable and hang on to my money. In addition, I may be able to flourish by enjoying pleasures that are not characteristic of my species, or avoiding pains that are characteristic of it. Suppose that I find that I do not suffer from pain in childbirth; this freedom from pain surely makes my life go better, even though it is certainly not characteristic of my species.

These examples suggest that I can improve my flourishing in ways that are not connected to the four ends, and I can contribute to the four ends without flourishing. To secure a connection between the virtues and self-interest, Hursthouse must appeal to a reciprocally moralized conception of self-interest. But, even with this in place, it is far from clear that the character traits that will contribute to my (moralized) self-interest will also contribute to my achieving the four ends and vice versa. Of course, achieving some of those ends is likely to benefit me, but it is very likely that there will be tension between achieving the two 'other-regarding ends' (the survival of my species and the good functioning of my social group) and my own self-interest, even when my conception of my self-interest is moralized. So at best there is a very loose connection between the character traits that encourage flourishing and the traits that make their possessor a 'good human' according to Hursthouse's methods of evaluation.

## 4. Virtue Egoism

Virtue egoism begins with a fully non-moral notion of flourishing that includes survival, health, the achievement of your goals, the enjoyment of goods such as money and prestige, skill in one's chosen activities and success at them, and so on. From this conception of non-moralized flourishing, virtue egoism derives a conception of the 'egoist virtues'.

*Egoist virtues.* The egoist virtues are the traits of character that (for the most part) promote non-moralized flourishing better than any other character traits.

The virtue egoist can give a definition of what you have reason to do that parallels the previous account of the link between virtue and right action.

*Rational virtue egoism.* Everyone has reason to do what the person with the egoist virtues would characteristically do in the situation, and avoid doing what she would characteristically refrain from doing in the circumstance, precisely because this is what the person with the egoist virtues would do (or for the reasons why this is what the person with the egoist virtues agent would do). There are no other reasons for action.[29]

When we understand flourishing in a non-moralized way, the traditional virtues divide fairly naturally into self-regarding virtues, which primarily benefit the agent, and other-regarding virtues, which primarily benefit others. If you are temperate, for example, you do not overindulge in food, drink, or other sensual pleasures; this self-control saves you from the illnesses and embarrassments that result from overindulgence. Of course, other people may well benefit too: they won't have to nurse you through your sickness, or put up with your bad temper when you have indigestion. But the primary beneficiary of temperance is you. By contrast, if you are just, you give to other people what you owe them, even at considerable cost to yourself. If you are benevolent, you will give money, time, and other assistance to people who are in need. Of course, you may benefit from being benevolent and just. You may feel pleased with yourself for acting in a way you know to be right. You may gain a good reputation,

---

[29] This definition of rational virtue egoism has a similar problem to that affecting Hursthouse's definition of right action. Suppose that in your circumstances you could gain significantly by being untruthful. The person with the egoist virtues would characteristically lie in your situation. But you are very bad at lying, and if you tried to lie you would get found out and lose out badly. You would be best advised not to lie, even though it is what he would do himself in the circumstances. You might instead do what the virtue egoist would advise you to do. But it is problematic, because the virtue egoist will no doubt advise you on the basis of whatever is in his interests, rather than your own. Instead, we might appeal to the following connection: what you have reason to do is what you would do if you had the virtues that would promote your own non-moral flourishing, assuming that your other abilities are fixed. This implies that, if you are very poor at lying and cannot improve at it, you will rarely have reason to lie.

and find yourself with more friends. You can get genuine benefits from other-regarding virtues. But the primary beneficiary of these virtues is not you.

It is possible that in different circumstances and for different agents, different character traits will count as the egoist virtues. But it is likely that there will be some core egoist virtues that parallel the traditional core moral virtues. Here I briefly sketch the form that these egoist virtues are most likely to take.

### Temperance

Temperance is the virtue of moderation in one's appetites for food, drink, and sex. The egoist will be happy to indulge his appetites, but with an eye for his future interests. He will make sure that he does not damage his health or his ability to enjoy these pleasures in the future. Since temperance is a self-regarding virtue, it will take more or less the same form in the morally virtuous and in the egoist.[30]

### Egoist Courage

Courage is the virtue of facing up to fear and to danger. It is a matter of taking appropriate risks in a good cause. Courage may mean risking your life, perhaps even losing your life, so courage understood in the traditional sense is unlikely to be an egoist virtue.

Nevertheless, courage is one of the so-called 'executive virtues' that tend to be useful whatever your plans. It can be worth having whatever your ends are; even if you are determined to promote your own interests, you may need courage to take a risk that could be disastrous for you but might bring you a great reward. So an egoist version of courage, the disposition to face danger for the sake of your own interests, is likely to be one of the egoist virtues. The distinctive feature of egoist courage is the circumstances in which dangers are worth facing. Someone with the virtue of moral courage will face danger when either his own or others' interests are at

[30] The moral agent who has the moral virtue of temperance may modulate his appetites for the sake of the interests of others as well as himself; for example, if it is particularly important to others though not to himself that he is sober, he will make sure that he is. The egoist who has the egoist virtue of temperance will only control his appetites for his own sake. So there may be some differences between temperance in the moral agent and the egoist.

stake, when it is just to do so, and so on. Someone with the egoist virtue of courage will do so only to protect his own (non-moralized) interests.[31]

A very nice example of egoist courage in action is the career of Harry Flashman. Flashman describes himself as cowardly, and he is constantly shirking combat (whilst being happy to allow others to take his place and to benefit from their self-sacrifice), but in fact he is prepared to face danger if he sees that doing so gives him the best chance of survival. Moreover, he is keen on conspicuous displays of aggression when he calculates that the real danger is low. Through this, and a considerable amount of luck, he acquires a reputation for genuine bravery and is awarded countless medals and honours.

When someone else's interests are at stake, the moral agent will be prepared to face danger, and both the coward and the egoist will not. But the egoist and the coward act for different reasons. Cowards are simply not willing to face their fear. They may be overcome by terror, or they may cunningly calculate how to avoid danger. But in either case they avoid danger even when they have (and they know that they have) good reason to take a stand. The egoist is not necessarily overcome by terror; he may be prepared to face danger when the benefits to himself are sufficiently great. He simply refuses to do so for the sake of others.[32] As Flashman says: 'Why other, unnamed lives, or the East India Company's dividend, or the credit of Lord Aberdeen, or the honour of British arms, should be held *by me* to be of greater consequence than my own shrinking skin, I've always been at a loss to understand.'[33] He lacks moral courage but he is not a coward; he exemplifies the egoist virtue instead.

## Egoist Beneficence

Beneficence is the virtue of giving to others what they need. It is obviously other-regarding: you give to someone because of their needs not because of your own (non-moralized) interests. Beneficence involves considerable

---

[31] 'Someone who does not see the relief of others' suffering as a good worth pursuing, something it is worth facing danger to achieve, lacks the virtue of courage (though without, thereby, being cowardly)' (Hursthouse, 1999: 154). The person she describes lacks the moral version of courage, but may have the egoist version instead.

[32] Assuming that the effects of reputation are not significant enough to make this worth his while.

[33] Fraser 2006: 190.

sensitivity to others in terms of recognizing when they need help (which even they themselves may not appreciate) and understanding of suitable ways to offer help; it also involves a willingness actually to give help, even at some cost to yourself.

The egoist is of course not responsive to the interests of others for their own sake. But, on the other hand, she is interested in getting other people to help her and in having a good reputation. She is willing to help others when those things are at stake. The egoist virtue of beneficence is a disposition to help when help will be noticed and reciprocated and will not be too costly. It is very different from the moral virtue of beneficence, to help when help is needed. The egoist will be concerned about the appearance of good will. She will be interested in the opportunity for making emotional public speeches about the importance of charity, rather than anonymous donations to the needy. She will be prepared to give some real help to others (for the sake of her reputation and in the expectation that they will reciprocate) and she may even find some enjoyment in this assistance. But, for the most part, her real concern is not the welfare of others, but the effect on herself.[34]

### Egoist Justice

Justice is the virtue of giving to others what you owe to them. Justice may require you to give up substantial goods if you have promised to do so, or if not doing so would be unfair. Justice as it is traditionally conceived will obviously not be an egoist virtue.

Nevertheless, the egoist is once again likely to have concerns about reciprocity and reputation. If you respect other people's property, it is more likely that your own property will be respected in return; if you keep your promises and honour your contracts, it is more likely that promises made to you will be kept and so on. If others know that you break contracts and fail to live up to your promises, they may prefer not to cooperate with you at all. If you are known as honest and reliable, others will be happy

---

[34] It is of course possible that caring for others for their own sake and doing things for them for their sake will be the traits of character that most promote one's self-interest (in a non-moralized sense). But since it is likely that these traits will lead you to benefit others at a cost to yourself, it will be rare for this sort of unselfish concern for others to be the trait that most promotes your self-interest understood in the egoist's sense. It is more likely that the egoist virtue of beneficence will at most include a concern for others for their own sake that you act on only when helping them is in your (long-term) self-interest, and this is very different from the moral virtue of beneficence.

to rely on you. Every time you break a promise or act in ways that others think are unjust, you run the risk of damaging your reputation.

Someone with the egoist virtue of justice will be sensitive to what other people think is fair and honest, the probability that non-compliance will be noticed, and the effect of it on her reputation. The egoist will be concerned about the appearance of justice, that is, about doing what others think is just, rather than thinking about what she really owes to others; and about appearing to live up to these standards, rather than actually doing so; whereas the moral agent with the moral virtue of justice will try to do what really is just.

## Naturalism

Can a virtue egoist endorse the link between the virtues and the 'naturalistic' conception of what is good for man? We have already seen that it was difficult, given Foot's conception of their connection, to prove that either the moral virtues or the egoist virtues were those genuinely characteristic of humans. But it is certainly open to an egoist to argue that it is egoist justice (keeping promises out of self-interest, for example) not the moral virtue, which is distinctive of human society.

There are obvious links between the egoist virtues and the two 'individualistic' ends that Hursthouse identifies: survival and characteristic pleasures. Anything that contributes to my survival and my pleasure should also contribute to my flourishing.[35] It is less likely that the egoist virtues also contribute to the two 'social ends': the survival of the species and the good functioning of the social group.

A virtue egoist who wanted to endorse naturalism might well question whether those particular ends had the importance claimed for them.[36] Alternatively, she could argue that we should interpret these ends in egoist terms. Part of what it is to be a good human is to be a good member of the social group, contributing to the good functioning of the group. But what is it for a human group to function characteristically well? Hursthouse assumes that the social group functions well when members of the group are altruistic: honest, loyal, and benevolent. Foot assumes that a human

---

[35] Though other things may do so too: such as enjoying pleasures that are not characteristic of my species.

[36] Hursthouse acknowledges that humans may not adequately be able to flourish well themselves, as well as being good members of the social group (Hursthouse 1999: 250–65).

group functions well when members of that group are just. But the egoist will claim that humans characteristically are egoists who are ultimately
interested only in their own welfare, but who are prepared to take the interests of others into account for strategic reasons, for the sake of reciprocity,
and reputation. A well-functioning social group might be characterized by
reciprocity, but not by genuine benevolence or justice. In favourable conditions, it is likely that a social group of people with the egoist virtues could
survive and function reasonably well. Such a group might be less stable than
one consisting of the morally virtuous, but this would depend on a number
of contingent factors, such as the extent to which people notice and object to
'free-riding'. People with the egoist virtues are unlikely publicly to endorse
that view as their own, for it is usually better for an egoist that no one knows
what she is like. But this secrecy need not undermine the functioning of
their society. Up to a point, a virtue egoist can agree with Hursthouse
that the four ends she picks out, when understood in the right way, are
important; but insist in contrast to Hursthouse that the egoist virtues, as well
as contributing to non-moralized flourishing, also contribute to those ends.

What kind of dispute is this? Hursthouse and Foot have suggested that
claims about human nature and what it is for a human society to function
well is an empirical question. If this is right, then the disagreement between
them and virtue egoists is ultimately empirical. But, as we have already
seen, it is not as clear that these are genuinely empirical questions, or
at least questions that we could settle by empirical investigation. There
are two obvious empirical methods of determining what is characteristic
for humans, either individually or in a society. The first is to discover
what is statistically average for humans, and there are well-understood
methods of statistical sampling and analysis to discover this. But this is not
what Hursthouse and Foot mean by what is 'characteristic' for humans: it
might turn out that most people had the egoist virtues rather than their
moral counterparts, but they would not regard that as evidence that it is
characteristic of humans to have the egoist virtues. The second method is
to turn to evolutionary biology, and human functioning considered within
that scientific discipline. But Foot is quite explicit that this is not what she
means by the characteristic functioning of humans.[37] It is not clear that

---

[37] Foot 2001: 32. Hursthouse too suggests (1999: 228) that the evaluation of humans will not be
primarily based on biology.

there is an alternative empirical method to settle these questions, and so it is tempting to think that the dispute is not an empirical disagreement about what humans really are like, but a normative disagreement about what they should be like. In any case, whether or not we call these questions empirical, there is no obvious method of empirical investigation that we can use to settle them, and it is not at all clear that the dispute could be settled by *any* means, empirical or otherwise, to the satisfaction of both sides.

## 5.  Virtue Ethics and Virtue Egoism

According to rational neo-Aristotelian virtue ethics: *Rational virtue ethics*: everyone has reason to do what the virtuous agent would characteristically do in the circumstances, and avoid doing what the virtuous agent would characteristically refrain from doing in the circumstances, precisely because this is what the virtuous agent would do (or for the reasons why this is what the virtuous agent would do).

And the virtues are characterized as follows.

*Reciprocally moralized egoism.* What is a virtue is constrained by which character traits for the most part promote self-interest, and at the same time what is in your self-interest is constrained by the virtues.

Although this leaves open the possibility that some surprising traits of character might turn out to be virtues (depending on what turns out to contribute to flourishing), we expect the traditional moral virtues, including justice, beneficence, and courage to be among them.

According to rational virtue egoism: *Rational virtue egoism*: everyone has reason to do what the person with the egoist virtues would characteristically do in the circumstances, and avoid doing what she would characteristically refrain from doing in the circumstances, precisely because this is what the person with the egoist virtues would do (or for the reasons why this is what the person with the egoist virtues agent would do). There are no other reasons for action.

Where the egoist virtues are characterized as follows.

*Egoist virtues.* The 'egoist virtues' are the traits of character that (for the most part) promote non-moralized flourishing better than any other character traits.

Given that different traits of character may promote self-interest in different circumstances, a range of qualities might count as egoist virtues. But it is likely that there will be some core egoist virtues, including egoist justice, egoist courage, and egoist beneficence.

In some circumstances, the morally virtuous agent and the virtue egoist will do the same: both will keep their promises and help the needy when other people are watching. It is likely that many societies would generate social sanctions against acting solely in your own non-moralized interests. With these social sanctions in place, it may be rare for a virtuous egoist to act wrongly. But, of course, there will be limits to these sanctions: when they would benefit greatly by breaking a promise, without too much damage to their reputation, the virtue egoist will break his promise, the morally virtuous agent will not.

But, even if the egoist helps people and keeps his promises he may not act in the ways characteristic of the virtuous agent. On one interpretation, all that is needed to act in that way is to perform the same outward action as the virtuous agent. In that sense, virtue egoists may well act in ways characteristic of the morally virtuous. But, on another interpretation, more is required: the virtuous agent does not simply do the right act; she does the right act for the right reason.[38] The virtuous agent keeps her promises and helps others because she owes it to them and because they need help. By contrast, the egoist does so because he wants to avoid sanctions or obtain benefits for himself and he may well regret that he has no opportunity to break his promise; the moral agent will be glad to keep her word. Even when an egoist does the same outward action as the just and beneficent agent, he is responding to different features of the situation, with different attitudes and emotions, so he does not act in the ways characteristic of the virtuous.

In many ways virtue ethics and virtue egoism are remarkably similar theories. According to both, reasons for action depend on the virtues.[39] Both link the virtues with flourishing. They disagree, however, about what it is to flourish, and therefore about which character traits are the virtues.

The structure of the disagreement between virtue ethics and virtue egoism is slightly different from that of the rational utilitarian★ and standard

---

[38] Hursthouse (1999: 121–60).

[39] Though virtue ethics, but not virtue egoism, leaves it open that there are reasons of other kinds as well.

egoist. Rational utilitarianism★ and standard egoism agreed on a source of reasons (happiness) and the kind of reasons (reasons to maximize) but disagreed on whether any of the reasons were other-regarding. Virtue ethics and virtue egoism agree on a source of reasons only in the sense that they call it by the same name: flourishing. They have different accounts of what it is to flourish. Nevertheless, when we consider conflicts between the characterizations of particular virtues, the parallel is stronger. For example, it is quite plausible that the difference between the moral virtue of courage and the egoist virtue is that according to the moral version you have reason to stand up to danger for the sake of the non-moralized interests (the survival, health, and so on) of all; according to virtue egoism you have reason to face danger for the sake only of your own non-moralized interests. Similarly, the moral virtue of beneficence requires you to help others who are in need; the egoist version requires you only to attend to your own needs. At the level of individual virtues, the moral theory includes other-regarding reasons where the egoist theory includes only self-regarding reasons; so the conflict between virtue ethics and virtue egoism may be quite similar to that between rational utilitarianism★ and egoism after all.[40]

## 6. Conclusion

The purpose of Part I of this book is to explore in more detail the egoist's challenge to the practical authority of morality. In the last few chapters, I have sketched three theories of egoism and some variations on them. Each of the three parallels a major moral theory, and each is very different

---

[40] The most obvious exception to this is the virtue of justice, of giving to others what you owe to them. It is not obvious whether this can be characterized in terms of a source of reasons that generates other-regarding reasons, with egoist justice a parallel virtue that includes only self-regarding reasons from the same source. It might be described as follows: the just agent recognizes other-regarding reasons to give to anyone what she owes to them; the egoist recognizes only self-regarding reasons to give to herself what she owes herself. But this is not very helpful unless we have an account of what we owe others as a matter of justice. Hursthouse gives only a very brief discussion (1999: 5–7) of the virtue of justice, and does not attempt to characterize what we do owe to others in this regard, so it is not possible to say whether, on her account, justice fits the schema. A further difference between moral and egoist virtue plays a role in the argument of Part III: I suggest that it is part of moral virtue (but not egoist virtue) that you should be an authority on what to do: you should be able to give good advice on the basis of your own judgement.

from the others. Standard egoism is based on the promotion of happiness, and is closely connected to utilitarianism. Kantian egoism is based on a requirement to treat yourself as an end, not as a mere means, and has strong similarities with the moral law. Virtue egoism claims that you have reason to act as the virtuous egoist would act—that is, to act on the virtues that would overall promote your flourishing in a non-moralized sense.

It is clear from reflection on these three that egoism can take a great variety of forms. It can, but need not, have anything to do with happiness. It may, but may not, include reasons to promote your own good; egoist reasons may be of a completely different type, reasons to respect yourself, or reasons to act in the way that people with certain virtues would act.

Furthermore, these three theories are only a handful of the many that are possible. It is plausible that one could formulate an egoist shadow to any moral theory, taking the view of one's interests or of the good that the moral theory endorses, and the type of reasons relating to that good, and devising a theory claiming that all reasons are reasons of that kind relating to your own good or your own interests.[41] These egoist theories differ from the parallel moral theory: they include only self-regarding reasons for action, whereas the moral theory includes impartial or other-regarding reasons (based on the interests or good of all).[42] Most of us accept that morality is authoritative and reject all of these egoist theories. But we would like to be able to respond to egoists of any type with an argument that shows that they too must recognize the authority of morality. In the remainder of the book, I investigate what kind of argument against egoism is available to us.

---

[41] And of course there will be many possible egoist theories that do not parallel any extant moral theory.

[42] In addition, egoist theories claim that these reasons, based on your own good, are the only reasons for action. Several of the moral theories considered here, by contrast, do not claim that moral reasons are the only reasons for action: there may be aesthetic reasons, reasons based on the environment (which are separate from reasons based on human interests), and so on. The egoist theory does not allow parallels to these extra reasons.

II

Problems for Morality

# 5

# Ambitious Vindication

## 1. Ambitious Vindications of Common-Sense Morality

Morality presents itself to us as having a certain kind of practical authority, which is expressed by the 'Moral Authority' thesis.

*Moral authority*. Everyone has reason to do what is morally right and reason not to do what is morally wrong. The grounds of these reasons are either the action's moral rightness (or wrongness) or the features that ground the action's moral rightness (or wrongness).

Many people think that the thesis is true, but egoists like Hume's sensible knave deny that morality has any practical authority whatsoever.

*Rational egoism*. Everyone has reason to do what is in her own interests, and no other reasons for action. The grounds of this reason are the interests of the agent.

We have seen that egoism can take a wide variety of forms. Egoists may have reason to maximize their happiness. They may have reason to do what a virtuous egoist would do. They may have reason to respect their own rational nature. Every moral theory probably has its own egoist shadow, each with a different view of self-interest and a different conception of reasons for action. Egoism is protean, adaptable. Since it can take so many forms, it is a difficult opponent. Arguments against one type of egoism may simply not apply to another version of the theory.

Many of us who for the most part accept the authority of morality find ourselves wondering whether we really do have reason not to profit from wrongdoing. Ray Monk's biography makes it clear that Wittgenstein was not the kind of person who regularly told lies; in fact, he seems to have had an unusually strong devotion to the truth. But even he questioned whether he really had reason not to lie for his own benefit. Scepticism about the authority of morality is widespread, and affects not merely genuine egoists but from time to time almost all of us. Yet it is extremely important whether morality does have practical authority. We are confronted with moral questions all the time. Unlike other kinds of philosophical controversy, they are not matters that you can leave behind in your study whilst you distract yourself with backgammon.

Given that the Moral Authority thesis is so controversial, and pursuing one's own interests so tempting, it would be nice to have an argument that showed that egoism was false. We would like to be able to vindicate the authority of morality both to moral agents like ourselves and to egoists most of all. Of course, common-sense morality has many other opponents and challengers: nihilists, immoralists, and other kinds of amoralist, just for starters. Even if we could dispatch the egoist, we would not have fully vindicated morality; we would have to answer all of these critics. But we would have made some progress in its defence, against an opponent whose views have more than a little appeal.

We can attempt to give a more or less ambitious vindication of the authority of morality against the challenge of egoism.

*Ambitious vindication.* A valid argument based on premises that an egoist would accept that egoism is false.

How can an argument begin with premises that an egoist accepts and end up concluding that egoism is false? It would have to show that egoism fails to have the qualities essential to a theory of practical reason, or that it conflicts with some other claim that egoists already accept. For example, an argument showing that egoism was internally inconsistent should persuade everyone to reject egoism, because even egoists agree that an inconsistent theory of practical reason is unacceptable. Of course, it may not persuade anyone actually to reject egoism: egoists may be stubborn and refuse to listen to argument. But an ambitious vindication *should* persuade even an egoist that egoism is false.

An ambitious vindication of morality is what Glaucon asked Socrates to produce in the *Republic*; it is what Kant tried to provide and Sidgwick struggled to find. It is the Holy Grail of moral philosophy. Many have searched for the Grail, but few have met with any success. Such an argument is obviously not going to be easy to provide but many moral philosophers have made the attempt. I will not be able to address all of their arguments here, but I will look at some of the most prominent recent examples. Some criticisms of these arguments are already well known and it is widely accepted that they do not succeed, but I hope to bring out some general reasons why similar arguments will almost certainly fail too.

The first strategy I will consider is an argument that egoist reasons for action are illegitimate, or at least that no adequate theory of practical reason can include only egoist reasons. Nagel, Korsgaard, and Allison all offer different versions of this argument. Nagel claims that an egoist is guilty of 'practical solipsism' (Sect. 2); Korsgaard that egoist reasons are improperly 'private' (Sect. 3), and Allison, working within a Kantian framework, tries to show that only someone who acts for moral reasons can be autonomous (Sect. 4). The second strategy is to attack the metaphysical presuppositions of the theory. Parfit argues that egoism is inconsistent with the most plausible metaphysics of the self. I discuss his argument in Section 5. In Section 6, I assess the implications of these failures.

## 2. Nagel on Practical Solipsism

Nagel draws a distinction between two kinds of reason for action that has become well known.[1] Agent-relative reasons give different agents different aims, agent-neutral reasons give different agents the same aim.[2] According to egoism, all reasons for action are based on the agent's own interests. For example, according to standard egoism, I have reason to maximize my happiness and you yours. These are different aims. Kantian egoism states that each of us has reason only to treat ourselves as an end. Virtue egoism implies that each of us has reason only to promote our own (non-moralized) flourishing. Egoist reasons are all agent-relative.[3]

---

[1] Nagel 1978. He uses the terms 'subjective' for 'agent-relative' and 'objective' for 'agent-neutral'.

[2] More precisely, a reason is agent-relative if and only if it is specified by a principle which refers ineliminably to the agent for whom it is a reason (Nagel 1978: 90); for example, egoist reasons are agent-relative because the specification of the reason ineliminably refers to the agent herself (each agent has reason to promote her own happiness). Agent-neutral reasons do not refer ineliminably to the agent. For example, hedonic utilitarian reasons are agent-neutral because they do not refer to the agent herself; rather, any agent has reasons to promote anyone's happiness. See also McNaughton and Rawling 1993; McNaughton and Rawling 1995; Skorupski 1995.

[3] According to Moorean egoism, the reasons to maximize happiness are agent-neutral: everyone has the same aim: to maximize my own happiness. We can restate the problem for Moorean egoism

Most moral theories include at least some agent-neutral reasons. Accord-ing to rational utilitarianism★, each of us has reason to promote the general happiness. In that regard, we should have the same aim. Of course, what we can do towards this aim depends on our own capacities and circumstances (in this sense all reasons are relativized to each person), but the crucial point is that we all should, as far as we can, try to make people happy.

By contrast, all egoist theories of practical reason involve only agent-relative reasons. If it is illegitimate for a theory of practical reason to include only agent-relative reasons, then every version of egoism must be false.

In *The Possibility of Altruism* Nagel actually defends a much stronger claim. He argues that agent-relative reasons are not genuine practical reasons at all. It follows that any theory of practical reason that includes any basic agent-relative reasons (that are not derived from agent-neutral reasons) cannot be correct. This is a rather surprising conclusion, since many moral theories include agent-relative reasons for action as well as agent-neutral reasons. Rational utilitarianism★ of course includes only agent-neutral reasons. But any 'dual source' or multiple-source theory that includes reasons to help others for their own sake as well as special reasons to look after oneself (that are not derived from reasons to promote the interests of anyone) will include both kinds of reason. Virtue ethics includes the requirement to promote your own (moralized) flourishing, which certainly seems to be an agent-relative reason for action. Kant's moral law is usually interpreted as including 'side constraints'—for example, a requirement to refrain from lying to other people, whatever the consequences.[4] Side-constraints are agent-relative reasons for action of a different type, constraints or restrictions that require the agent not to perform a specific type of action in any circumstances.[5] If agent-relative reasons are not genuine reasons for action, egoism will have to be rejected, but so will many moral theories.

Nagel argues that genuine reasons for action must be able to explain and to justify action. Egoist reasons—'it would make me happy'—can obvi-ously explain action. Some explanations of action are not justifications—for

in these terms: it is difficult to see why everyone should have agent-neutral reasons to maximize my happiness when no one else's happiness grounds any reasons at all. According to the version of egoism in which we are interested, there are no agent-neutral reasons, only agent-relative reasons.

[4] Though this has in fact been denied; for example, Cummiskey (1996). Cummiskey interprets the moral law as including agent-neutral other-regarding reasons, but no side-constraints.

[5] Scheffler 1994: 2–5, 80–114.

example, a reason based on a false belief of mine may explain but not justify what I did: it would not be a genuine reason to act as I did. But egoist reasons need not be based on false beliefs, or mistakes in reasoning. Nagel claims, however, that only agent-neutral reasons for action can justify actions adequately.

A solipsist does not believe that anyone else exists. A practical solipsist has a somewhat similar belief that manifests itself in action; he does not believe that others exist in the same way that he himself does, in the sense that he does not accept that reasons which apply to them also apply to him, and he is not motivated by those reasons as he would be by reasons that apply to him.[6] Nagel illustrates this by describing the 'person-neutral' perspective—that is, the perspective from which one does not know which person one is. As an egoist, I am motivated to perform action A because action A will maximize my interests. Considered from the person-neutral perspective, all I know is that action A will maximize Alison's interests. But since I do not know that I am Alison—it is precisely that information that is not available in the person-neutral standpoint—I am not motivated to perform it. According to Nagel, the practical solipsist is, in a sense, 'dissociated' even from her own reasons for action because she does not recognize them as reasons and is not motivated by them from the person-neutral perspective, whereas a genuine justification for an action must be accessible (and must motivate) from the person-neutral perspective.[7] Since egoist reasons—and agent-relative reasons quite generally—cannot move anyone from that perspective, they cannot justify action and they therefore cannot be genuine reasons for action.[8]

As we have seen, this argument, if correct, would rule out many moral theories. It is worth noting, too that the argument does not secure the authority of morality: some non-moral theory that included only agent-neutral reasons might be the correct theory of practical reason. But, the most important point is that if the argument is sound egoism must be false. Is it sound?

---

[6] Nagel 1978: 107, 113–15.

[7] Nagel puts the point in terms of motivation, that the practical solipsist is dissociated because he is not motivated by reasons from the person-neutral perspective. But the practical solipsist does not unfortunately happen to lack the motivation to act for reasons that he acknowledges, but rather he fails to recognize these reasons as binding on him at all.

[8] Sturgeon 1974: 374–402; Darwall 1983: 117–29; Nagel 1986: 167.

Nagel is right that it is an attractive feature of a theory of practical reason, and possibly a requirement of any such theory, that a rational agent should be able to justify his conduct to any other rational agent.[9] It follows that reasons must be understandable by other rational agents and exchangeable with them. Reasons must, in a sense, be universal.

Egoism may seem to make an arbitrary distinction between my interests and those of anyone else. It seems to be committed to my interests, which give me reasons to act, being entirely unlike yours, which do not. This would be very implausible. But in fact there need be no difference between my interests and yours: according to egoism, each person's interests grounds reasons to act for her, but for no one else. There is no normative difference between the kinds of reasons generated by my interests and by yours. Egoism implies that I have reasons relating to my interests but not yours; you have reasons relating to your interests but not mine: my interests are of exactly the same normative significance as yours.[10] Egoist reasons are universal in the relevant sense.

Nagel claims, very plausibly, that a reason for action must be able to justify that action. But he understands what it is to justify an action in an unusual way. He thinks that not only must others be able to follow my reasoning and see that I have made no factual or inferential mistakes, not only must they be able to see that I am acting for good reasons, but they must also recognize that *they themselves* have a reason to promote my aim.[11] For example, if I have a genuine reason to add to my collection of interesting paperclips, everyone must have a reason to promote my expanding my collection. Perhaps they have reason to encourage me in my quest for interesting paperclips, perhaps to hunt for such things themselves on my behalf. I am justified in adding to my collection only if everyone else is justified in assisting me.

---

[9] The argument presented here has been much criticized, and is no longer endorsed by Nagel (see Nagel 1986: 159), but it is a very important attempt to argue against egoism. For criticisms of Nagel, see Sturgeon 1974; Darwall 1983: chap. 10.

[10] Egoism might seem to distinguish arbitrarily my interests and yours as values: my own interests contribute to the value of the world—it is good if I do well—but yours do not—it is a matter of indifference if you do well. But egoists typically make no claims at all about the value of the world. Egoism is a thesis about reasons for action, not about value. An egoist who wanted to make a claim about value could regard everyone's interests as valuable, but only in the sense that they are a source of (agent-relative) reasons for action, not in the sense that they contribute to the value of the world.

[11] Nagel 1978.

Egoist reasons cannot justify action in this way, but this sense of justification is plainly not essential to the concept of a reason. It is obviously one thing for me to have a reason to add to my paperclip collection, and quite another for others to have a reason to help me. Other people have no reason to care about my collection, even though I do. Practical reasons can be genuine though they do not justify action in this stronger sense of justification.

From the 'person-neutral' standpoint, egoists can recognize reasons only under descriptions such as 'Alison's reasons for action', not under the kind of description—'my reasons for action'—by which they are motivated to act. So they are not motivated by their judgements about reasons made from the person-neutral standpoint, and as a consequence they are guilty of 'practical solipsism'. This certainly sounds bad. But must an egoist really regard this as a problem? The question can be put in another way: is the person-neutral standpoint really so important? From that standpoint, the egoist cannot recognize any reasons for action. But why should reasons be identifiable from that perspective? If anything, the standpoint seems to abstract from exactly the sort of features that are relevant to practical reasons. Who you are and where you are situated are obviously relevant to what you have reason to do. The person-neutral standpoint makes this information unavailable. An egoist may well respond that there is nothing wrong with failing to be motivated by practical reasons when they are considered from the person-neutral standpoint. The problem is with the standpoint itself.

Nagel's argument can be summarized as follows:

(1) Any practical reason must be able to justify action.
(2) Egoist reasons (more generally, agent-relative reasons) cannot justify action.
(3) Therefore, egoist reasons (and all other agent-relative reasons) are illegitimate.

But (1) is plausible only on a weak reading of 'justification'. It is perhaps a condition on reasons for action that they can be exchangeable with other rational agents, who can thereby appreciate that you had good grounds for your action. But agent-relative reasons can justify action in this way, so (2) is false. They cannot justify action in a stronger sense: other agents will not necessarily be motivated to act by them. But on the stronger reading of justification (1) is false, or at best begs the question against egoism. In other words, Nagel's argument either fails to establish its conclusion, or it begs the question. Either way, it is clearly not an ambitious vindication of morality.

## 3. Korsgaard's Private Language Argument

In *The Sources of Normativity* Korsgaard gives a different argument for a similar conclusion to Nagel.[12] Making an analogy with Wittgenstein's private language argument, she argues that only 'public' reasons are acceptable. Korsgaard sets up the analogy by dividing reasons for action into private and public reasons. Private reasons are reasons that have normative force for the agent alone. Public reasons are shared, in the sense that they have normative force for everyone. In other words, private reasons are agent-relative reasons, and public reasons are agent-neutral.[13]

Korsgaard argues that

> if these reasons really were essentially private, it would be impossible to exchange or to share them. So their privacy must be incidental or ephemeral: they must be inherently shareable . . . what enables us and forces us to share our reasons is, in a deep sense, our *social nature*.[14]

She claims that it is essential to a consideration counting as a reason at all that it is possible to exchange and share that consideration with other agents. As a consequence, all reasons must be public in the sense that the reason *can* have normative force for everyone. Reasons can be private to an agent only in the sense that no one except for the agent is affected by the

---

[12] Korsgaard 1996b: 132ff. Korsgaard defends Kant's moral theory in an extended argument composed of several parts. The first part of her argument centres on the claim that to act for a reason requires an agent to value humanity. I will not focus on this section of the argument, for, as she admits, it only shows that an agent must value his own humanity. Nevertheless, she believes that she can defend the moral law against rival theories of practical reason, and she attempts to do so in the later sections of the work. Korsgaard's argument is critically discussed by Nagel and Geuss in Korsgaard 1996b; Skorupski 1998; Gibbard 1999; and Kerstein 2001, who raise objections to the first part of the argument, as well as to its later sections.

[13] Korsgaard 1996b: 133. Since Korsgaard intends to defend the moral law which includes agent-relative side-constraints, she must intend 'private' reasons to include only self-regarding agent-relative reasons. Public reasons must include both agent-neutral reasons and agent-relative side-constraints.

[14] Korsgaard 1996b: 135.

reason—for example, because no one except the agent is placed so that he can act on the reason. Any genuinely private reason, that had force for the agent alone, could not be a real reason.

The connection between this argument and the private language argument is not at all clear. A private language can only be used by one person and cannot be communicated to others. It is plain that, even if we were to accept Wittgenstein's controversial argument that such a language is impossible, we would not be able directly to draw any conclusions about whether egoism is correct. Egoist theories of reasons for action do not depend on the possibility of a private language.[15] Egoist reasons for action are not incommunicable; indeed, it is quite conceivable that there could be a society of egoists, all of whom know that each is an egoist, who tell each other what they are doing and why. If egoists are in situations in which it is in their interests to conceal that they are egoists they may well not tell other people their reasons for action, but it does not follow that their reasons are not communicable. It is still possible for them to share their reasons for action with others. In fact, an egoist *would* communicate his egoist reasons for action if it were in his interests to do so.

The private language argument attempts to show the impossibility of a language in which the meanings are determined by a single person and the standard of correctness of applying a term depends solely on that agent's judgement. The standard of correctness for using a term cannot be like this; it must at least be possible for others to judge whether or not the agent has used the term correctly. But, egoists can recognize when someone has acted, in their terms, for good reasons—for example, a standard egoist will consider that someone has acted for good reasons when she has maximized her happiness. It may be perfectly open and public when this is the case. It is not true that in acting for egoist reasons 'whatever is going to seem right to me is right'.[16]

---

[15] As Nagel succinctly remarks: 'The invocation of Wittgenstein doesn't help, because egoism doesn't violate publicity' (Korsgaard 1996b: 208). See also Gert 2002.

[16] Korsgaard makes a somewhat different argument against private reasons in her most recent work (2009: 188–206). She argues that shared deliberation is possible for us, and that it requires public, shared reasons. She acknowledges that this sort of interaction with other people may be optional, but argues that you must interact with yourself (e.g., yourself in the future) in this mode of shared deliberation if you are to be a unified agent. If this is right, though, it seems that a Kantian egoist could be a unified agent (by treating himself, now and in the future, as an end in himself) who refuses to accept the moral law and to treat others as ends in themselves.

Korsgaard does have other arguments against egoism. She thinks that any rational agent must be committed to there being at least some agent-neutral reasons.[17] For example, she claims that we think of our own goals, or at least some of them, 'under the guise of the good'—that is, as grounding agent-neutral reasons for everyone to help us to achieve them.[18] If this is right, then we are committed to there being some agent-neutral reasons for action.[19]

It is, however, controversial whether we do view our goals 'under the guise of the good' at all. We certainly do not believe that there are agent-neutral reasons for everyone to promote all of our goals. Perhaps it is true that many of us think that there are agent-neutral reasons for everyone to promote some of our goals but it is certainly open to the egoist to reject

[17] Others have made similar claims. Hursthouse (1999: 177), for example, following Hare, asks us to consider the situation of a parent who is deciding how to bring up her child. She thinks that most of us try to teach our children to have the moral virtues of justice, benevolence, courage, and so on, for their own sake: 'Contemplating the lives of, say, those who are wealthy and powerful, and, apparently at least, perfectly happy, but who lie and cheat and ruthlessly sacrifice some others when it suits them, we may find that we do not regard them as enviable or desirable at all.' In other words, we think the good life is a life of moral virtue. But, as Hursthouse is perfectly well aware, some parents do not bring up their children to be virtuous. Unlike Korsgaard, however, Hursthouse is not trying to give an ambitious vindication of morality. She makes it clear that she is not attempting to prove to the egoist that he should be moral, and indeed she does not think such a proof is possible. Modest vindications of morality are discussed further in the following chapters.

[18] 'What you make good by means of your rational choice must be harmonious with what another can make good by means of her rational choice—for the good is a consistent, harmonious object shared by all rational beings' (Korsgaard 1996a: 123).

[19] This is just part of Korsgaard's well-known 'regress' argument for the moral law. She begins by distinguishing conditional values (which are valuable in some circumstances but not others, which are valuable only when certain conditions hold) and unconditional values (which are valuable in all circumstances) (1996a: 16; see also 106–32). Korsgaard claims that if there were only conditional values there would be a 'regress of justifications': we could ask of each conditional value, 'why is that valuable?' The answer would be some value that was also conditional. We could ask the same question again, and again the answer would be a conditional value. If nothing were of unconditional value, we would never get a satisfactory reply to the question: 'why is that valuable?' To halt the regress, we need something of unconditional value (Korsgaard, 1996a: 16–17). For example, suppose that all values are instrumentally valuable, valuable only as a means to something else. It is very plausible that this is not in fact possible: not everything can be valuable as a means to something else. If some things are instrumentally valuable, there must be some non-instrumental values. Since the rational will is the source of value, Korsgaard claims, if anything is unconditionally valuable, it must be. So, she concludes, 'The good will is the only thing that has its "full worth in itself" (G 4: 394) and it is the only thing whose value is in no way relative to its circumstances or results . . . it is in the strictest sense intrinsically good.' (Korsgaard 1996a: 117). This argument that there could not be only instrumental value is convincing. We might concede that, if the rational will is the source of value, it must be non-instrumentally valuable. But it does not follow that it must be valuable in such a way that everyone has reasons to treat any will as an end in itself. The rational will might be valuable for its own sake, even though each agent had agent-relative reason to protect his own rational will. The rational will might be the source of all value and therefore all reasons for action, but all those reasons might be agent-relative.

this claim and to deny that others have reason to help him do anything.[20] I do not see my goal of collecting paperclips under the guise of the good, in the sense of giving reasons for others to act. No one else has any reasons of any kind relating to my paperclips. Yet they still can ground reasons for me.

Paperclips may not ground agent-neutral reasons, but perhaps other goals do. The prevention of suffering, for example, may ground reasons for anyone. Korsgaard argues that, under certain circumstances, even someone who claims to be an egoist would acknowledge this. If someone were to torture her, she would not just want them to stop, Korsgaard claims, she would resent what they did and would believe that her torturer had a reason to desist. She is therefore forced to accept not only that she has a reason to avoid being tortured but that there are reasons for someone else not to torture her, even if it is in his interests to do so. There is at least one non-egoist reason for action, so egoism is false.[21]

An egoist might agree with Korsgaard that she would prefer not to be tormented, and she would wish that his tormentor would refrain. She might find herself with vivid and persistent feelings of resentment towards him, where this includes the feeling that he is not just doing something that she does not like, but something that he *ought not* to do. Does the very fact that she has this feeling show that she is committed to at least one agent-neutral reason? Not necessarily. She would be committed to agent-neutral reasons if she *endorsed* her resentment, in the sense that she regarded it as warranted. She may feel resentment, without actually believing that her torturer has a reason to stop. She has a reason to try to get him to stop, of course, but he would have a reason, she may think, only if it is in his interests to do so. She may do her best to think of a way of making his interests align with hers without acknowledging, even in these terrible circumstances, that he has an agent-neutral reason not to cause her pain.

Is it not very implausible that an egoist could maintain this position when she is in agony? Perhaps in those circumstances everyone thinks that anyone who can help them should do so; no one can avoid thinking that their pain

---

[20] An agent might regard that he has agent-neutral reasons to promote his goal because he might be concerned to justify his action to other rational agents. But, as we have seen, all he needs to do to justify his action is to show the other agents that he really did have a reason to act. That reason need not be shared with the other person, giving both a reason to act. It might be an agent-relative reason instead.  [21] Korsgaard (1996a: 277) makes the same argument.

grounds agent-neutral reasons. But an egoist could quite reasonably say that no one thinks very clearly under torture. When you are suffering so much that you desperately want the pain to end, it is very understandable, perhaps even inevitable, that you end up thinking—erroneously—that there is a reason for others to make it stop. But, this is just not so, and in less stressful circumstances egoists will claim they can clearly see that there is no such reason.

Suppose that someone has just lost a fair competition for a job that she very much wants. She feels very frustrated and begins to resent the person who got the job, feeling that he must have just got lucky, he did not deserve to win, that the appointments committee has made a terrible mistake and should re-run the competition. Many people have probably experienced similar feelings, but no sensible moral person would endorse them. The competition was, after all, fair. No one has any reason to do anything in response to her feelings: she has no reason to try to undermine his position; he has no reason to resign in her favour; the appointments committee need not reconsider the post. A sensible moral agent will regard her resentment as unwarranted, if understandable and perhaps inevitable, given her bitter disappointment. The fact that many people would feel resentment in those circumstances does not show anything at all about the reasons for action that anyone has. In those circumstances, no one thinks very clearly, and, in a while, once her feelings have subsided, she will see that too. If she recognizes all of this at the same time as feeling resentment she is not really committed to there being a reason for the committee to reconsider her application.

Of course, we think it obvious that torture is quite different from a job competition. The torture victim's resentment is warranted; the torturer does have a reason not to cause her pain whereas the job applicant's resentment is unwarranted since her treatment is fair. We think that in the terrible torture situation the truth about reasons for action is thrown into relief by our feelings. But the egoist disagrees: she thinks that it is obscured by them.

More generally, moral agents and egoists are likely to disagree about the circumstances in which our feelings and our beliefs about reasons are reliably formed. If we knew when our judgements about reasons were most reliable, we could find out which theory was right after all. But how can we determine which kind of environment is best without antecedently finding in favour of one of the theories? Without a shared conception of what is a reliable and what is an unreliable process of forming judgements about reasons, we can insist that the situations in which people tend to make judgements that support the authority of morality are the situations in which our judgements about reasons are reliable. But, the egoist will remain unmoved, and reasonably complain that we are just begging the question against her.

## 4. Kantian Autonomy

Korsgaard tried to defend a Kantian ethical theory by appealing to the idea of public reasons, but Kant's own defence of morality is quite different. Kant claims that there is 'reciprocity' between freedom and the moral law: an agent is free if and only if he accepts the moral law. It seems that we can use this to construct an argument in favour of the moral law.[22] Freedom is the kind of thing that even egoists may regard as important. So if it were true that egoists were not and could not be free, this would be a reason that many egoists would acknowledge as genuine to reject egoism. It seems that it should be fairly straightforward to provide an ambitious vindication of the moral law, provided that we are entitled to make use of Kant's theory of freedom.[23] The only serious question is whether Kant's conception of freedom, as requiring choice that is independent from desire, is tenable: if it is, then even egoists will have to accept that the moral law binds us.

[22] Sussman 2003: 362–3. There is some evidence that Kant himself saw the autonomy argument of *Groundwork III* as the justification of the moral law. For when the formula of humanity is introduced in *Groundwork II* Kant suggests that it is easier to see that your own humanity (rational nature) should be treated as an end in itself ('This is the way in which a man necessarily conceives his own existence' G 4: 429) than that you should treat others' humanity as an end. Indeed, he says of the requirement to treat *other* rational agents as ends in themselves: 'This proposition I put forward here as a postulate. The grounds for it will be found in the final chapter' (G 4: 429 n.). This interesting remark suggests that Kant recognized the problems of justifying duties to others and that he thought the considerations about freedom would solve the problem.

[23] There is some dispute whether autonomy is simply defined by Kant so as to include accepting the moral law: 'Autonomy of the will is the sole principle of all moral laws and of duties in keeping with them' (CPrR 5: 33, see also CPrR 5: 43; 5: 87). If this were the case, it would not be possible for an agent who accepted Kantian egoism to be autonomous, by the definition of autonomy. Allison (1990; 1996), however, interprets Kant as offering an argument that only an agent who accepts the moral law can be autonomous, and it is his reconstruction of this argument which is criticized here. In the remainder of this chapter the term 'autonomy' will be used, as Allison uses it, for a property which must be shown to be identical with acceptance of the moral law.

Kant's difficult argument has been set out very clearly by Henry Allison (1990; 1996).[24] According to Kant, a will has 'negative' freedom if it is 'able to work independently of determination by alien causes' (G 4: 446). By 'alien causes', Kant includes anything that is *outside of the will*, including, for example, desire, pleasure, or happiness. A will is positively free, or autonomous, if its maxim is determined by a law that is not derived from anything external to the will.[25] A positively free will is therefore not determined by the agent's desires. But a positively free will cannot be completely randomly determined, for it could not then genuinely be acting for reasons. So, it must be determined by a law.[26]

Kant identifies a positively free or autonomous will with a will which has adopted the moral law. Autonomy and acceptance of the moral law are not obviously identical. A will is autonomous if it adopts any principle which is law-like and is independent from external influence; perhaps different autonomous agents could act according to different laws. But Kant claims that in fact the moral law is the only law that a positively free will could adopt.

Suppose that Kant is correct that an autonomous agent will act on a law, and that the law would be determined by the will itself, independently of her desires. If the will is not determined by desire, it cannot be determined by the content of particular maxims, for, we may assume, an agent would choose a maxim with a particular content only if she wanted to act on that maxim. Instead of choosing maxims according to their content, autonomous agents must choose them on the basis of the *form* of the maxim. Maxims must be chosen on the basis that, when suitably generalized, they have the right form to be laws of practical reason, laws that all rational agents could adopt. A maxim must therefore be law-like in the sense that it is *universally applicable* (in other words, *it could be adopted by all rational agents as a law*). This is very close to one of the formulations of the moral law,

[24] In her most recent work, Korsgaard (2009: 72–83) makes a similar argument, identifying autonomy with acting on the moral law, but she fails to acknowledge the possibility of an autonomous Kantian egoist (a possibility I defend later in this section). She supplements this with considerations about private reasons that I discussed in the previous section.

[25] A positively free will is therefore also negatively free, since if the will determines itself independently of alien causes, it clearly must have the capacity to determine itself independently of alien causes.

[26] This is another point at which Kant's argument has been questioned—perhaps a free will could be random, or, at least, not determined by a law, but I will assume that Kant is correct here for the sake of argument.

the formula of universal law, which states: '*Act only on that maxim through which you can at the same time will that it should become a universal law*'. But it is not equivalent: the moral law includes the extra requirement that the agent must be able to *will* the maxim as a universal law.[27]

It is easy to see that the two requirements are distinct by considering a version of standard egoism, that it is rational for an agent to do what will best satisfy her desires. A standard egoist can certainly affirm that this theory is universally applicable, since she can accept that it is rational for any agent to do what will best satisfy that agent's desires. But arguably she *cannot will* that standard egoism become a universal law, because if everyone were a standard egoist she would have much more difficulty in satisfying her desires (no one would help her unless he wanted to do so). So, standard egoism has universal applicability but cannot be willed as a universal law. Similarly, Kantian egoism has universal applicability—you could accept that it is rational for each agent to treat herself as an end—but you cannot will that other agents fail to treat you as an end.

Allison notices the 'gap in the derivation' of the reciprocity of freedom and the moral law.[28] He argues that if we look more closely at the requirements of autonomy, we can see why standard egoism cannot be a law of practical reason. In particular, the requirement that you choose a law of practical reason in virtue of its form rather than its content can close the gap:

if I am required to adopt a maxim at least in part because of its conformity to universal law . . . then, clearly, this maxim must be able to include itself as a 'principle establishing universal law'. In other words the intent expressed in the maxim must be compatible with the universal law produced by the generalization of that maxim.[29]

You might be able to accept a principle of always making promises that you do not intend to keep because that principle has universal applicability. But this could not be your *reason* for adopting it. For if you adopted that maxim because it was universally applicable you would have to be able to will the law produced by the generalization of the maxim, and you

---

[27] See Allison 1990: 205–6; Wood 1999: esp. 82.

[28] Allison 1996. This 'presumed gap' is also noted by Copp (1992) and Hill (1992). Neither recognizes the possibility of a non-desire-based law of practical reason that is distinct from the moral law.

[29] Allison 1996: 152–3.

cannot will as a law that everyone makes promises that they do not intend to keep.[30]

Is it possible for you to accept standard egoism on the basis of its form rather than its content? Standard egoism is universally applicable, and you might accept it precisely because it is universally applicable, in which case you would be accepting it in virtue of its form rather than its content. But, lots of principles of practical reason are universally applicable. You cannot claim that your reason for accepting standard egoism rather than those principles is that it applies to everyone, as those other principles have that feature too. You must have some further reason for choosing standard egoism rather than a different universally applicable principle—for example, the law of counter-egoism (the law to minimize your own happiness). If you accept standard egoism rather than counter-egoism, the grounds of this decision must be something like: you prefer to be happy than unhappy. But this is a reason based on your happiness or on your preferences, not on your will. If you make your choice on the basis of that kind of reason, you would not be autonomous.[31]

But the moral law, Allison claims, is different. For the moral law, unlike standard egoism, has nothing to do with your desires or your happiness, or indeed anything external to your will, so you can choose the moral law above other universally applicable principles of practical reason on grounds that are not external to your will—and if you choose it for those reasons you will be autonomous. The autonomy argument against egoism can be set out as follows:

---

[30] 'This property of the maxim [universal applicability] or, equivalently, its conformity to universal law, cannot function as the reason for adopting it. If its conformity to universal law were the reason, then the agent, considered as rational legislator, would have to be able to will the law produced by the generalization of the maxim' (Allison 1996: 153). According to Allison, that a maxim conforms to universal law is a reason for adopting it. This is crucial to his argument that the moral law is the only acceptable theory of practical reason, but it is not a generally accepted interpretation of Kant's requirement that an agent must adopt a maxim which conforms to universal law. Usually this is taken to mean that a maxim which does not conform to universal law, such as a maxim of false promising, must be rejected (e.g., Paton 1963: 141; Sullivan 1989: 50; Wood 1999: 78), *not* that that a maxim conforms with universal law is a reason for accepting it. Nevertheless, even if Allison's interpretation is accepted, his argument for the moral law still fails.

[31] Allison 1996: 153. Furthermore, even if the agent adopted the law for this reason, the reasons for action derived from rational egoism are clearly desire-based, and therefore external to the will. This argument for the reciprocity thesis is put forward by Reath (1993: 428).

(1) If you accept a law of practical reason on grounds that are external to your will, you are not autonomous.

(2) Any egoist theory of practical reason can be accepted only on grounds that are external to the will.

(3) Therefore, if you accept an egoist theory of practical reason, you are not autonomous.

The first and most obvious objection to the argument is that egoists will simply embrace the conclusion. Why should it matter to an egoist that she is not autonomous? It is quite plausible that practical reasons must be universally applicable, and egoist reasons are universally applicable. By contrast, it is not at all obvious what is wrong with an agent's accepting a law of practical reason on grounds that are external to her will. Why must a putative law of practical reason that does not meet this standard be rejected? Many egoists will remain unmoved.

But, suppose that they are sympathetic to Kant's conception of autonomy. The argument against egoism is still not conclusive, for premise (2) claims that an egoist theory cannot be accepted except on grounds that are external to the will. As we have seen, it may be true that standard egoism cannot be accepted on grounds that are external to the will, because choosing to pursue your own happiness for the sake of your happiness or because you prefer to do so is to choose on grounds external to your will. But as we know from Part I of the book, standard egoism is not the only version of egoism that there is, and premise (2) may not be true of all versions of egoism.

And, indeed, premise (2) is false. Consider the egoist theory introduced in Chapter 3, Kantian egoism, according to which you are rationally required to treat humanity in your own person as an end, never merely as a means. I interpreted this as meaning that it is never rational for you to undermine your own rational nature—your own will—for the sake of anything else. Kantian egoism is a self-regarding version of the moral law (recall that the formula of humanity requires you to treat humanity in yourself or in another person as an end, never merely as a means).

Clearly, Kantian egoist reasons are universally applicable: I can accept that it is rational for each of us to treat our own humanity as an end not as a mere means. But why would you choose to adopt and act on Kantian egoism rather than any other universally applicable principle of practical reason?

The obvious response is that you choose it for the sake of your rational nature or, in other words, for the sake of your will. Are you thereby choosing on the basis of something *external* to your will? Obviously not. If you choose for the sake of your will, you are not doing so on grounds that are external to the will. Moreover, if you are autonomous when you choose the moral law as your principle of practical reason then you surely *must* be autonomous when you accept Kantian egoism. For you can choose the moral law or Kantian egoism on more or less exactly the same grounds. So a defender of the moral law is faced with a dilemma. Either choosing on those grounds does not make you autonomous (in which case you are not autonomous when you accept Kantian egoism but you are also not autonomous when you choose the moral law) or choosing the moral law or Kantian egoism for the sake of rational nature makes you autonomous. So an egoist—a Kantian egoist—can be autonomous.[32]

Kant does not after all have an argument against egoism. First of all, an egoist can reasonably claim that he cares nothing for autonomy. Why should it matter whether he has accepted a theory of practical reason on grounds external to the will? But, more interestingly, *you can be an egoist and still be autonomous*. Kant cannot show that we must choose the moral law above Kantian egoism for reasons relating to autonomy. So there is no ambitious vindication of morality on Kantian grounds.[33]

---

[32] Could a defender of Kant argue that there is a significant difference between the moral law and Kantian egoism? When you choose Kantian egoism, you must do so for the sake of *your own* rational nature. When you choose the moral law, you may do so for the sake of rational nature generally. This is clearly true, but it is not clear why it should have any implications at all for the autonomy of anyone choosing Kantian egoism over the moral law. If I choose for the sake of my own will, surely I am not choosing on grounds external to my will—so I must be autonomous. It is hard to see any reason for denying that a Kantian egoist is autonomous if a Kantian moral agent is autonomous. However, I think that there may be a problem for Kantian egoism here. Is autonomy really part of your self-interest? It is not obvious that it is, in which case a theory that requires an agent to be autonomous is not a form of egoism (I discuss this further in Chapter 11). As a consequence, it may be best for a Kantian egoist to deny the importance of autonomy, rather than to defend a version of the theory that requires agents to be autonomous.

[33] Kant's considerations about freedom do *not* prove that there are some duties to others rather than none at all. Why is it so often assumed that freedom plays this role in Kant's ethics? Many commentators assume that the only alternative theories of practical reason are versions of Humean desire-based theories, or the moral law (Allison 1990) and Korsgaard's (1996a: 159–87) 'Morality as Freedom'. If these were the only two options, and one could rule out Humean theories by the freedom argument, then one could conclude that the moral law was the only acceptable theory of practical reason. Everyone would have to accept that he had duties to others. But they are not the only two available options.

## 5.  Parfit on Persons

Nagel, Korsgaard, and Allison all attack the egoist's conception of reasons. Parfit criticizes the theory in a very different way.[34] He claims that egoism conflicts with the best conception of personal identity. According to egoism, all of your reasons for action are based on *your own* interests. You have reason to care about a person and to make sacrifices for her only if that person is *you*. Egoism is committed to the practical importance of identity.

Parfit has a number of arguments against egoism.[35] But his most important attempts to establish that personal identity is not practically significant. The argument depends on a thought experiment in which your brain is divided.[36]

Suppose that your brain has been split into two and each half has been transferred into a new body. Call the two resulting bodies, each of which

[34] In *Reasons and Persons*, Parfit argues against the 'Self-interest theory' or 'S'. Parfit first introduces S as a theory that makes claims about what aim it is rational to have. According to S, 'for each person, there is only one supremely rational aim, that his life go, for him, as well as possible' (Parfit 1984: 4). He later restates S as the conjunction of two claims, that each of us has most reason to do whatever would be best for himself and it is irrational for anyone to do what he believes will be worse for himself (ibid. 8). S is not equivalent to egoism. Whereas, according to egoism, each person has no practical reasons except to maximize his happiness, according to S, there may be other reasons for action, but they never outweigh one's own interests and one would be open to rational criticism if one acted for reasons not based on one's own interests when doing so conflicted with self-interest. In order to make it clear how Parfit's arguments apply to egoism, I will use my terminology of reasons rather than Parfit's terminology of what it is rational or irrational to do. This should make no difference to Parfit's arguments.

[35] Parfit conceives of egoism as a 'hybrid' theory in the sense that an egoist believes that reasons for action are agent-relative: she, but no one else, has reasons to promote her own happiness and she has no reasons to promote that of anyone else. Parfit interprets the egoist as regarding these reasons as time-neutral, however. She has exactly the same reason to pursue a benefit or avoid a harm that will occur tomorrow as she has to pursue an equivalent benefit or avoid a similar harm that will occur in many years' time. Egoist reasons are 'time-neutral', but 'person-relative'. Parfit argues (1984: 140–7) that there is an analogy between the terms 'I' and 'now', so that any theory should treat them in the same way. In addition, Parfit argues that since egoism is temporally neutral, it implies that past pain should matter as much to us as present or future pains, and the satisfaction of past desires, even those that we do not now have, should matter as much as the satisfaction of the desires we now have or will have in the future. It is very implausible that I should try to satisfy the desires that I now longer have. But the egoist can avoid this problem by claiming that it is not in her interests that past desires that she no longer has are satisfied: so egoism does not imply that she has reason to try to satisfy them (in other words, she can change her theory of self-interest, rather than denying that her reasons are time-neutral). Moreover, Parfit interprets S as time-neutral, with the proviso that sometimes it is less certain what will happen in the further future. It is not clear to me, however, that egoism must be committed to time-neutrality. The basic egoist claim, as I understand it, is that all reasons are based on self-interest. It does not follow that an equal benefit or harm at any time in one's life grounds the same strength of reasons. So I would regard time-neutrality as a claim that egoists can and often have made, but not one that they are necessarily committed to as egoists.    [36] Parfit 1984: 253ff.

has half of your brain, X and Y. Each of X and Y can now remember some of what happened to you, each shares many of your beliefs, desires, and your character traits. Each can carry out your intentions. But each goes on to lead a very different life: X is rich, famous, and successful; Y is not. Of course, this sort of division is not something that actually ever happens. But it does seem to be conceivable. Many people have quite strong intuitions about such cases, and Parfit claims that we can use these to assess theories of personal identity and its significance. The division of your brain and the transplant raise intriguing questions. Which of X or Y is identical to you? If you are an egoist, which of their lives should matter to you: do you have reason to make sacrifices now for the sake of X or Y?

Let us start with identity. After the division, who are you? There seem to be three possibilities. First, X and Y might both be identical to you. In some ways this is quite plausible. Both of them will claim to be you. Both of them will remember what you did, believe what you believed, want what you wanted, and do what you intended. So perhaps you are now two people. But, on reflection, this is very peculiar. If each of X and Y was identical to you, they would be identical with each other. But they cannot be identical to each other. One becomes rich, the other poor; they are in completely different places at the same time, and so on. So you cannot be both X and Y.[37]

Secondly, one or the other, but not both, might be identical to you. If you were an egoist, you would have reason to make sacrifices now for the sake of X, say, but not Y, because X but not Y is you. Again, on reflection, this does not make much sense. Both X and Y will say that she is you, both have your memories, desires, intentions, and so on. Each has half of your brain. In so far as either of them has a claim to be you, each has an equally good claim. It is hard to believe that one of them is you and the other one is not, when there are no other differences between them.

The third possibility is that neither of them is you. You did not survive the surgical procedure of division and transplant, and in your place two new people were brought into existence. But, after the surgery, there are

---

[37] Perhaps they could both be identical to you because you become a single person who happens to have two bodies and two minds. But this is so far from how we normally conceive of personhood—as involving one body and one mind—as to be very implausible.

people with the same memories, beliefs, and intentions as you. This does not sound very much like your death. And as far as an egoist is concerned you would have no reason to care about either of X or Y, and no reason to sacrifice anything on their behalf. But surely this is just wrong. It would be reasonable for you, even as an egoist, to be interested in what happened to X and to Y.

The division case is puzzling because it appears that each of the three possible descriptions of the outcome—that you are identical to one, both, or neither of X and Y—encounters strong objections. There are very good reasons to reject each of them. Parfit suggests that in this sort of case it is simply an empty question whether you are X or Y, both, or neither. There is no deep metaphysical fact about personal identity that would settle the case. We could choose to describe it in different ways. Nevertheless, some of these descriptions are better than others, according to Parfit, and best is the description: 'division is not as bad as death, and yet neither X nor Y will be you'. It follows that in cases of division it is not identity that matters. Something else must be important.

It is reasonable for you to be concerned about what happens to X and Y after your division. Why? The obvious reasons are: they have your memories, hopes, fears, and dreams. They will carry out your intentions. They will have your character. Parfit defines what he calls 'relation R', which consists in psychological continuity and/or degree of connectedness. Psychological connectedness is the holding of particular psychological connections—for example, memory, the continued holding of beliefs, desires, carrying out of past intentions, and so on. Psychological continuity is the holding of overlapping chains of strong psychological connections. X and Y are both psychologically continuous with you and there are many strong psychological connections between each of them and you (at least initially). In the division thought-experiment, it would be reasonable for you to have a special concern for X and for Y because they each stand in relation R to you.

Why is this a problem for egoism? According to egoism, all reasons for action are based on *your own* interests. So identity is of the utmost practical significance: it determines whether you have reasons for action or not. But, in the division case, it is most plausible—at least if Parfit is right—that you are not identical to X and Y but you do have reasons for action relating to them.[38] So, egoism is wrong; there must be reasons for action that are not based on your own interests.

An egoist might not be too worried at this stage. She might simply concede that in the highly unusual, not to say bizarre, circumstances of division, you would have reason to sacrifice your interests for X and Y, even though neither of them is you. In normal, non-division circumstances, all reasons for action are based on your own interests; in division cases, you have reasons for action based on your psychological relations to X and Y. This is a revision to egoism, but not a very damaging one. After all, the second clause is relevant only if you divide (which has never happened and probably never will) and the egoist has thereby made no concessions to morality or to its practical significance.

But the egoist is not entitled to be complacent. This divided theory may not be stable. Why should identity matter under some circumstances and relation R matter in others? In non-division cases, the egoist has simply assumed that identity is important, but there is a better candidate: relation R. Personal identity, according to Parfit, just is relation R held uniquely. If only X (or only Y) survived the transplant, you would be identical with X (or Y). If both survive, you are identical with neither; relation R does not hold uniquely: both are R-related to you. If identity were practically important, it would have to be important that R held uniquely. And surely it is not. If anything, it is better if there are more people around who are like you, who can carry out your intentions, and satisfy your desires. Parfit concludes that it is relation R that matters in all circumstances. Egoism is wrong that identity as such is *ever* important. Reasons for action cannot be based on *self*-interest.

Moreover, there is an additional problem for egoism. Parfit initially defines relation R as 'psychological continuity and/or connectedness', but

---

[38] It is possible that, since X and Y are very similar to you, they will satisfy some of the desires and intentions that you had before the division (of course, they can only satisfy desires which do not essentially refer to yourself—for example, a desire that a book about moral philosophy is written, rather than a desire that such a book is written *by you*). If so, you might have reasons of self-interest (grounded in your pre-division desires and interests) to be concerned about what happens to them. This is true, but the same is true of other people who might decide to satisfy some of your desires (such as your siblings or children or friends). As an egoist, you should have no special concern for X or Y over these other people who might carry out your desires after your division (except in so far as some are somewhat more and others somewhat less likely to carry out your pre-division desires). But, contra-egoism, it seems plausible that you have much stronger reasons than this to be concerned about X and Y.

later he argues that connectedness must be part of what matters. This has two problematic implications for egoism. First, it casts doubt on whether egoism can be time-neutral.

You today are strongly psychologically connected with yourself tomorrow, you tomorrow are strongly psychologically connected with you the day after, and so on. There are overlapping chains of psychological connectedness throughout your life (unless, for example, you suffered from an episode of severe amnesia). But the degree of psychological connectedness between you now and your future states typically diminishes through time. You are more strongly psychologically connected with you tomorrow than you in twenty years' time, when you have many different beliefs, desires, and values. If psychological connectedness is part of what is practically important, then typically you have less reason for concern about your further future than your nearer future.[39]

Secondly, though in normal circumstances, you are psychologically continuous only with yourself (you do not have strong overlapping chains of psychological connectedness with anyone else) you typically are psychologically connected with other people. You can share memories, beliefs, desires, and so on with others. So if psychological connectedness is practically important, in normal circumstances, you have reason to be concerned about others to some extent (though not so strongly concerned as you are with your own near future). So reasons for action cannot be entirely based on your own interests: you must have some reasons for action based on the interests of other people (and not just those who are as closely related to you as are X and Y). This is obviously a very damaging admission for egoists. Even if they do not go as far as to accept the practical significance of morality, it is an important step in the right direction—perhaps in acknowledging, for example, reasons to help (some) other people who are in need.

How should an egoist respond to Parfit's arguments? There are many points with which she could take issue.

Her first response might be to deny that psychological connectedness is of practical significance. This claim is crucial to the arguments that egoism is not time-neutral and that the egoist will have to acknowledge some

---

[39] Strictly speaking, it is not that some benefit or harm happens in the near or further future that matters, but the strength of the psychological connections between you-now and you-then. In other words, reasons are relative to connectedness, not to time.

reasons to benefit others. Since in normal cases we are only psychologically continuous with ourselves, and we are equally psychologically continuous with all parts of our life, if psychological continuity alone mattered, egoism could retain time-neutrality and the claim that, in normal circumstances, we have no reasons for action based on the interests of others.

In the division case, you are both psychologically connected and psychologically continuous with X and Y. It could be true that you have reason to care about each of them because continuity matters alone, or because connectedness and continuity matter.[40] The division case, therefore, does not settle whether connectedness or just continuity matter. An egoist might well argue that the fact that in normal circumstances it seems perfectly reasonable to be concerned about your further future as much as your nearer future, and that in division cases it is reasonable to care about what happens to X and Y later on, not just immediately after division occurs, strongly suggests that psychological connectedness does not make a difference here.[41] So Parfit's argument at most shows that psychological continuity grounds reasons for action. An egoist might be

[40] If psychological connectedness alone mattered, you would have no reason whatsoever to be concerned about your further future, which, I assume, is very implausible.

[41] Parfit does have some arguments that psychological connectedness matters. He points out that it would matter to us if we were not psychologically connected to our future selves. For example, it would be unfortunate if you were only able to recall things that happened to you in the previous twenty-four hours. In a week's time, you would have no idea what happened to you today, though you would be psychologically continuous with yourself now. Similarly, if your strongest desires or character traits were constantly in flux, each held for very short periods of time, this would be regrettable. So it is reasonable to care about psychological connectedness. Of course in ordinary life we do forget most of what happens to us quite quickly, and we do sometimes change our mind about what is important: this is neither unusual nor regrettable. Psychological connectedness does not matter all that much. But, more importantly, this is the wrong sort of argument to support Parfit's conclusion. Living a unified life might be worth doing; something that egoists should strive for, just as happiness is something that they perhaps should strive for. But it does not follow that if you are not strongly psychologically connected to your future self, right now you have less-forceful reasons for action based on the interests of your future self than if you were more strongly psychologically connected. Similarly, it does not follow that if in the future you will be less happy you have less-forceful reasons based on the interests of you-later than if you were happier then. The phrase 'Z matters' is ambiguous. It might mean: Z is part of a person's interests; part of what it is to live a good life. Or it might mean: given the correct theory of practical reason, Z is relevant to whether this person's interests ground reasons for action for you. In other words, Z partly determines whether you have reasons for action relating to that person at all. Parfit's arguments concern psychological connectedness in the first sense—whether it is part of a person's interests—but he draws a conclusion about the second sense—whether it partly determines whether you have reasons relating to that person. An egoist can and should reject this.

prepared to accept this, dropping the claim that it is identity that matters, for example:

*Psychological continuity-related standard egoism.* Each agent has reason to maximize the happiness of anyone who is psychologically continuous with her; and no other reasons for action. The grounds for this reason are the happiness of those who are psychologically continuous with her (or that their own happiness is good for them).

In normal circumstances, anyone who accepted that theory would act in exactly the same way as a standard egoist; in the unlikely event of division, she would acknowledge reasons to promote the happiness of X and Y. The egoist may be forced to make revisions to her theory, but not in such a way as to accept the authority of morality.

Parfit might argue that once we reject the significance of identity and acknowledge that psychological continuity is what matters, egoism even in its revised form no longer looks very plausible. He describes his own reaction to accepting his theory: 'There is still a difference between my life and the lives of other people. But the difference is less. Other people are closer. I am less concerned about the rest of my own life, and more concerned about the lives of others.'[42] But it is one thing to have this reaction, and another for it to be justified. The difference between yourself and others is still pretty clear: in normal circumstances, no one else is psychologically continuous with you. It is certainly open to the egoist to insist on acknowledging reasons for action based only on that relation. Parfit has no argument against that claim that the egoist must accept.

Can an egoist make a less concessive reply to Parfit, by defending her original claim that identity is practically significant? There are a number of ways that she might. First, she might claim that after division she is not identical with either X or Y. In virtue of the fact that identity is practically significant, she might claim, it follows that she has no reasons for action relating to their interests. Of course, many people, on hearing the example, think that they would have reasons relating to X and Y. But the egoist can make two responses. First, that anyone who is psychologically continuous

---

[42] Parfit 1984: 281.

with you is likely to carry out some of your intentions and satisfy some of your desires (at least those desires that do not require you to satisfy them). Certainly she is more likely to do so than anyone who is not psychologically continuous with you. So you do have some special reasons to be concerned about X and Y, for the satisfaction of any of your desires after your division is likely to be up to them. You may have reasons regarding them relating to *your own* (pre-division) interests. Secondly, the egoist can point out that their intuitions about this kind of case may not be particularly reliable. It is hard to make sense of division and it would not be at all surprising if people's initial reactions to the case were mistaken.

On the other hand, the egoist might accept that even though she is not identical with X or Y, she does have reasons for action relating to X and Y, but suggest that what is true in this unusual case has no implications for what is practically important in ordinary life.[43] Identity normally matters; but when there is no identity, psychological continuity matters. For example, standard egoism might be revised as follows.

*Disjunctive standard egoism.* Each agent has reason to maximize her own happiness, and no other reasons for action, unless there is no one identical with her but there are people who are psychologically continuous with her (in which case she has reason to maximize the happiness of anyone who is psychologically continuous with her, and no other reasons for action). The grounds for this reason are the happiness of those who are identical with or are psychologically continuous with her (or that their happiness is good for them).

Parfit argued that this kind of disjunctive theory could not work, because identity was simply psychological continuity plus uniqueness, and uniqueness was not particularly valuable—in fact, it could be more valuable to have more than one person around who was psychologically continuous with you. But an egoist could reasonably deny this. She might defend a different theory of personal identity, according to which it is not simply psychological continuity plus uniqueness, and argue that that conception of identity is practically important. Or she might argue that personal identity supervenes on psychological continuity, uniquely held, but that the value of identity is not the same as the value of psychological continuity plus the value of uniqueness.[44]

---

[43] Sosa 1990.    [44] Johnston 1992; Johnston 1997.

A third strategy for an egoist is to claim that after division she would be identical to either X or Y, but that it is *indeterminate* which, and therefore it is indeterminate what reasons for action she has relating to them. This strategy raises difficult questions about vague existence, and does not fit with many people's intuitions that they *definitely* would have reasons relating to each of X and Y in a case of division. But an egoist might reasonably cast doubt on the reliability of these intuitions.

Finally, an egoist might claim that she is identical with *both* X and Y and it is because of this that she has reasons relating to each of them.[45] Just as a road or a railway line can divide, and the same line can continue to two different towns across two different parts of the country, a person can divide and the same person can continue in two quite different lives. Again this strategy raises difficult metaphysical questions. For example, before you underwent division, is it really possible that you were two people in one body? Is each of us really two different people because it is possible that we might undergo fission (or, more than two, if we could undergo fission multiple times)? If sustainable, this strategy would allow the egoist to retain all her original theory: that identity is practically important and that all reasons for action are based on self-interest.

The metaphysical issues raised by cases of division and personal identity are too complex to be pursued here in any more depth. But it is clear that the egoist has many potential lines of response to Parfit. At worst, she will have to revise her theory to a form of psychological-continuity-related egoism, a theory which would not differ interestingly from egoism in ordinary circumstances. She might instead prefer a disjunctive theory, which in normal circumstances entails that all reasons for action are based on self-interest. Or, more radically, she might accept egoism in its original form—that all reasons for action are based on self-interest in all circumstances—and develop one of the two approaches sketched above, that identity in division cases is indeterminate, or that you would be identical to both X and Y.

There is undoubtedly a cost to the egoist in modifying her theory in some of these ways to meet Parfit's arguments. The cost is that the egoist theories no longer look particularly natural: there was an attractive simplicity to the idea that you have reason to do what is in your interests which is lost. But

---

[45] See Lewis 1976; Sider 1996.

the egoist may respond that in normal circumstances her core claim is still true: everyone does have reason to do only what is in her interests. In the very strange division cases the issue is more complicated, but perhaps that is just what we should expect. Moreover, many moral theories would have similar problems when faced with Parfit's arguments, and would have to be modified in ways that make them more complicated and less intuitively appealing. The egoist can insist that whichever response she chooses she can retain the core of her theory, and certainly has no need to concede that morality has any practical authority.

## 6. Companions in Guilt

Sidgwick found that he could not give an ambitious vindication of rational utilitarianism⋆. He could not prove to an egoist that she had reason to maximize everyone's happiness rather than her own. This problem turns out to be quite general, applying to all the major theories of ethics. We can construct an egoist theory of practical reason that parallels the candidate moral theory, and it is then very difficult to show that everyone has reason to do what is morally right rather than to do what is in her interests, without begging the question against egoism. Even Kant's moral theory that so emphasizes the links between practical reason and morality does not have the resources to prove that morality is authoritative.

In this chapter, I have surveyed a number of recent attempts to refute egoism. None of these arguments establishes that egoism is false without begging the question against it. Several of them have a further difficulty, in that if successful against egoism they would condemn equally some plausible moral theories too. Of course, just because some arguments against egoism fail it does not follow that no ambitious vindication of morality will succeed. There are, however, good reasons to be sceptical that we can successfully refute egoism.

An ambitious vindication might question the nature of egoist reasons for action:

(1) There are certain qualities any practical reason must have if it is to qualify as a genuine reason at all.

(2) Egoist reasons do not have these qualities.

(3) Therefore egoist reasons are not genuine reasons and egoism must be rejected.

Nagel and Korsgaard argued that any practical reason must be agent-neutral if it is to justify action and therefore to count as a genuine reason for action at all; egoism is not. Allison claimed that a principle of practical reason must be autonomous; egoism is not. The problem with all these arguments is similar. To refute egoism (1) and (2) must both be true. But it is extremely difficult to establish them both without begging the question against egoism. Either some version of egoism actually has the quality that is required in a theory of practical reason or it is not at all plausible (and the egoist can certainly deny) that the quality is essential to a theory of practical reason.

On the other hand, we might, following Parfit, question egoism's commitment to the practical importance of identity. But it is hard to see an argument along these lines refuting all forms of egoism. An egoist can modify her theory to a disjunctive form or to psychological continuity-related egoism whilst retaining the core of her theory and refusing to accept the authority of morality.

But, if we cannot reject egoism for its conception of reasons for action or its commitment to personal identity, in what other way could an argument against egoism possibly proceed? We might have good reasons to reject one or other *type* of egoism. For example, if we were convinced by Kant that happiness could not be the basis of a theory of practical reason, we might reject standard egoism. But rejecting one version of egoism is not the same as proving that all forms of it are untenable. The arguments in this chapter against all forms of egoism fail, and it is hard even to imagine where to turn next to do any better.

The task at the start of this book was to try to find the 'Holy Grail', a response to a sensible knave proving in terms that he himself would accept that he has reason to be moral. But we have no ambitious vindication of the authority of morality. The arguments of this chapter have not proved conclusively that there can be no such thing. But no attempt at presenting such an argument has so far succeeded and the prospects of finding a non-question-begging argument for the authority of morality seem bleak.

The focus on arguments against egoism here could be mistaken as a sign that I take the burden of proof to be on defenders of the authority of morality—that egoism is the default view, which we should all accept unless we have compelling reasons to reject it in favour of morality. Of course, this is not so. There is no presumption in favour of egoism. The lack of a refutation should not be taken as any sort of endorsement of the theory. There are plenty of false and even absurd theories that we cannot refute in terms that their defenders will accept. Nor is there any reason to doubt, and much reason to think, that an attempt to vindicate egoism in terms that moral agents accept would fail just as ignominiously.

Consider the distinctive claims of egoism: that all reasons for action are agent-relative and all are based on self-interest (in other words, that identity is of supreme practical importance). According to most moral theories, there are agent-neutral reasons for action as well as (or instead of) agent-relative reasons. How can an egoist prove that agent-neutral reasons are not legitimate? Agent-neutral reasons for action can explain and justify action in the strongest sense: they have all the requisite properties for a genuine reason for action. It is very difficult to see how an egoist could argue that they are not real reasons. In addition, whilst Parfit's arguments do not establish that identity cannot be practically significant, this certainly does not imply that we have no reasons to act on behalf of other people, with whom we have no connections whatsoever. How can an egoist argue that each of us has reasons for action relating only to ourselves? It is difficult to see what kind of argument she could give, except an appeal to intuitions like: no one has reason to sacrifice her own interests for anyone else. And this appeal simply begs the question against common-sense morality.

Although this chapter and indeed the whole of the book is focused on whether we can find a good argument against egoism, the failure of attempts to vindicate morality is in no way a defence of egoism. Egoism and morality are most likely on a par, in the sense that it is extremely unlikely that there is an ambitious vindication of either.

Does it matter if we cannot show the egoist that he has reason to be moral? Philosophers often feel that they should be able to engage with and answer satisfactorily anyone who expresses a view about an issue. But, even if this is a noble ambition, in practice it may be much too demanding. We should not expect to produce such a powerful argument that it will convince everyone, whatever their initial views. There are many areas in which we normally think that our beliefs are justified, though we cannot refute someone who disagrees with us in terms that he himself accepts. Most of us form beliefs about the world through perception and induction. A sceptic may point out that we can suffer from illusions and hallucinations and that it is possible for the future to be entirely different from the past; he may deny that beliefs formed by perception or induction are justified at all. It is notoriously difficult to produce an ambitious argument that refutes an inductive sceptic or a sceptic about perceptual knowledge in terms that he himself accepts. If the moral agent cannot give an ambitious vindication of her beliefs about moral reasons for action then she has several 'companions in guilt', including anyone who has beliefs formed by perception and induction (and, of course, anyone who holds a controversial philosophical view).[46]

The 'companions in guilt' strategy raises the stakes for affirming that the moral agent is unjustified in accepting the authority of morality, given the lack of an ambitious vindication of it. If she is not justified, many of us are not justified in many of our beliefs. But, though raising the stakes can be an effective rhetorical move, it leaves open the possibility for a sceptic of simply denying that our beliefs are justified in these other areas. Perhaps many of our beliefs are not really justified after all.[47]

The 'companions in guilt' strategy claims that we should not be too worried that we have no ambitious vindication of morality since it is not unusual for us to be unable to refute a sceptic without begging the question against her. But we might be able to make some kind of response to egoism. We might be able to give a modest vindication of morality—that is, an argument that establishes to our own satisfaction that egoism is false.

But, the very idea of a modest vindication is rather puzzling. The egoist has a consistent and coherent view that everyone has reason to promote

---

[46] The 'companions in guilt' strategy is suggested by Mackie (1977) and employed by Shafer-Landau (2003).

[47] If there is no ambitious vindication of morality, one might think that this poses problems for common-sense morality. For example, if a perfectly rational person can fail to acknowledge moral reasons for action, do such reasons really apply to her? In other words, the lack of an ambitious vindication of morality may cast doubt on whether the Moral Authority thesis itself is true. I think this can be answered, however, by distinguishing between procedural rationality and substantive rationality. An egoist can be procedurally rational (because she makes no mistakes in reasoning) but, if morality does have practical authority, she is not substantively rational (because she does not acknowledge reasons for action that apply to her).

her own interests. She will deny all the claims that the moral agent makes. Without an ambitious vindication of the authority of morality, how can the moral agent defend herself? In the next chapter I consider arguments that all modest vindications of morality are fatally flawed and cannot be used against egoism.

# 6

# Modest Vindication

## 1. Modest Vindications of Common-sense Morality

Perhaps it is not possible to construct an argument showing that egoism is false without begging the question. Suppose that, instead of attempting to prove egoism false in the egoist's own terms, we tried to defend the authority of morality to our own satisfaction, appealing to premises that we, as moral agents who believe in common-sense morality, accept. This is clearly a more modest vindication.

*Modest vindication.* A valid argument based on premises that an egoist would not accept (but that a defender of common-sense morality would) that egoism is false.

As a first try, we might consider the following.

THE LIE
L1: I have reason not to lie.
L2: If L1, then egoism is false.
L3: So, egoism is false.

HELP
H1: I have reason to help those in need.
H2: If H1, then egoism is false.
H3: So, egoism is false.

But these will not do. Plenty of egoists will accept that I sometimes (maybe frequently) have reason not to lie and that I sometimes and perhaps often have reason to help those in need, because from time to time it is in my interest to do those things. It is even possible, according to egoism, that I always have reason not to lie, and reason to help those in need (provided that it is always in my interest to do so). So, H2 and L2 are false.

We need a different first premise. There are a number of possibilities. According to some moral theories, our reason not to do what is morally wrong is grounded precisely in the fact that doing so is morally wrong:

> THE LIE (moral rightness)
> L1: I have reason not to lie because lying is morally wrong.
> L2: If L1, then egoism is false.
> L3: So, egoism is false.

But according to other theories our reason not to do what is morally wrong is grounded in other properties of the action—for example, that it makes people unhappy. But, of course, moral agents will disagree about the relevant properties.

> THE LIE (happiness)
> L1: I have reason not to lie because lying makes other people unhappy.
> L2: If L1, then egoism is false.
> L3: So, egoism is false.

> THE LIE (respect)
> L1: I have reason not to lie because lying expresses a lack of respect for the other person.
> L2: If L1, then egoism is false.
> L3: So, egoism is false.

All three arguments set out not just a reason for action but a ground for that reason. According to egoism, you may have a reason not to lie, but only on very specific grounds: when doing so is in your interest. Egoism is not consistent with the ground of your reason not to lie being that lying is morally wrong, or that it makes other people unhappy, or that it expresses a lack of respect for others. So in each of these arguments L2 is true.

Different moral theories would support different first premises, and it is not clear which, if any, is part of common-sense morality. So we might try for an argument that is neutral between these different moral theories, but which avoids the problems of the original arguments.

> THE LIE (moral reason)
> L1: I have moral reason not to lie.
> L2: If L1, then egoism is false.
> L3: So, egoism is false.

According to egoism we have no specifically moral reason not to lie (where this is understood as a reason grounded in the kinds of considerations made explicit in the other LIE arguments) provided that we clearly distinguish moral reasons from reasons of long-term self-interest (as I have already argued that we should, in Chapter 2). So L2 of this argument is true too.

Similarly, we can envisage different versions of HELP, corresponding to different moral theories.

HELP (moral rightness)
H1: I have reason to help those in need because doing so is morally right.
H2: If H1, then egoism is false.
H3: So, egoism is false.

HELP (happiness)
H1: I have reason to help those in need because doing so makes them happy.
H2: If H1, then egoism is false.
H3: So, egoism is false.

HELP (virtue)
H1: I have reason to help those in need because doing so is generous and kind.
H2: If H1, then egoism is false.
H3: So, egoism is false.

And, again, a version which avoids taking a stand on these moral controversial questions.

HELP (moral reason)
H1: I have moral reason to help those in need.
H2: If H1, then egoism is false.
H3: So, egoism is false.

It proved to be very difficult to give an ambitious vindication of the authority of morality. But, proving that egoism is false—a first step in a defence of common-sense morality—seems to be much easier, provided that we can begin from premises accepted by moral agents, those who already believe common-sense morality. But there looks to be something not quite right about these arguments. In this chapter—and indeed the remainder of the book—I assess whether modest vindications of morality like THE LIE (moral reason) and HELP (moral reason) can be genuine vindications of common-sense morality. In Section 2, I set out two problems with the arguments. In Section 3, I develop a similar objection in more detail, the problem of 'cogency', in the course of which I compare arguments like HELP (moral reason) with 'Moorean' arguments defending common sense against sceptics and idealists. In Sections 4–6, I set out three possible responses to the problem of cogency. The first appeals to an idea of an 'entitlement' to believe that egoism is false. I argue that this response fails, but the other two—reliabilism and dogmatism—may succeed. The purpose of this chapter is not so much to defend one of these strategies, but rather to show that there are a number of ways that the problem may be solved, and there is no reason to think that in principle an argument like HELP (moral reason) cannot be cogent.

## 2.  Problems with Modest Vindication

Both THE LIE (moral reason) and HELP (moral reason) are valid arguments for the conclusion that egoism is false. Many people would accept their premises. And their premises may well be true, in which case the arguments are sound too. So far, so good. Of course, modest vindications are much less ambitious than the arguments that we were considering in the last chapter, which tried to show that the egoist could be defeated in her own terms. But perhaps it was a mistake to aim so high. We should be content with defeating her to our own satisfaction. So are there any problems with arguments like THE LIE (moral reason) or HELP (moral reason)?

A modest vindication is of limited dialectical assistance. No egoist would accept the first premise of either HELP (moral reason) or THE LIE (moral reason). We cannot prove to an egoist's own satisfaction that she had reason to be moral. Modest vindications *beg the question* against their opponent. In fact, the problem is worse: neither argument seems likely to convince a doubting or open-minded moral agent. When the nine-year-old Wittgenstein asked himself if he had reason not to lie, he was, at least at that time, taking seriously the possibility that egoism might be true. He surely would not have been satisfied if he had been offered THE LIE (moral reason) as a response. Modest arguments seem to be an *expression of our belief* in the authority of morality, rather than in any sense a *vindication* of it.

A second problem is that egoists seem to be able to respond in kind, with a modest vindication of their own views.[1]

SELF-HELP

SH1: I have reason to help those in need only when doing so will benefit me.

SH2: If SH1, then common-sense morality is false.

SH3: So, common-sense morality is false.

Of course, we are not particularly impressed by this argument, as we do not accept the first premise SH1. But, now putting forward modest vindications does not seem to have got us very far. Initially, the egoist said that we had only reasons based on self-interest. We disagreed. Now each of us has elaborated slightly on our original position, but surely no one has made much of an advance.

Of course, our positions may not be symmetrical: one of HELP (moral reason) or SELF-HELP may have a false premise whilst the premises of the other are all true. In other words, one of the arguments may be sound whilst the other is not. But we knew already that at most one from common-sense morality and egoism could be true, so once again we do not seem to have moved on by attempting a modest vindication of each.

Another way that the symmetry could fail is that the first premises of one might be epistemically justified, and the first premise of the other, not. This is different from a question of soundness—for premises can be true but epistemically unjustified, or false but epistemically justified. So it may not seem to help us very much to consider this question—for were we not concerned with whether common-sense morality or egoism was *true*?

But if there is a difference of epistemic justification between the premises of HELP and SELF-HELP, such that we are justified in accepting the first premise of HELP but an egoist is not epistemically justified in accepting the first premise of SELF-HELP, then there is an important difference

---

[1] This kind of argument has been offered for egoism. Brink, for example, suggests (though he does not endorse the claim) that we may think that it is reasonable to make a sacrifice only if you will later be compensated for that sacrifice. If I sacrifice my own happiness for yours, I will not be compensated; the benefit to you does not compensate me for my sacrifice (Brink 1992: 207–12; see also Brink 1997b: 102–5). This is clearly a claim that a moral agent will not accept, so it cannot be the basis of an ambitious vindication of egoism, but it could be the first premise of a modest vindication.

between us relating to the epistemic standing of each of us. This is not to say that one is true and the other is not; rather it is to say that one of us is justified in believing what we do, and the other is not. So a difference in epistemic justification for their premises would be an important difference between the two arguments. As we shall see, however it is not at all clear that either the egoist or moral agent is epistemically justified in accepting the first premises of their respective arguments. I set out this problem, the problem of disagreement, in the following chapter, and addressing it will take up the last part of the book.

First, however, I want to consider a related objection to modest vindications. Crispin Wright has written extensively about a similar argument, and he has a distinctive account of what is wrong with it. In the remainder of the chapter I will set out the problem as Wright conceives of it, and then see whether there is any way of rescuing modest vindications from this difficulty.

## 3. Cogency

In introducing the third potential problem with THE LIE (moral reason) and HELP (moral reason), it is useful to compare them with another apparently similar argument, Moore's defence of common sense. According to common sense, there is an external world, full of ordinary material objects like tables and chairs, people and other animals. And we know quite a lot about this world. But some people reject common sense. Idealists question whether there are any ordinary material objects: they think that tables and chairs are really collections of ideas. Sceptics cast doubt on whether we have any knowledge (or even justified beliefs) about the external world. It would be nice to have an ambitious vindication of common sense, an argument that addressed the sceptic and the idealist in their own terms proving that there is an external world as we ordinarily think of it (that is, a world as presented to us by perception, not the worlds, whatever they are like, that brains in vats and evil demons live in) and that we have knowledge of that external world. G. E. Moore famously defended common sense by pointing to his hands and making the following argument.[2]

---

[2] Moore 1959.

MOORE

M1: I have a hand.

M2: If M1 then common sense is right that there is an external world.

M3: So common sense is right that there is an external world.

Moore claimed to be more certain that he had a hand than he was certain of the truth of the premises of any sceptical argument attempting to show that he had no knowledge of the external world. In other words, he used the MOORE argument against scepticism, as well as against idealism.

There are important differences between scepticism as a rival to common sense, and egoism as a threat to common-sense morality. Egoists believe that common-sense morality is false, that there is no moral reason to help others and no moral reason not to lie. Sceptics do not necessarily believe that the world is different from the way that common sense presents it. They typically do not argue that we are wrong about the nature of the external world: they argue that we are mistaken when we claim to *know* anything about it. Sceptics point out that the world *might* be very different from how we think it is: you might be being fooled by an evil demon, or you might be a brain in a vat tricked by an evil scientist. Sceptics argue that in order to know the premises and conclusion of MOORE we must be able to rule out these relevant alternatives. For example:

SCEPTIC

S1: I might be a brain in a vat.

S2: If S1, then there might be no external world as I normally conceive of it.

S3: So, there might be no external world as I normally conceive of it.

Sceptics argue that since you cannot rule out S1 as false you cannot know that the conclusion S3 is false, and so you cannot know that there is an external world as you normally conceive of it.

By contrast, idealists have a positive view about the world; they think that it is made up of ideas, not mind-independent material objects. However, there is a similar problem with using MOORE against idealism as there was in using THE LIE against egoism. The idealist might well accept that Moore has a hand. But whereas according to common sense Moore's hand is a material object, according to the idealist it is not. So we can set out a new version of the argument that makes this explicit.

MOORE*
M1: I have a hand that is a mind-independent material object.
M2: If M1 then common sense is right and idealism is wrong: there is an external world which includes mind-independent material objects.
M3: So common sense is right and idealism is wrong: there is an external world which includes mind-independent material objects.

But now the idealist can produce a 'symmetrical' argument against common sense for his own views.[3]

IDEALISM
I1: I have a hand which is not a material object but a collection of ideas.
I2: If M1 then common sense is wrong about the external world.
I3: So common sense is wrong about the external world.

The relationship between MOORE* and IDEALISM is similar to that between HELP and SELF-HELP—more similar than the relationship between MOORE* and SCEPTIC—but it will help us to consider both the idealist and the sceptic as a threat to common sense.

Modest vindications such as MOORE* and HELP can be both valid and sound, but as arguments they seem to lack a crucial quality, which Wright calls *cogency*. If an argument is cogent, it can be used rationally to resolve doubt about its conclusion or rationally to convince anyone about the truth of its conclusion. A successful or 'cogent' argument must be able to *transmit justification* from the premises to the conclusion.[4]

Wright primarily discusses Moore's argument as a response to scepticism. Is it cogent? The evidence that I have for the first premise of MOORE*, M1, is my experience of having a hand. But this evidence is compatible with my being fooled by an evil demon, or my being a brain in a vat

---

[3] An idealist might insist that his theory is not contrary to common sense, either because common sense is neutral on whether hands are material objects or collections of ideas, or (more implausibly) because common sense supports the view that hands are collections of ideas. But, for the purposes of my argument, I will discuss only idealists who are prepared to accept that their theory conflicts with common sense.

[4] Wright 2002; Wright 2004. One might take issue with the idea of cogency. In what sense can justification 'transmit' from premises to conclusion? Does it really matter if an argument is not cogent? But, rather than raise these questions about cogency here, for the sake of argument I will assume that Wright's objection is legitimate, and I hope in this chapter to answer it by showing that modest vindications can be cogent.

with no hands, and there being no external world (or at least, none that corresponds to my experiences). If I were in one of these 'sceptical scenarios' my experience of having a hand would be radically misleading. In order to be justified in taking my experience to be evidence for my having hands, I need a justification for thinking that my experiences are reliable guides to the external world.[5] I need a justification for believing that there is an external world that my experiences accurately represent. In order to accept the first premise of MOORE*, I need already to have a justification for the conclusion. Wright claims that for these reasons MOORE* is not cogent.

Wright's diagnosis of the flaw in MOORE* can be applied to the arguments against egoism, HELP (moral reason), and THE LIE (moral reason). Let us say that my evidence that I have reason to help those in need because of their needs is that it seems to me that I have such a reason, and this fits with my other views about what reasons I have. But this is compatible with the possibility that I was taught as a child to help others and not to lie for the convenience of my parents, when in fact I have only reasons for action based on self-interest. My intuitions about reasons for action may not be in touch with reality. If I am to take what seems to me to be the case as evidence for what reasons I actually have, I need a justification for thinking that there are reasons for action not based on my interests that are accurately represented by what seems to me to be true: I need a justification for thinking that there are some reasons for action that are not based on my interests—that is, that egoism is false.[6] HELP (moral reason) cannot transmit justification from its first premise to its conclusion, because to have a justification for the first premise you already need to have a justification for the conclusion. HELP (moral reason) is not cogent.

Recall our first problem for our modest vindications: that they beg the question against egoism. We can now put this problem into Wright's terms: these arguments beg the question against egoism because any justification

[5] I could, for example, claim that I am justified in thinking that I have a hand that is a material object, because I perceive a hand and my perception is reliable: when I see a foot, a foot is there; when I see an arm, an arm is there; and so on. But, of course, this 'track record' argument *presupposes* that there is a material world and that when perception represents it in a particular way it does so accurately.

[6] Again, I might appeal to a 'track record' argument, that when I think that I have moral reason to do A I have such a reason, and so on, so my intuitions about morality are reliable. But, again, this argument *presupposes* that there are moral reasons for action and that when intuition represents them in a particular way, it does so accurately.

that you have for the premises (that you have a moral reason not to lie) presupposes that you have a justification for your conclusion (that egoism is false). In other words, it is rational for you to accept the premises of the argument only if you already accept the conclusion. Since the egoist does not already accept the conclusion, it is not rational for her to accept the premises. So it seems that no modest vindication of morality can be used to convince an egoist that her theory is false, or to resolve doubt in the mind of a moral agent. Modest vindications of the authority of morality seem not to be justifications at all.

## 4. Entitlement

Perhaps there is something especially problematic with trying to justify the basic methods that we use to form beliefs. It is very hard to see how to defend induction or perception or any other basic method of forming beliefs without using that method itself and therefore without presupposing that they are justified—in other words, without arguing in a circle. The same may be true of our reliance on our intuitions about what is morally right and what reasons for action we have.

These methods may need no justification at all: we can simply say we just do form beliefs by perception and induction, and there is no further question about whether we are entitled to do so. But that does not seem good enough: we can imagine many basic methods of forming beliefs that we might have had that are hopeless: counter-induction, for example (that is, forming beliefs on the basis that the future will be completely different from the past); or counter-perception (forming beliefs on the basis that the outputs of our sense organs are completely mistaken). Surely there must be something to be said about the difference between perception and counter-perception?

One obvious thing to say is: anyone who forms beliefs by counter-perception is not going to do very well in life. It will not be too long before they stroll onto a motorway and get run over or wander off a cliff. In most circumstances, your life will go better if you use induction and perception than if you use any other method of forming beliefs. Perhaps this is one way in which we can defend our use of perception or induction. Of course, this is not an argument that these methods are reliable. But we have already seen the problem in offering that kind of justification. This is a completely different sort of defence, one that gives us an 'entitlement' to accept that they are reliable: a warrant that does not require any evidence.[7] Perhaps the moral agent can claim a similar kind of entitlement to accept that she has reason to be moral.

Suppose that Robinson Crusoe is stuck alone on his island with nothing to eat except some odd-looking fruit that he has never seen before. He has no evidence that the fruit is safe to eat (and no evidence that it is unsafe). But if he does not eat it he will starve. What should he do? Obviously he should eat the fruit. If he doesn't eat the fruit, he will die slowly and painfully of starvation. If he does eat it and it is safe, then he will survive for a little longer. If he eats it and it is poisonous, he will die—but in that case he is no worse off than if he had not eaten it in the first place (assuming that it is no worse to die of poison than through starvation). Accepting that the fruit is edible and eating it is, for Crusoe, a dominant strategy. Accepting that p is a dominant strategy for you if you will either do better by accepting p or do no worse by accepting it than by accepting any of the alternatives open to you, whether or not p is true.[8] What does it mean for an outcome to be 'better' or 'no worse' than an alternative? If Robinson Crusoe eats the fruit and lives, he gets what he wants, for he has no desire to die. Survival is good for him and, arguably, it is also good overall that he carries on. Any of these measures—achieving your aims, self-interest, and moral value—could be used to assess outcomes, and, according to all of them, eating the fruit is a dominant strategy for Crusoe.[9] Following Crispin Wright, we can define strategic entitlement as follows: an agent X

---

[7] The concept of entitlement is introduced by Crispin Wright as a potential solution to the problem of answering scepticism. He suggests (2004) we have an 'entitlement' to believe that perception or induction is reliable: a kind of rational warrant whose possession does not require the existence of any evidence, a priori or empirical. He does not consider whether this strategy could be extended to defend our moral beliefs. In previous work (1985), Wright had given a different solution: suggesting that certain key propositions, like the proposition that there is an external world, are not actually truth-evaluable. Wright's claim was that, since these propositions are not truth-evaluable, there may be no need to provide a justification for them. Applied to the argument against egoism, this strategy implies that no argument against egoism is necessary, rather than that vindication of the authority of morality is possible. I will not therefore discuss Wright's earlier view.

[8] Wright 2004: 178–88. In Wright's view, 'acceptance' of p is connected to thought and action—you act as if you believe that p—but, unlike a belief, it is not rationally controlled by evidence. Wright also describes this as an entitlement to trust that p.

[9] Wright himself puts the matter this way (2004: 184): an outcome is good if we lead secure, happy, and valuable lives.

is strategically entitled to accept p iff it is a dominant strategy for X to act as if he had a justified belief that p and he has no sufficient reason to believe that p is false.[10]

A strategic entitlement is rather like a kind of practical reason that we have for not doubting certain propositions. Normally, we distinguish between having a pragmatic justification for accepting propositions on the grounds that doing so will have good consequences for us, and having an epistemic justification. A belief can be pragmatically justified without being epistemically justified when it is useful but we have no good evidence that it is true. Of course, someone who is sceptical that perceptual beliefs are justified is interested in epistemic justification: what kind of evidence you have for these beliefs. The success of the sceptic's challenge may be in showing that there are limits to the traditional conception of epistemic justification. But this might merely prove that we have good reason to allow pragmatic considerations to supplement traditional epistemic justification. This would give us some sort of response to the sceptic, though admittedly not one that engages directly with his original challenge. So can we use the concept of strategic entitlement to answer a sceptic about perception? Consider two strategies.

(1) Form beliefs about the external world on the basis of perception.
(2) Form beliefs about the external world on some other basis (e.g., by guessing what the world is like).

If perception is generally reliable, then obviously you can use it to make your way round the world and you will do much better by forming beliefs by perception than by any other strategy. But, if perception is not reliable, no method of forming beliefs about the world, certainly not guesswork, is going to be any better. Whatever we do, our lives are not going to be very successful. Since we have no reason to think that perception is unreliable, we seem to have a strategic entitlement to trust it.[11]

This is only a sketch of a response to the sceptic who doubts that we are justified in trusting our senses. It would need to be developed in much

---

[10] Strictly speaking, Wright defines a strategic entitlement in a context. X has a strategic entitlement to accept that p in a context of in that context it is a dominant strategy for X to act as if he had a justified belief that p, and he has no sufficient reason to believe that p is false (Wright 2004: 184).

[11] It is a dominant strategy for you to act as if perception is reliable because you will either do better by accepting that it is reliable (and forming perceptual beliefs) or do no worse by accepting it than by accepting any of the alternatives open to you, whether or not it really is reliable.

more detail. But, even so, it has a number of drawbacks, which Wright points out. First of all, he suggests that it could only be an answer to a certain type of sceptic. All we are entitled to conclude, on the basis of that argument, is that the world is open to perception when our sense organs are properly engaged—and they may not be engaged right now (you may be dreaming now, for example). Secondly, and more importantly, Wright insists that the argument establishes only that *if* there is a material world, our sense experience represents it reliably, not that there is in fact such a world. This is because the argument that using perception is a dominant strategy *assumes* that there is a material world: using perception is our best strategy to find our way around material objects. Since the argument presupposes that there is a material world that we need to navigate, it cannot be used to establish that there is one.[12] In other words, this argument can be used to counter (some forms of) scepticism, but it cannot be used against idealism, which denies that there is a material world. This is of course a problem for us. We saw earlier that the disagreement between egoists and defenders of common-sense morality is more similar to the disagreement between idealists and defenders of common sense than between the latter and sceptics. An argument that fails against idealism is unlikely to be helpful to us. And, indeed, we cannot use strategic entitlement to defend a modest vindication of common-sense morality.

The moral agent accepts that she has reason to be moral, on the basis, we may assume, of her intuitions that she has moral reason to help others, that she has moral reason not to lie, and so on. Suppose that the moral agent forms beliefs about her reasons for action using the following method.

Accept that your intuitions about reasons for action are reliable and therefore accept that you have reason to be moral.

When you decide what to do, you are not compelled to trust your own intuitions about reasons for action.[13] If you doubt the reliability of your

---

[12] Ibid. 188. Wright distinguishes between methodological scepticism (about whether perception should be used as a method to form beliefs) and ontological scepticism (about whether there actually is an external world). Scepticism about the external world, however, includes both methodological and ontological concerns, and whilst the strategic entitlement answers the former, it cannot address the latter. We have an entitlement to trust our senses, but we still cannot answer a sceptic who doubts that there is a material world—someone like the idealist.

[13] This is a significant difference between trusting sense perception and trusting our normative intuitions. If you do not use your sense organs to find out about the world, what could you use instead?

own normative intuitions, there are many other ways in which you might form beliefs about what you have reasons to do. You might find a guru and simply do whatever he or she told you to do. You might find a text that could guide you. You might do whatever your peers do. You might imagine what an egoist would do in her situation and choose to do that. So consider a different way of deciding what to do.

Ignore your own intuitions about reasons for action, accept that all your reasons for action are based on self-interest and emulate an egoist.[14]

Is there a dominant strategy with regard to forming beliefs about reasons for action? Suppose that the moral agent could either trust her own intuitions about reasons for action, or she could emulate what an egoist would do in her circumstances. In many circumstances, the egoist and the moral agent will agree about which reasons for action they have (though they will disagree about the grounds of these reasons) and, as a consequence, they are likely to end up doing the same thing. In those circumstances they are, presumably, equally good strategies.

There are, however, circumstances in which the moral agent would form different beliefs if she trusted her intuitions than if she accepted egoism, and as a consequence is likely to act differently too. An egoist would think

Of course, if you think that one sensory mode may be unreliable (e.g., your eyesight) you can use other modes instead (e.g., touch). But if you doubt the reliability of all of them, you cannot ask someone else, or consult a textbook, for you would still be relying on the reliability of your senses to find out what they thought. It does not follow that sense perception must be reliable, but it does mean that it is much more difficult to think of a realistic form of 'counter-perception' other than mere guesswork.

[14] Is this just a complicated way of relying on your own intuitions? If you emulate an egoist, must you at the same time judge that they tend to get the answers right; in other words, use your own judgement after all? It is certainly possible to follow advice or do what you think someone else would do because you think doing so is a good idea. But this is not essential. It is possible to decide to follow a guru on a whim, not because you think that what he says is always or even frequently right. On the other hand, there is a difference between deliberating about what to do and deciding to emulate an egoist, for example, and simply acting without any thought at all. In so far as deliberation, rather than merely opting for one way of action, implies responding to what you think are reasons, then you must at the very least decide that you have reason to emulate an egoist or a moral agent, or that doing so is in some sense justified. You must, therefore, rely on your intuitions to some extent. But it makes perfect sense to judge that you have reason to emulate an egoist, even if, like the moral agent, you tend to think that we have reasons to be moral. The egoist might have persuaded you, for example, that your own intuitions about reasons for action are unreliable and that he is the better judge. Now you might be mistaken about that; but the fact remains that you can deliberate about how to act without accepting that you have reasons to be moral, and without relying on your own intuitions when they tell you that you have reason to be moral. So the moral agent has no entitlement to trust her own intuitions, on the grounds that that is essential for rational deliberation (the entitlement of rational deliberation is discussed by Wright (2004: 197–203)).

that she had reason to fake some qualifications on her CV to get a better job or to invest the money she might have given to charity buying the shares of a weapons manufacturer. A moral agent would argue that she had moral reasons not to do these things that in at least some cases would be more forceful than the competing reasons of self-interest.

When the two strategies call for different responses, which is better? The crucial question here is: better in what sense? There are several ways in which we can judge whether a strategy is better or worse. Suppose that we think of good outcomes as ones in which we live valuable lives: this could be a life that the egoist would regard as good, or a life that the moral agent would regard as good (recall, for example, the two conceptions of flourishing distinguished in Chapter 4). We could measure whether a strategy is 'no worse than' another in distinctively moral terms: on its impact on others as well as oneself, on the morally relevant consequences.[15] Unless she is exceptionally poor at carrying out her intentions, it is likely that, judged in moral terms, a moral agent's trusting her intuitions will be better than other strategies, if her intuitions are reliable.[16] And, if they are not reliable, no other strategy of forming beliefs about reasons for action is likely to be any better. Since the moral agent has no sufficient reason to think that her intuitions are mistaken, she is strategically entitled to accept that her intuitions about reasons for action are reliable.

But this assumes that it is legitimate to judge the different strategies in moral terms. But, suppose that the moral agent's intuitions are unreliable and there are no reasons to be moral. A rational agent need not take into account moral issues when deciding what to do. But, if moral matters are practically irrelevant, why should strategies of accepting reasons for action be judged in moral terms? There are situations in which you could make money from telling a lie, and are not likely to be exposed. In terms of your (non-moral) self-interest—your desires, aims, pleasure, and so on—you would do better to lie. Similarly, there will be other occasions where you could profit by doing something that you have moral reason not to

---

[15] There is a hint of this kind of assessment in Wright's suggestion that we judge strategies in terms of whether we lead secure, happy, and valuable lives (ibid. 184).

[16] It is possible that the moral agent's trusting her intuitions will sometimes produce a worse outcome, even in moral terms, than using some other strategy: a moral agent may make many people very unhappy by her patronizing and clumsy attempts to help them. So, even if we judge strategies in straightforward moral terms, trusting her intuitions may be worse than other strategies for a moral agent.

do. You would miss out on these benefits if you act on common-sense morality. But you can enjoy them if you emulate an egoist. Of course, you have to be careful not to lose the benefits of (apparent) cooperation and trustworthiness. But it is most likely that, judged in terms of unmoralized self-interest, the following strategy will be most successful.

Ignore your own intuitions about reasons for action, accept that all your reasons for action are based on long-term self-interest, and emulate a sophisticated egoist.

It is likely that the methods of the moral agent are sometimes worse than other strategies, if 'worse than' is understood as a measure of the agent's own unmoralized interests. Even if you are in the fortunate position that the cost to you of doing what is morally right is not very high and you are never called on to give up your life, or the people you love, or substantial amounts of your income, nevertheless, you may still do worse in terms of your own self-interest if you accept, as the moral agent does, that you sometimes have reason to sacrifice your interests for others.[17]

Trusting her intuitions is a dominant strategy for a moral agent only if the strategies open to her are judged in moral terms. But that is appropriate only if she is right that there are reasons to do what is morally right and not to do what is morally wrong. But that is exactly what is at issue between the moral agent and the egoist. So the argument is not neutral between the two strategies: it presupposes that the moral agent is correct that there are reasons to be moral in order to judge whether it is a dominant strategy. It begs the question against egoism.[18]

There are two main problems in our claiming a strategic entitlement to reject egoism. First, there are realistic alternatives to deciding what to do other than trusting your intuitions and accepting that you have reason to be moral. It is far from absurd that someone might choose to ask advice

[17] You are likely to do worse in terms of self-interest if you accept that you have reason to sacrifice your own interests for those of others, provided that it is not in your unmoralized self-interest to act on the basis of commonsense morality. Since you can sometimes achieve significant benefits through wrongdoing, it is unlikely to be in your unmoralized self-interest to follow common sense morality.

[18] The challenge from the egoist to the moral agent is of two kinds: a methodological challenge about whether she should trust her normative intuitions about reasons for action and a metaphysical challenge about whether there really are reasons to be moral. If we use moral terms to judge strategies, then the moral agent trusting her intuitions and accepting that there are reasons to be moral is a dominant strategy. This would settle the methodological question, but not the metaphysical one. The moral agent would be entitled to accept what her intuitions told her about moral reasons to act, but only if there were any. So it is unclear that this strategy really could be used against egoism in any case, since the egoist denies that there are reasons to be moral.

from someone else, or even emulate an egoist, rather than relying on her own intuitions about what to do.[19] Secondly, the argument that the moral agent's strategy is dominant relies on the moral agent being right that there are reasons to be moral, which is exactly what the egoist denies. This is similar to the problem that Wright sees in claiming an entitlement to accept that there is a material world: the argument that through perception you can successfully navigate the material world presupposes that there is material world, and so begs the question against idealism. The moral agent would have an entitlement to accept the Moral Authority thesis, but only if it were true. And that was the question at issue from the start. We are once again back where we began.[20]

## 5. Simple Reliabilism

Perhaps we were too swift to give up on the possibility of epistemic justification for premises like: I have a hand (that is a material object) or

[19] By contrast, it is hard to conceive of viable ways of forming beliefs about the external world except by perception that have any prospect of success—so we do have an entitlement to use perception (though perhaps not an entitlement to accept that there is a material world).

[20] Wright distinguishes some other forms of entitlement, including an *entitlement of cognitive project*: 'If a cognitive project is indispensable, or anyway sufficiently valuable to us—in particular, its failure would at least be no worse than the costs of not executing it, and its success would be better—and the attempt to vindicate (some of) its presuppositions would raise presuppositions of its own of no more secure an antecedent status . . . then we are entitled to . . . the original presuppositions without specific evidence in their favour' (ibid. 192). Does the moral agent have a cognitive project that it is indispensable or sufficiently valuable, for which she needs to use her own intuitions about reasons for action? The moral agent may well have a cognitive project of the following kind: working out how to live and what she and others have reason to do. Whether or not this project is indispensable, however, arguably it is very valuable, in the sense that 'its failure would at least be no worse than the costs of not executing it, and its success would be better'. Moreover, perhaps carrying out the project of thinking about how to live could be no worse than not doing so in terms of its *epistemic* consequences—that is, in terms of the moral agent believing more true propositions and fewer false ones. So the project of thinking how to live and what to do is of the right kind to generate entitlements. But, according to Wright, a cognitive project generates entitlements only if it includes presuppositions that must be taken for granted. Must the moral agent trust her intuitions in order to think about how to live and what reasons for action she has? We have already questioned whether the moral agent must rely on her own intuitions—instead she might do what she imagines an egoist would do or follow someone else's advice even if her own normative intuitions oppose this. Furthermore, it is questionable whether carrying out a project of working out how to live by trusting one's intuitions will result in believing more true propositions and fewer false ones. After all, if the egoist and the moral agent both trust their intuitions, they will end up believing opposing theories. So, trusting your intuitions, whatever they are, is not always a route to believing more truths. Does the project of thinking what to do require you to presuppose that there are moral reasons for action? Clearly not, since the egoist can carry out that project too, without the presupposition. So it is not clear that a moral agent is entitled, in this sense, to presuppose that her intuitions are correct and morality does have practical authority.

I have moral reason to help those in need. Perhaps we can overcome the problem of cogency without resorting to claiming an entitlement to believe these propositions.

Suppose that perception is in fact a reliable method of forming beliefs about the external world. Moore looks down and sees his hand. Then, according to what I will call *simple reliabilism*, he is justified in believing that he has a hand.[21] He does not need to know that perception is reliable. He does not even have to have reason to think that it is. So he doesn't need evidence that there is an external world in order to accept the first premise of the MOORE* argument. The MOORE* argument is cogent. Moreover, the idealist cannot make a similar modest argument in response because his method of forming beliefs is not reliable—it keeps resulting in false beliefs, so he is not epistemically justified in accepting the first premise of his modest argument IDEALISM. And, similarly, the sceptic keeps forming false beliefs (that we have no knowledge) and so his method is unreliable too and he is not justified in accepting scepticism. Only the defender of common sense has justified beliefs and only he can use a modest argument against his opponents.

Suppose that your method of forming beliefs about reasons for actions is reliable. You judge that you do have moral reason to help others because of their needs. According to simple reliabilism you don't need to know that your beliefs are reliably formed: you are justified in accepting the first premise of the HELP argument anyway and you can use that argument to conclude that egoism must be false. Nor can the egoist use SELF-HELP against you, because she is not justified in accepting the first premise (because she is forming her beliefs by an unreliable method, one that regularly results in false beliefs).

There are, however, problems, some for simple reliabilism as a theory of justification, some particularly with simple reliabilism in a defence of

---

[21] There are other more sophisticated forms of reliabilism, according to which if your belief is to be justified, it needs to be formed by a reliable method, but you also need some justification for thinking that it has been formed by a reliable method—or at least no strong reason for thinking that it has not been formed by an unreliable method. It is not clear that these extra conditions can be met when we form our belief about reasons for action, since the existence of so much disagreement suggests that many of us, at least, are forming our beliefs by unreliable methods (I discuss further whether our beliefs are formed by a reliable method later in this section). In addition, it is questionable whether the argument would be cogent, if in order for the initial premise to be justified, it was necessary to dispel doubts about the reliability of your methods of forming beliefs. So I will not discuss sophisticated versions of reliabilism further here.

morality. The problems for simple reliabilism are well known and I will not discuss them further here; I will turn instead to the problems in using it in defence of morality. According to reliabilism, the HELP argument is cogent only if the moral agent's belief in the first premise—that she has moral reason to help people—is reliably formed. Of course, you do not actually need to know that your method is reliable in order to be justified, according to this theory.[22] So the question need not be of urgent interest to an agent; no one has to delve into her methods of belief formation in order to form justified beliefs. But it is nevertheless of interest to a theorist who wants to know whether moral agents do indeed have justified beliefs. And there are some quite good reasons to think that our methods are not reliable.

In the first place, moral agents frequently disagree with one another over what is morally required and why, and, as we know, egoists regularly disagree with all of them about reasons for action. At least one of an egoist and a moral agent must be using an unreliable method, and what reason do we have to think that his method is flawed and ours is fine? Moreover, it is possible that neither of them is reliable. And there are in fact good reasons to doubt that any of us forms our beliefs about reasons reliably.

It is easy to give at least a rough outline, if vague and very general, of why our perceptual beliefs might be reliable. Creatures that can move around and manipulate their environment are more likely to survive than creatures that do not, and to do that they need accurate information about the location and nature of the objects around them.[23] This theory of how

---

[22] Though if our methods are reliable, we may be able to use a 'track record' argument to prove to ourselves that they are, even if we have no account of how this can be so.

[23] See Street 2006. Evolution will select methods of perception that are reliable, so it is not unreasonable to expect creatures like ourselves to have them. Can we give a similar account of why we might have evolved to have correct beliefs about moral rightness and about reasons for action? Suppose that there are facts about moral rightness and wrongness and reasons for action, such that we generally have reason not to do what is wrong and reason to do what is right. When they are considered in such an abstract form, it may not be obvious why it would be useful for us to form true beliefs about these matters. But in particular cases it is easier to see. For example, suppose that we do have reason to help other people when they are in need; suppose that we do have reason not to lie even when it is in our own interests. Having true beliefs about these matters may influence our actions in a way that is overall conducive to our survival and the survival of others. Of course, this account is just a rough outline and it may not be easy to fill in the details. But in any case it is likely to face two strong objections. First, there is a disanalogy between this account of why we have true beliefs about practical reasons and the sketch of why we have true beliefs about the objects around us. It is useful for us to have true beliefs about those objects whatever the facts are: it is useful for us to track the truth about them. It may be useful for us to believe truly that we have reason to help others when they are in need, but we have

perceptual justification is reliable is of course circular, in the sense that the evidence that we have for that theory, concerning the function of our sense organs and their causal connection to the world, was itself gathered through those sense organs, and therefore presupposes their reliability. But there is no similar account for our beliefs about reasons, not even one that is circular.[24]

Moral 'intuition' is sometimes described as if it were a special kind of telescope through which we are supposed to be able to survey moral reality from our armchair, where the only way of checking whether your observations are correct is to use the same telescope in exactly the same way. But, clearly, that is not so. Empirical information, your experience, the advice and example of others can all play a role in your forming beliefs about what you have reason to do. But it is nevertheless true that they ultimately rely on your judgement about morality, its authority, and your reasons for action. For all your careful reflection, it could be no more than a coincidence that you have true beliefs about reasons for action; worse still, your beliefs might be false. How can it be that reflecting on our reasons for action, forming theories about them, making judgements about real and imaginary situations is a good way of forming beliefs about practical reasons?

no explanation of why it might be useful for us to track truths about reasons. Suppose that we actually had reason to cheat and lie and destroy one another. Then it would not be conducive to the survival of all if we had true beliefs about reasons. So there is no reason, after all, to think that a mechanism to form beliefs about reasons that is responsive to the facts would be selected. This problem is not quite as difficult as it first seems. We must concede that if the facts about our reasons for action were very different from what they actually are, we would not have tracked them. If human life was altogether morally bad, and we all had most reason to kill ourselves immediately, we might not have tracked the truth about reasons. But if the objects around us had all been too big or too small for us to navigate or manipulate, it would not have been useful for us to track the truth about them either. On the other hand, smaller changes in human life and in what is valuable might be usefully tracked. For example, if we no longer needed to be nurtured for such a long time as babies and children, the ethics of child-rearing would be quite different as would our reasons for action. It would clearly be useful then to track the truth about reasons for action in these cases, and we might expect such an ability to be selected. A second worry is more serious. There is a rival account of why we form the beliefs about reasons that we do. We might have formed beliefs about reasons for action that are directly conducive to survival, independently of facts, if there are any, about reasons for action (Street 2006 presses this worry). We have to concede that this is true. The sketch offered here does not show that an ability to form beliefs about reasons by a reliable method must have been selected. It can only show that it might have been selected.

[24] These same questions can also be raised for our mathematical and logical beliefs, and have clearly connections to the Benacerraf problem for mathematical knowledge—namely, how could we have reliable beliefs about mathematical entities when they are not causally efficacious (Benacerraf 1973)?

The link between our beliefs and the facts could be causal. For example, we might quite literally perceive, when confronted with someone in need, that we have reason to help him. Of course, it is not at all plausible that all of our beliefs about reasons are causally linked to the facts: we make judgements about reasons for action in the future and in hypothetical situations. We might, however, be in some kind of causal contact with at least some of our reasons for action. But we have no detailed account of this causal connection, the nature of the facts about reasons for action, or our receptivity to those facts. We have no explanation of why some people (such as egoists) are worse than others at detecting the facts. An appropriate causal connection *might* exist between our beliefs and the facts, but as yet we have no good reason to think that it *does*.

Alternatively, there could be a different kind of reliable connection between our beliefs and the facts. Truths about our reasons for action might be conceptual truths: it might be part of the concept of lying, for instance, that we have reason not to lie. However, it is not very plausible that the most important facts about reasons are conceptual truths. It does not seem to be a conceptual truth that we have reason to help others who are in need because of their needs. It is not a *conceptual* mistake that the egoist is making, but a *substantive* mistake about which reasons for action there are.[25]

There is much more to be said about both these suggestions, and it might be possible to overcome their well-known difficulties. There is, however, an important third possibility. The outcome of our reflection, whatever it is, might determine the truth about our reasons for action. That would certainly secure a reliable connection between our beliefs and the facts. The problem with this sort of anti-realism, however, is that we were trying to give a defence of common-sense morality, according to which there is no simple connection between our beliefs about reasons for action and the reasons themselves: believing that you have reason to help others does not make it the case that you do have such a reason, and you may have moral reason not to lie whether you realize it or not. Common-sense morality

---

[25] Of course, it is not easy to distinguish clearly between conceptual and substantive mistakes. So I do not intend to rule out completely the possibility of defending a conceptual account of at least some moral knowledge. But, once again, there is no plausible and detailed account of this kind and as yet no reason to think that one could be provided.

is perhaps compatible with a sophisticated form of anti-realism, however, and this might be the most promising way of explaining how there could be a reliable connection between our beliefs about reasons for action and the reasons themselves.[26]

Simple reliabilism does not require an agent to know, or even reasonably to believe that her beliefs are reliably formed. So the fact that moral agents have no idea whether they have a reliable connection to the facts about moral reasons does not matter, provided that it nevertheless exists.[27] But, nevertheless, it is hard to be satisfied with the mere possibility of the HELP (moral reason) and THE LIE (moral reason) arguments being cogent, when we have little idea of what kind of reliable connection there might be between the facts about reasons for action and our beliefs about them. Rather than explore these theories further, however, I want to look elsewhere. There are other options for defending modest arguments. We might appeal to a different variety of externalist theory.[28] Instead of that, however, I want to consider a completely different approach, which I call moral dogmatism.

## 6. Moral Dogmatism

Suppose that you try to give a modest vindication of the authority of morality with the argument HELP (moral reason).

> HELP (moral reason)
> H1: I have moral reason to help those in need.
> H2: If H1, then egoism is false.
> H3: So, egoism is false.

---

[26] This is not to say that there are no further problems with anti-realism. For example, given the amount of disagreement between moral agents as well as between moral agents and egoists, there are problems for the claim that there is a close connection between what we believe about reasons for action and what is true (there is a danger of an unattractive form of relativism, according to which reasons for action are different depending on what the agent believes her reasons for action are). It is unclear whether a sufficiently sophisticated form of anti-realism could successfully avoid relativism.

[27] Therefore, anyone who formed perceptual beliefs without having an account of perception could still have justified beliefs.

[28] That is, one that does not require us to rule out 'sceptical scenarios' in order to be justified in thinking that we are not in one of them, but does not require a reliable connection to exist between our beliefs and the facts in order for our beliefs to be epistemically justified.

The egoist asks you to defend that first premise. Surely the most natural thing to say is: it is just obvious that we have a moral reason to help those in need—we should help them because they need help, not because ultimately doing so will rebound to our benefit. H1 needs no further argument or defence. Anyone who understands it and is at all thoughtful will immediately be able to see that it is correct.

Call this sort of account of H1 *moral dogmatism*. It is inspired by a 'dogmatic' response to scepticism about the external world (I will call this *perceptual dogmatism*).[29] Perceptual dogmatism is particularly well placed to solve the problem of 'transmitting justification' from the premises to the conclusion. Consider again the argument MOORE*.

MOORE*
M1: I have a hand that is a mind-independent material object.
M2: If M1 then common sense is right and idealism is wrong: there is an external world which includes mind-independent material objects.
M3: So common sense is right and idealism is wrong: there is an external world which includes mind-independent material objects.

The perceptual dogmatist says that when I look at my hand I have an experience of a special kind. I seem to ascertain that I have a hand that is a mind-independent object. Having an experience of this nature, with this phenomenology, gives me a prima facie justification for believing that I do indeed have a hand. So I am justified in accepting M1, without needing any justification for thinking that there is an external world. The conclusion of MOORE* does not have to be justified prior to the premise, and MOORE* is a cogent argument after all.[30]

[29] This is a modification of Pryor's account of dogmatism as a response to scepticism about the external world in Pryor 2004 and Pryor 2000. Pryor sets out the argument in response to scepticism rather than idealism and he does not explicitly say that the experience is of a mind-independent material object (and it is not clear to me whether he would accept this). Pryor does not endorse or even consider extending the strategy to justify our moral beliefs.

[30] It is a good question—one I cannot address here—whether one can have perceptual experiences of this content (this goes beyond what Pryor explicitly claims as the content of the relevant experience in his presentation of perceptual dogmatism). Are things really presented to you in perception as mind-independent material objects? If they are, then Moore can use his argument against idealism. If not, you nevertheless have a perceptual experience as of having a hand and so, *ceteris paribus*, you are justified in believing that you have a hand. You therefore have an answer to the sceptic (who claims you are not justified in believing that you have a hand) though not the idealist (who claims that you are justified in believing that you have a hand, but that it is not a mind-independent material object).

Suppose that when I see someone who needs my help, whom I could help very easily; or when I simply reflect on whether I have moral reason to help others in need, it strikes me very forcibly that I do. I have an experience of the following kind: I seem to ascertain that I have moral reason to help others.[31]

The moral dogmatist claims that my seeming to ascertain a moral reason to help is a prima facie justification for my believing that I do have a moral reason to help. This justification does not require me to have independent evidence that I have some reasons for action that are not based on my own interests. Instead it depends on the phenomenology of 'seeming to ascertain a moral reason'. If this is right, I have a prima facie justification for the first premise of the HELP (moral reason) argument that does not depend on my having a justification for its conclusion. The argument is cogent after all.

Moral dogmatism might be a strategy that appealed to an epistemological intuitionist. According to intuitionism, some basic moral propositions are known non-inferentially. Intuitionists characterize this non-inferential knowledge in different ways. According to one version, it actually is available to us through a kind of moral perception.

If you round a corner and see a group of young hoodlums pour gasoline on a cat and ignite it, you do not need to conclude that what they are doing is wrong; you do not need to figure anything out; you can see that it is wrong.[32]

The phenomenology of moral experience supports the claim that we sometimes 'just see' the moral properties, like the property of wrongness, when we see that setting light to a cat is wrong. The wrongness of the action is represented to us in a perceptual-like experience, just as we see that the cat is ginger and feel that the fire is hot.[33] We might in addition *just see* that the

---

[31] Once again, we might ask whether we have experiences of this content: are we struck by seeming to have a reason at all, and, if we are, are we struck by having reasons of certain kinds? I think it is not implausible that we are sometimes (though not always) struck by having reason to do something, and that sometimes we are struck by its being a moral reason. For example, suppose that you pass near to an old lady who has fallen over and needs to be helped up. It is not implausible that you just 'see' that you have a moral reason to help.

[32] Harman 1977: 4. Harman himself does not think we actually gain moral knowledge through perception. See also McGrath 2004.

[33] It is a significant question which properties are represented in perception. An opponent of intuitionism might argue that all we see in perception is natural properties and that we infer moral properties from these (Väyrynen 2008). But I will leave this problem aside and assume for the sake of argument that we have some kind of perceptual-like experience in which moral properties are directly represented.

boys have a moral reason not to set light to the cat. It is not very plausible that we get all our moral knowledge through a kind of perception.[34] But an intuitionist may well accept that not all our moral knowledge is gained in this way, but insist that some of it is. The remainder may be inferred from our basic moral knowledge, or have some other source.

This version of intuitionism, explicitly linking moral knowledge to perception, is obviously very similar to perceptual dogmatism. With alternative versions of intuitionism the connection is not as clear, for, according to this theory, some basic moral propositions are known a priori: they are 'self-evident', known on the basis of reflection alone.[35]

The very idea that some moral propositions are self-evident faces obvious difficulties. If anyone who understands the proposition is justified in accepting it, why is there so much disagreement in ethics amongst people who know perfectly well what they are talking about? But a proposition that is self-evident need not be obvious. Even if understanding the proposition is a sufficient justification for believing it to be true, it does not follow that everyone who understands it actually does believe it.

There may be some analytic moral truths that we know a priori: wrongful killing is wrong, for example. But intuitionists typically claim that we also know some moral propositions that are not analytic—for example, that we have moral reason to help those in need. It is not very plausible that this is a conceptual truth.[36] These intuitionists are therefore committed to our having synthetic a priori knowledge. It is notoriously difficult to understand how this sort of knowledge is possible. Their claim that the justification for our believing these propositions is that they are 'self-evident' is not very helpful. How can we settle whether a proposition like 'I have moral reason not to tell lies' is self-evident, whereas 'I have reason to tell lies when doing so benefits me' is not?

Intuitionists have not given detailed explanations of what it is for a proposition to be self-evident, but one way to understand their claim is the

---

[34] If we take the possibility of this kind of perception seriously, we can have non-inferential knowledge of particular moral propositions (e.g., that particular action is wrong) or of propositions about reasons for action, but not of general propositions (setting light to cats is wrong) nor of the wrongness of future actions or actions performed in hypothetical circumstances, since these are not and cannot be represented in perception.

[35] That is, they are known on the basis of reflection, and not by being inferred from propositions that were already known in another way.

[36] Stratton-Lake 2002: 18–19, 22; see also Shafer-Landau 2003: 247–66; Audi 1996; Audi 1997. Roger Crisp (2002: 59) attributes this view to Sidgwick.

following. Though at first glance it may not be obvious to me whether or not I have a reason to help others, if, on reflection, I seem to ascertain a reason to help others because of their needs, this 'seeming to ascertain a moral reason' is a prima facie justification to believe that I do in fact have a moral reason to help others.[37] This is a kind of dogmatism that appeals to what presents itself to us on reflection rather than through perception, but in other relevant respects it is similar to perceptual dogmatism.

Can moral dogmatism of either type vindicate the authority of morality? Suppose that you do seem to ascertain a reason to help others because of their needs. According to moral dogmatism, this is a prima facie justification for believing that you do have such a reason. So you are justified in accepting H1 independently of any justification you might have for believing that egoism is false. The HELP (moral reason) argument is cogent, and you can use it to reject egoism.

Can the egoist respond with a cogent modest vindication of her own? Recall the SELF-HELP argument.

SELF-HELP

SH1: I have reason to help those in need only when doing so will benefit me.

SH2: If SH1, then common-sense morality is false.

SH3: So, common-sense morality is false.

Suppose that the egoist seems to ascertain a reason to help others only when doing so is in her interests. If she does have an experience of the right phenomenology then it seems that she is justified in accepting SH1 and she does have a cogent argument against common-sense morality.[38]

---

[37] There may be other strategies of justification to which an intuitionist might appeal. In addition, some intuitionists would reject moral dogmatism. According to moral dogmatism, our justification for these propositions is based on the phenomenology of the experience we undergo when we reflect on them. This kind of justification might not count as a priori (depending on what it means for a justification to be a priori).

[38] It is possible that the egoist might think she had an experience of the right kind even though she did not, in which case she would not be justified in accepting SH1 after all. But it certainly seems possible for an egoist to have an experience of the right phenomenology even if egoism is false. Compare your experience when you look at an optical illusion like the Müller-Lyer illusion. You have an experience of seeming to ascertain that there are two lines in front of me that are not equal in length. According to perceptual dogmatism, this is a prima facie justification for taking there to be two lines in front of you that are not equal in length—but they really are the same length. Suppose that the egoist does have an experience of the right phenomenology, an experience of seeming to ascertain a reason to help others only when doing so is in her interests. It follows, according to moral dogmatism, that

## 7. Conclusion

Modest vindications can be cogent: they are if either dogmatism or simple reliabilism is the correct theory of justification of these matters, and there may be other possibilities too. Of course I have not attempted to defend any particular account of moral justification, and all of them may have further problems not yet considered here; but the problem of cogency seems to be solvable, at least in principle.

Does that mean that we can at last rest satisfied? Unfortunately not. We can in principle have a modest vindication of the authority of morality against egoism that is cogent. But modest vindications still have a serious problem, which is the subject of the next chapter. There is a good reason to think that no one is epistemically justified in accepting the first premises of HELP (moral reason) or THE LIE (moral reason). All of us should in fact suspend judgement on whether our reason to help others is based on self-interest or not—and similarly whether our reason not to lie is a moral reason or not—and so we cannot use HELP (moral reason) or THE LIE (moral reason) or any similar argument against egoism.

she is epistemically justified in accepting SH1 and the conclusion SH3 that common-sense morality is false, and her argument is valid and cogent.

# 7

# Disagreement

## 1. The Problem of Disagreement

It is easy to construct an argument against egoism if you can begin from an explicitly moral premise.

> HELP (moral reason)
> H1: I have moral reason to help those in need.
> H2: If H1, then egoism is false.
> H3: So, egoism is false.

In the last chapter, I found that there were standard approaches to epistemic justification, including dogmatism and simple reliabilism, according to which HELP (moral reason) was cogent. I did not defend either of these as the correct theory of justification, but I have established that modest vindications of morality can at least in principle be cogent.

There remains, however, a serious problem for arguments like HELP (moral reason). In brief, the problem is this. When there is disagreement of a certain type over whether a proposition is true, it is epistemically rational to suspend judgement about its truth. There is disagreement of this type over the first premise of HELP, so it is not rational for the moral agent to accept that premise, and she cannot use the argument against egoism. She cannot vindicate morality, even modestly. This problem of disagreement proves to be much more intractable than issues of cogency, and ultimately my defence of morality against this problem will take up the remainder of the book. In this chapter, I will set out the problem in detail.

There are widespread, persistent, and apparently irresolvable disagreements about morality, with regard to both its content and its authority. In the past, many people thought slavery was acceptable; in the present, most people do not. Even now, there are disagreements about whether abortion is ever permissible, whether eating meat is always wrong, whether capital punishment is just. This means that it is difficult to find a first premise for a modest vindication of common-sense morality on which everyone will agree. The following versions of HELP will be accepted by some but not all moral agents.

HELP (moral rightness)
H1: I have reason to help those in need because doing so is morally right.
H2: If H1, then egoism is false.
H3: So, egoism is false.

HELP (happiness)
H1: I have reason to help those in need because doing so makes them happy.
H2: If H1, then egoism is false.
H3: So, egoism is false.

H3: HELP (virtue)
H1: I have reason to help those in need because doing so is generous and kind.
H2: If H1, then egoism is false.
H3: So, egoism is false.

We devised versions of HELP and THE LIE to avoid this problem:

HELP (moral reason)
H1: I have moral reason to help those in need.
H2: If H1, then egoism is false.
H3: So, egoism is false.

THE LIE (moral reason)
L1: I have moral reason not to lie.
L2: If L1, then egoism is false.
L3: So, egoism is false.

But, of course, egoists do not accept this L1 or H1, and this poses a problem for THE LIE and HELP as vindications of morality.

Suppose that an egoist and I are confronted with exactly the same situation: we come across a homeless person who needs some money to buy food. It is clear to both of us that this person is very unlikely ever to be in a position to help us in return, and the effect on our reputation will be negligible—there is no one about and no one is likely to find out. Nevertheless, I judge that both of us have reason to help him—specifically a moral reason to do so. The egoist judges that she has no reason to help, since doing so is not in her interests. We both seem to be careful, sensible people, and I have no antecedent grounds—before we started to make opposing judgements about reasons—for thinking that either of us is better at appreciating what reasons for action there really are. One of us (or both) must have made a mistake. But either might attempt to explain the other's mistake in terms of the way that they have been brought up and encouraged to think about reasons and values. I may be convinced that I am right and the egoist wrong. But I cannot point to the egoist's mistake in a way that the egoist will concede to be correct. What should I do in response to this disagreement?[1] According to common-sense morality, the disagreement between an egoist and a moral agent is like a disagreement about a non-moral matter of fact.[2] The trouble is that it seems to be rational to suspend judgement in disagreements about matters of fact.

---

[1] This depends on what sort of disagreement it is. For example, consider a very simple subjectivism, according to which 'I have reason to X' means 'I believe here and now that I have reason to X'. According to this theory, the correctness of my judgement that I have reason to X entirely depends on my own current response to it. This suggests that I should not change my view at all in response to disagreement with another. A sophisticated version of non-cognitivism about reasons for action, on the other hand, may try to match the first-order statements of a realist. This kind of 'quasi-realist' may need to 'speak with the realist' about disagreements with egoists. If simple subjectivism were true, it would not be rational for moral agents to suspend judgement in response to disagreements with egoists. Does it follow that we would be in a position to vindicate morality? Unfortunately not. Our goal was to defend common-sense morality, and common-sense morality is committed to realism about reasons for action (or a sophisticated kind of anti-realism like quasi-realism), in the sense that there are truths about reasons for action that are not dependent in any simple way on whether we think that we have those reasons.

[2] The grounds for thinking that common-sense morality is committed to realism about morality and reasons for action, or at least to a sophisticated kind of anti-realism, are well-known: we talk about morality and reasons for action in statements that seem to be truth-evaluable and appear to express our beliefs (rather than other kinds of propositional attitudes). We take it that in disagreements about morality and reasons at least one of us must have made a mistake. I am not suggesting here that we must be moral realists; ultimately we might find that we have very good reasons to discard these features of common-sense morality. Nevertheless, I will assume that realism or a sophisticated anti-realism like quasi-realism is an assumption of common-sense morality, so that a supposed defence of common-sense morality that actually defends simple subjectivism or relativism is not adequate.

We can set out the problem as follows:

(1) When my judgements conflict with those of someone else, it is rational for me to suspend judgement.
(2) There are egoists who do not accept L1 or H1 — that is, they deny that anyone has moral reason to help those in need or moral reason not to lie.
(3) Therefore, it is rational for me to suspend judgement about L1 or H1.
(4) My argument that egoism is false depends on my accepting L1 or H1.
(5) Therefore, it is rational for me to suspend judgement on whether egoism is false.

A similar argument could be used to attack common-sense morality if premise 2 were replaced with a premise about the amount of disagreement amongst moral agents over the legitimacy of euthanasia, abortion, the killing of animals, and so on. We would have to suspend judgement about the content of morality, at least on these controversial matters, whenever there is rational disagreement. If (1) and (2) are true, however, we have to suspend judgement on the authority of any moral claim. Even if all moral agents speak with one voice that some profitable action is morally wrong and that we have moral reason not to do it, if (1) and (2) are correct, we must all suspend judgement about whether we have any moral reason whatever not to go ahead anyway.

The key to this argument is obviously premise (1), but the appropriate response to disagreement has recently become a matter of much debate.[3] I will argue that, given the two most plausible accounts of the rational response to disagreement (the Equal Weight view, discussed in section 2 and the Total Evidence view, discussed in section 4), we should suspend judgement on moral disagreements and disagreements about reasons for action. So it seems that (a suitably revised version of) premise 1 is true for the disagreement between ourselves and egoists. It follows that we should suspend judgement about the first premises of HELP, THE LIE, and any

---

[3] For example, Kelly 2005; Kelly forthcoming; Elga 2007; Elga forthcoming; Christensen 2007; Frances forthcoming; amongst others.

similar argument: no modest vindication of morality can succeed against egoism.

## 2. The Equal Weight View

Sidgwick argues that it is rational to suspend judgement in response to disagreements:

If I find any of my judgements, intuitive or inferential, in direct conflict with a judgement of some other mind, there must be error somewhere: and if I have no more reason to suspect error in the other mind than in my own, reflective comparisons between the two judgements necessarily reduces me temporarily to a state of neutrality.[4]

Sidgwick may be suggesting here that we in fact always do find ourselves suspending our judgements when we are in conflict with one another. But I will read the 'necessity' claim as a claim about what is rationally required of us.

> R1: It is always rationally required that we suspend judgement in response to disagreement.

This principle is obviously false. Suppose that you disagree with me about the answer to some maths problem. Are you rationally required to suspend judgement? Obviously not: you may be much better than me at maths. It may be extremely likely that you are right and I am wrong. But Sidgwick made it clear that he was not talking about disagreements of that kind. He was talking about disagreements in which 'I have no more reason to suspect error in the other mind than in my own'.

One way of spelling out this condition is in terms of an *epistemic peer*.[5] You and I are epistemic peers when, disregarding our current dispute, you regard that I am as likely as you to get the answer to your current

---

[4] Sidgwick 1907: 341–2.

[5] Peer disagreement is a special type of disagreement; you can also have disagreements with those whom you consider to be your epistemic superior or inferior. But, for simplicity, I will consider only disagreements between epistemic peers (the argument for suspending judgement would, I think, only be stronger if there were, as certainly seems possible, disagreements between moral agents and egoists, where egoists were the epistemic superiors of the moral agents).

question right.[6] Suppose that you and I reasonably regard ourselves as epistemic peers, and we share some evidence (E) on the basis of which I believe that not-p and you believe that p. At least one of us has made a mistake.[7] Should we both suspend judgement?[8] According to R2, we should.

> R2: It is always rationally required that we suspend judgement in response to disagreement with someone whom we reasonably believe to be an epistemic peer.

In support of R2, consider the following cases. I will start with an example in which we have not two people but two instruments whose verdicts are not in alignment.[9] Suppose that I test the temperature of a pan of water that I am heating up with one thermometer and it reads $40°$. Then I test it with another, which reads $50°$. If I have no extra reason to think that one is the more reliable (either in general or in this particular case), then surely the rational response for me is to suspend judgement on whether the temperature really is $40°$ or $50°$ (and perhaps wait for further confirmation).

[6] Kelly 2005 makes additional requirements on an epistemic peer—that we have the intellectual virtues: intellectual honesty, perspicacity, industry, carefulness, and so on to the same extent and we have equal access to the relevant evidence and the relevant arguments. This is not a necessary condition of an epistemic peer, according to my conception, though the evidence that we have and the epistemic virtues that we have will be relevant to our relative epistemic standing: whether you are my epistemic superior, inferior, or peer. It is likely to be extremely controversial when moral issues are at stake whether another person is an epistemic peer, but in at least some cases we disagree with others whom we regard as equally intelligent, perspicuous, and careful about moral questions.

[7] Unless there is genuine indeterminacy in the subject-matter, a possibility I am discounting for the purposes of this argument, though see Shafer-Landau for a defence of this view (1994; 1995; 2003: 218). It is of course possible for one of us to make a mistake in a given situation and the other not to do so, even if we have the epistemic virtues to the same extent (we are not psychological 'clones' of each other and we are not infallible), just as we may be equally good at chess, even though sometimes I beat you and sometimes you beat me. But, since we are epistemic peers, and given that we have equal access to the evidence, we have no reason to think that either of us is more likely to have made the mistake.

[8] It might seem obvious that we should not. Perhaps you simply began with very different views, and the evidence that you share has not moved either of us to change our views. For example, if initially you think that it is very likely to be sunny today, and I think it is very likely to rain, and we are both confronted by the same, somewhat ambiguous, weather report, you may well carry on thinking that it is likely to be sunny, and I that it is likely to rain. Why should either of us suspend judgement on the matter? This raises interesting questions about the rationality of having views about the weather or anything else, prior to having evidence for them. But these are questions that I cannot discuss here, so I will simply assume that in the cases of disagreement with epistemic peers both peers begin with similar views about the relevant probabilities.

[9] Similar examples are used by Kelly forthcoming.

In the same way, if two people disagree on some factual matter, and we have no strong reason to think that either is more reliable in general or is right about this matter, then surely again the rational response is to suspend judgement. Suppose that you and I disagree about our share of a restaurant bill. We know that we are both usually equally good at working out the answer to this kind of question. Obviously, initially I thought that my answer was right, but once I know that you disagree, it seems that the rational response to this disagreement for each of us is to suspend judgement on the matter.[10]

Consider a third example. We are both watching the 100 metres swimming final at the Olympics, and we are—and we reasonably believe that we are—epistemic peers.[11] It is a very close race, but it seems to me that swimmer A touched the wall first—that is certainly how it looked to me. But it seemed to you that swimmer B was first. Once again, it seems that the rational response for us both is to suspend judgement (and to wait for the slow-motion replay which should settle the matter). These examples suggest that R2 is true. R2 is supported by a view about the treatment of disagreements between epistemic peers known as the 'Equal Weight' view.

*Equal Weight view.* In a disagreement with an epistemic peer, it is epistemically rational to give equal weight to your peer's judgement and to your own, and suspend judgement (since an epistemic peer is someone whom, disregarding your current dispute, you regard as likely as you to get the answer to your current question right).[12]

If the Equal Weight view is correct, so is R2—that is, whenever we are in a disagreement with an epistemic peer we should both suspend judgement. What about disagreements between moral agents and egoists? What kind of epistemic standing do egoists have compared with moral agents: are any egoists our epistemic peers? It is difficult to say anything general about this, as of course both egoists and moral agents differ in how careful they are,

---

[10] This kind of example is used by Christensen 2007 and Elga 2007.

[11] A similar example of a horse race is used by Kelly forthcoming.

[12] The Equal Weight view is defended by Elga (2007). See also Feldman 2003; Feldman 2006; and Christensen 2007, all of which are sympathetic to it. In its more general form, the view is that in disagreements you should be guided by your prior assessment of your opponent's ability (given the conditions in which the disagreement takes place). In the special case where your prior assessment is that your opponent is your peer, you must give equal weight to her judgement and your own, and therefore suspend judgement on the question.

how biased they are—that is, in terms of their sensitivity to the relevant considerations.

One might argue that a moral agent is obliged to consider all egoists her epistemic inferiors, however, at least with regard to questions of practical reason and morality. Consider that the first premise of HELP is just one of the vast number of propositions about reasons about which you disagree. Even if you think an egoist is generally rational and is not guilty of wishful thinking, you must regard her as having terrible judgement about all matters to do with practical reason. She consistently gets important questions wrong.

But, to make a fair assessment of her epistemic standing compared with you, you have to discount the questions that you are currently disputing and decide independently of your disagreement how likely each of you is to get the matter right. But there is another problem now. If you discount all her judgements about reasons for action, surely there is very little you can say about the egoist's epistemic qualities with regard to making these judgements in comparison with yourself. Do you have enough evidence either way to judge your epistemic relationship to any egoist?[13]

This problem can be overcome. There are intelligible judgements that we can make about people who disagree with us, even when we argue about whole subject matters. It is possible to look at an egoist and judge whether, disregarding your current dispute, she is as likely as you to get the answer right. She may have the epistemic virtues—intellectual honesty, perspicacity, industry, carefulness, and so on—to the same extent as you, or to a greater or lesser extent. She may have thought about these questions as much as you have; she may have similar evidence on which she bases her views, including philosophical arguments, her 'intuitive' judgements, her experience of life and so on.[14] Insisting that any egoist must be your epistemic inferior, whilst tempting, does not take seriously the fact that we can see that some of these people are rational, intelligent, and in

---

[13] Elga makes the case that in cases of significant moral disagreement you need not regard your opponent as an epistemic peer, and so suspension of judgement is not required (Elga 2007). But whilst in some cases we do find it plausible that others who disagree with us on moral matters have poor judgement, or our disagreements with them are so deeply embedded in our beliefs that we cannot say whether or not they are our epistemic peers, many moral disagreements are not like that. At least some moral disagreements are between epistemic peers and in those circumstances it seems to be rational to suspend judgement.

[14] A further complication is that the importance of certain kinds of evidence—such as philosophical arguments—is itself a matter of dispute.

other respects seem to have good judgement.[15] We find egoists threatening precisely because some egoists do have the requisite epistemic virtues, and we have no independent grounds to think that our judgements about reasons are better than theirs. So *there are some egoists who are our epistemic peers*.[16] And in a disagreement with someone who is your epistemic peer, according to the Equal Weight view, *it is rational for you both to suspend judgement*.

## 3. Egocentric Bias

Is the Equal Weight view correct?[17] Perhaps you need not give equal weight to the judgement of your peer, because it is reasonable for you to think that there is something special about your own faculties. You may trust your own cognitive faculties more than mine—despite the fact that you thought we were epistemic peers—and simply assume that you are right and I must be mistaken. This is an 'Egocentric Bias'.[18]

*Egocentric Bias*. It is always rational to give extra weight to your own judgement above that of your peer, simply because it is your own.

---

[15] Of course, not all egoists will be our epistemic peers. Some may be guilty of wishful thinking. If they have succumbed to this bias we can reasonably ignore their views. On the other hand, whilst some egoists may have reached their view through mistakes, biases, carelessness, or lack of thought, some may not have done. It is perfectly possible for an egoist to be intellectually honest, perspicuous, careful, and so on, and still fail to believe that he has reason to do what is morally required.

[16] Suppose, for example, that we have different evidence, on the basis of which I believe that p and you believe that not p, but it is not clear to us whose evidence is better. For example, you have read twenty books about x and I have read a different twenty books about x. Neither of us knows which books are more accurate, more comprehensive, and with fewer substantial errors. Or I may have considered a set of arguments and you a different set, so that neither of us has encountered the argument upon which the other puts most weight. It may still be true that, disregarding our current dispute, you have no more reason to think that I am more likely to make a mistake than you, in which case, on the definition of epistemic peer which I previously gave, we are epistemic peers (though we would not be peers according to Kelly's definition).

[17] Kelly (2005) suggests an argument against it, indeed an argument for ignoring completely your own and your peer's judgements, and responding solely to the original evidence E. If you did take each of your judgements as relevant to p, evidence E would seem to be double-counted: once in its own right and again as you and your peer have responded to it. He suggests that this double counting may not be legitimate and therefore that these judgements should always be ignored. But it very implausible that it is illegitimate to take the views of your epistemic peers or superiors as confirmation of your own judgement of the evidence if you agree or conversely as disconfirmation when you disagree. This is simply sensible practice—and Kelly (forthcoming) has now acknowledged this.

[18] Egocentric Bias is considered by Wedgwood (2007: chap. 11) as a possible solution to the problem of disagreement.

If Egocentric Bias is true, it is never rationally required that you suspend judgement in response to disagreement with someone whom you reasonably believe to be an epistemic peer, because it is always rational for you to give extra weight to your own judgement.

Can it be rational to be biased towards oneself? If each of us has a set of beliefs that are internally consistent and coherent, and you have no grounds for claiming that yours are better justified than mine, how can it be rational for you, with no further evidence, just to assume that I am wrong? It certainly looks like a stubborn refusal to admit that you might have made a mistake. Of course, you may say that you are not in a special position, for each of us is entitled to hold on to our original opinion in disagreements with our epistemic peers.

Suppose that I have not witnessed the Olympic 100 metres swimming final and I have no evidence who won until you (who watched the race, and who is no more likely to get the answer wrong than me) tell me that swimmer B won. Obviously I would take what you say seriously; I would probably believe that swimmer B won (whilst bearing in mind that it can be difficult to discern the winner in close races). Of course, if I gained new evidence, such as testimony from other eyewitnesses that someone else won, then I might reduce my confidence that swimmer B won, and perhaps even suspend judgement on the matter. But I would still be giving your testimony and your beliefs some weight. I count your opinion that B won as evidence that B won, not as conclusive evidence, of course, but evidence none the less. So what happens when I watch the race too, according to proponents of the Egocentric Bias? Does your opinion suddenly become less reliable? Does it somehow become irrelevant to the matter in hand, now that I am watching too? Surely if your opinion that B won is evidence when I miss the race, then it is still evidence when I watch it. Consider a case where, in a close race, I think that swimmer A won and you agree with me. Surely it would be rational for me to take your opinion as some confirmation that I was right. So is your opinion evidence when I am not an eyewitness, evidence when I am an eyewitness and you agree with me, but lesser evidence or not evidence at all when you disagree with me?

It is hard to see a justification for this view. So an Egocentric Bias towards the verdicts of your own cognitive faculties must be a mistake: Egocentric Bias is false.

## 4. The Total Evidence View

There is, however, a rival to the Equal Weight view that is more plausible than the Egocentric Bias: the 'Total Evidence' view.

*Total Evidence view.* The rational response to a disagreement with an epistemic peer depends on what your total evidence supports: your total evidence includes your original evidence together with the evidence provided by your own judgement and the judgement of your epistemic peer.[19]

The Equal Weight view required you to give equal weight to the judgement of your peer and your own judgement, no matter whether the evidence on which you based your original judgement strongly supported you or not. The Total Evidence view takes into account the judgement of your peer, but also the strength of the original evidence (and whom it supports). This is a plausible account of how you should respond to disagreements. For if you are seeking knowledge or truth, surely it cannot be rational for you to ignore significant and relevant evidence—either the evidence of the other person's judgement (as the Egocentric Bias account would do) or the original evidence on which you based your initial judgement (as the Equal Weight view would do).[20] However, my

---

[19] A version of the Total Evidence view (specifically concerning epistemic peers) is defended in Kelly forthcoming. More generally, the view is that in a disagreement you should take into account the judgements of your opponents, weighted in accordance with your antecedent judgement about their epistemic standing, but also the original evidence on which you based your initial judgement.

[20] In Chapter 8, I defend further the claim that the best strategy for acquiring truth or knowledge is not to ignore significant and relevant evidence, and that regarding normal matters of fact it is rational for us to form beliefs as if we were aiming for knowledge (or truth). I believe that the best account of epistemic rationality for ordinary factual beliefs supports the Total Evidence view. Elga (2007) has an argument against a similar view, however. He claims that this kind of account of the rational response to disagreement could lead to an unjustifiable sort of 'bootstrapping', according to which you are entitled to discount the judgement of someone you antecedently judged to be your peer simply on the basis of your disagreement (and after a series of such disagreements you might judge them not to be your peer). He claims that this bootstrapping cannot be acceptable, so the Equal Weight view must be correct. But I do not think that Elga is right that unjustifiable bootstrapping is inevitable, according to the Total Evidence view. It is true that in response to a disagreement you might revise your initial belief that your opponent was your epistemic peer, but usually it is reasonable for you in addition to revise your initial belief in the strength of your evidence (that is, you will be less confident that your evidence supports p). After a series of such disagreements, it is as reasonable to conclude that your original evidence is weak or hard to interpret, and to suspend judgement on what it supports, as it is to downgrade the epistemic standing of your opponent. You might have reason to favour one of these rather than the other (that is, additional evidence that the case is hard, or that your opponent is not really your peer); in the absence of additional evidence, it is certainly not rationally required, and perhaps not even rationally permissible, for you to decide to downgrade your opponent rather than

main goal here is not to defend the Total Evidence view but to show that whether it or the Equal Weight view is correct it is epistemically rational for any moral agent to suspend judgement on the first premise of a modest vindication of morality.

According to the Total Evidence view, it is not always rationally required for you to suspend judgement in response to a disagreement with an epistemic peer. Consider the following case. Suppose that you and your friend both believe that you are epistemic peers and you share some evidence, E. But as a result of E you believe that p and she believes that not-p. Your judgement that p is some evidence that E supports p. Her judgement that not-p is some evidence that E supports not-p. Your *total evidence* includes: your original evidence E, plus your judgement that p and her judgement that not-p.

How should you respond? That depends on the weight of each component of your evidence. You might have more or less evidence that you and she are epistemic peers—that is, that (antecedently to your disagreement) she is no more likely than you to get the answer wrong. The evidence that you have regarding what your opponent believes also may be stronger or weaker. She may have told you that she believes that p is true, but you may have reason to believe that she is lying or misleading you. Or that, though she does indeed believe p to be true, she has been careless in forming her beliefs, and, with more care, she would change her mind.

But aside from these you might have stronger or weaker evidence for p. There is a spectrum of cases, from the 'hardest' (in which p is a very difficult question that either of you might easily have got wrong) to the 'easiest' (where your evidence is very strong). The strength of the evidence for p makes a crucial difference to the rational response to your disagreement, according to the Total Evidence view.

Suppose that our original evidence is very strong, and it supports p (as you correctly noticed and I did not). Now we also have the evidence of our judgements: yours that p is true, mine that p is false, together with our (shared) view that we are epistemic peers.[21] My judgement that E does not

conclude that your original evidence was weak. Kelly (forthcoming) has a further defence of the Total Evidence view.

[21] Of course, even if we are epistemic peers, our positions are not completely symmetrical. Typically, you are in a better position to judge whether there are any features of the situation that might undermine the reliability of your judgement than you are to judge about mine. Of course, you may make a mistake

support p is some evidence that it does not do so after all. You should as a result become less confident that our total evidence supports p. Since your belief in p depends on this evidence, you should become less confident that p. But it does not follow that you should suspend judgement. Since our original evidence was very strong, you should become less confident that p but *you are not rationally required to suspend judgement.*

What about me? My original judgement was a mistake. I thought that E supported not-p but it does not. It is rational for me to change my views completely.[22] My new evidence of E plus our two judgements actually supports p—so that is what I should believe.

If the Total Evidence view is correct, we are not always rationally required to suspend judgement in response to a disagreement with an epistemic peer. In general, the stronger your original evidence, the more confident of p you should be initially and the less significant the disagreement is in terms of your total evidence. But in some cases we should still suspend judgement. If our original evidence is weak, once we discover our disagreement our total evidence no longer supports p over not-p. So it is rational for both of us to suspend judgement on the matter.[23]

about this too: no one is infallible about her own mental processes. And you may gain convincing evidence that we have been equally careful, in which case our positions are symmetrical once more. But, in normal circumstances, you are in a better position to assess how you formed your beliefs than how I formed mine. If you think that you have been careful, and that if you are careful, you are usually right, it may be reasonable for you to think it more likely that I made the mistake, even if we are epistemic peers. I will assume, however, that you know that we have been equally careful.

[22] We need here to distinguish between two kinds of epistemic rationality. You are *objectively epistemically rational* if your beliefs are appropriate given the actual strength of your evidence, and you formed them in response to your evidence. Note that it may be objectively epistemically rational for you to believe that p even though p is false, for your evidence can support p—and support it strongly—despite being misleading. You are *subjectively epistemically rational* if your beliefs are appropriate given the strength of the evidence that you *believe* that you have. It is, for example, subjectively epistemically rational for you to believe strongly that p if you think that your evidence supports p strongly, whether or not it in fact does. I will focus on what it is objectively epistemically rational to believe in these cases.

[23] Sometimes your evidence is not weak, but you have too much of it; it would take too long for you to survey it and to take it all in. Sometimes your evidence is too complex and difficult for you to understand. One might say in this type of case that you have 'conformed' your belief to the evidence that you have, but your evidence is less than it seems. Your evidence is not a mathematical proof that conclusively supports the theorem but which you cannot understand, for example, but something less than this, perhaps a proof 'as you understand it'. If so, you would have only weak evidence that the theorem is true, and it would be rational for you to suspend judgement in response to the disagreement. Alternatively, we might say that you have strong evidence that the theorem is true that you have failed to understand or appreciate properly. Nevertheless, it is not legitimate to expect a normal person to appreciate her evidence properly. If this is the right interpretation of this kind of case, you cannot be objectively rational—you have not formed your beliefs on the basis of the (very strong) evidence

To sum up, if the Total Evidence view is correct:

> R3: When you are in a disagreement with someone whom you reasonably believe to be your epistemic peer, the rational response depends on the strength of your original evidence. Where your evidence is sufficiently strong, neither of you need suspend judgement. Where your evidence is weaker, you should lose confidence in your original judgement, and where your evidence is sufficiently weak, it is rational for you both to suspend judgement.

The strength of your original evidence is obviously very significant, given this view. How can you tell whether your evidence is strong or weak?

Sometimes we get a strong feeling of certainty about our judgement, or the converse. Watching the 100 metres final I find myself feeling rather unsure who won, though I think that it possibly was swimmer B. By contrast, when I see the person standing in front of me, I feel absolutely certain that there is someone there. But, although these feelings of certainty may sometimes be correlated with the strength of my evidence they can be misleading and it is important not to take them too seriously. A strong feeling of certainty can accompany weak evidence, and you can feel less certain or have no particular feelings either way even when your evidence is strong.

The strength of evidence is better measured by looking at what type of situation you are in, what kind of evidence you have, and, if possible, a history of success or failure by yourself and others in similar cases in similar

---

that you have—but it would be unfair and unreasonable to blame you. Your failure is *excusable*. It follows that *you cannot reasonably be expected to form your beliefs in an objectively epistemically rational way*. For, even if you believe that p when your evidence actually supports p, you did not form that belief *on the basis of the evidence*. What should you believe? Even if your failure to be objectively rational is excusable, it is not excusable for you to form just any beliefs. When you cannot be sure what your evidence supports, it is reasonable to expect you not to jump to a conclusion about what it shows, simply to have a guess; instead, you should form beliefs reflecting the fact that you are not sure what your evidence supports, and so form only a weak belief that it supports p (or not p). And when you encounter disagreement with your epistemic peer you should lose confidence in even that weak belief and so suspend judgement on the matter. This is similar to the kind of cases we have already considered, where your evidence does not strongly support p over not p. But there are some important differences. Here, it is not rational for you to suspend judgement, for your evidence strongly supports p. But it is excusable for you to suspend judgement when you cannot be sure what your evidence supports and it is not excusable for you to form your beliefs in another way. For the sake of simplicity, I will ignore this possibility for the most part, mentioning it only when it is relevant to the overall argument.

circumstances. Cases with strong evidence tend to be characterized by a history of getting the answer right, with general agreement and only the odd disagreement or mistake. We might call these *easy cases*. If, in similar cases, you find people make a lot of mistakes about what the evidence supports, and there are persistent disagreements between people of similar abilities about what the right answer is, then you probably have a case in which your evidence is weaker.[24] These are questions that are *harder* to answer.

Are questions about practical reason and the authority of morality easy? If you are struck by the *obvious* truth of a premise like H1.

> H1: I have a moral reason to help those in need.

Then it must be tempting to say that they are. Surely you can be confident of the truth of that, if you can be confident of anything?

But we should be cautious in drawing conclusions about the strength of our evidence from our feelings of certainty. I have focused here on disagreements between egoists and moral agents. But this is far from the only kind of disagreement here. Moral agents themselves often disagree about the authority of morality. Are moral reasons always overriding? Do they silence other reasons? What is the source of morality's authority—is moral rightness itself the ground of practical reasons? Do other properties ground both moral rightness and practical reasons? There is a lot of disagreement not just between moral agents and egoists but also amongst moral agents, and I have yet to mention disagreements about the content of morality. Moreover, since many people take opposing views about these matters, many people must be making mistakes, about both the authority of morality and its content. So moral questions *must* be very hard.

Did we not devise, however, a premise for our 'modest vindication' of morality to which all moral agents would agree?

> H1: I have a moral reason to help those in need.

Can we not say that there is considerable agreement about this, and (presumably) few people making a mistake about it? And so the question of whether we have moral reason to help those in need is easy? Or, at least, it is relatively easy.

---

[24] Or more difficult to interpret.

This might be easier than some moral questions (such as familiar disputes about abortion and euthanasia), but I do not think that it is right to class it as easy. For it is worth remembering that the agreement amongst moral agents about H1 appears to be *superficial*, in the sense that they each think that it is true for different reasons. Recall that it was designed to offer common ground between moral agents who accepted different claims such as:

> H1 (moral rightness). I have reason to help those in need because doing so is morally right.
> H1 (happiness). I have reason to help those in need because doing so makes them happy.
> H1 (moral virtue). I have reason to help those in need because doing so is generous and kind.

If asked to elaborate on why they think that I have moral reason to help those in need, some moral agents will think it basic, others will cite these alternative versions of H1 as above. But each of these is controversial. This suggests that, despite the fact that moral agents agree that I have moral reason to help those in need, the question is not really that easy after all.[25]

So consider again a dispute between an egoist and someone who accepts common-sense morality.

An egoist and I are confronted with exactly the same situation: we come across a homeless person who needs some money to buy food. It is clear to both of us that this person is very unlikely ever to be in a position to help us in return, and the effect on our reputation will be negligible—there is no one about and no one is likely to find out. Nevertheless, I judge that both of us have reason to help him because he needs help. The egoist judges that she has no reason to help. We both seem to be careful, sensible people, and I have no antecedent grounds for thinking that either of us is better at appreciating what reasons for action there really are.

---

[25] Given that these questions are hard, and there is so much disagreement about them amongst moral agents who are epistemic peers, it is rational for moral agents to suspend judgement about the truth of each of these alternative versions of H1 (or excusable to do so, and not excusable to do otherwise). But if they think that there is moral reason to help those in need *because* doing so makes those people happy (or whatever), it is rational (or excusable) for them to suspend judgement on that as well. Underlying their apparent agreement is considerable disagreement, and this should lead them to suspend judgement on the apparently uncontroversial H1. Only if they have some separate ground for H1 could it be rational for them not to suspend judgement. Disagreements amongst moral agents, as well as disagreements with egoists, can ensure that suspending judgement is almost always rational even for relatively uncontroversial moral claims (or it is excusable, and it is not excusable to do otherwise).

Let us say that neither of us has any (antecedent) reason to think that the other is more likely to get the answer wrong. I have argued that moral disagreements and disagreements about reasons for action are usually hard, and this one is too. Generally, when I have a disagreement with someone who is my epistemic peer, and the issue is hard, it is rational for me to suspend judgement.[26] And so this is what I should do here. *I should suspend judgement about whether I have moral reason to help others, as indeed I should on any question of reasons for action that is at issue between me and the egoist.*

Recall that we were interested in arguments like the following:

> HELP
> H1: I have moral reason to help those in need.
> H2: If H1, then egoism is false.
> H3: So, egoism is false.

The problem is that whilst I (along with other moral agents) believe that H1 is true, many egoists do not. I have argued that, according to the two most plausible accounts of disagreement—the Equal Weight view and the Total Evidence view—we should all suspend judgement in response to this disagreement.[27] So I cannot use HELP—or any similar argument—in defence of morality.

## 5. Vindicating Egoism?

In focusing on attempts to vindicate morality once again, it might seem as if the burden of proof has been unfairly placed on moral agents. Of course, our original question was whether the authority of morality could be defended against egoism, so it is hardly surprising that we are concentrating on such attempts and their failure. But, if anyone who used to accept the authority of morality must now suspend judgement, is an egoist in an

---

[26] Or—if the evidence is strong but hard to interpret—it is excusable to suspend judgement and not excusable to do otherwise. In other words, I should suspend judgement in any case.

[27] I have not argued in defence of either of these views, though I am inclined to favour the Total Evidence view. The key point is that once it is acknowledged that the egoist's beliefs count as evidence regarding the truth of egoism and that questions about practical reason are hard (the evidence is weak or hard to interpret), it is hard to think of any plausible account of disagreement that will not advocate suspending judgement.

epistemically better position? Fortunately not. Recall the egoist's attempt at a modest vindication of egoism.

SELF-HELP
SH1: I have reason to help those in need only when doing so will benefit me.
SH2: If SH1, then common-sense morality is false.
SH3: So, common-sense morality is false.

The argument is valid but is the egoist rational to believe the first premise? Questions regarding reasons for action are hard. The egoist is in dispute with moral agents, some of whom are her epistemic peers. So, whether the Equal Weight view or the Total Evidence view is correct, she should suspend judgement on SH1, and therefore on whether common-sense morality is false.[28] In fact, if, as seems likely, there are more moral agents than egoists (i.e., there are more people who accept H1 than SH1) the case for suspending judgement is even stronger for the egoist than the moral agent, since disagreements with many others are even better evidence that she has made a mistake.

## 6. Conclusion

It was perhaps not surprising, if disappointing, that we could not give an ambitious vindication of the authority of morality, an argument that would persuade the egoist that she had reason to be moral. It was reasonable to hope that we might succeed by aiming for something less ambitious, a merely modest vindication, an argument against egoism that satisfied ourselves at least.

The last two chapters have raised some problems for a modest vindication. In Chapter 6, I discussed whether these vindications were 'cogent': whether they simply begged the question against egoism. I argued that in principle modest arguments against egoism could be cogent.

The arguments of this chapter are harder to answer. It seems that the moral agent, faced with an apparently rational egoist who disagrees with

---

[28] More precisely, it is either epistemically rational for the egoist to suspend judgement, or it is excusable to suspend judgement and not excusable to do otherwise.

her, will simply have to suspend judgement on whether she has reasons to be moral. It is hardly a consolation that a rational egoist ought to do the same. Not even to be able to give a modest defence, in terms that the moral agent herself can accept, is very disheartening.[29]

If the argument here is correct, we cannot give a modest vindication of the practical authority of morality. Of course, this was our original task, and so that has been the main focus of this chapter. But, it is worth noticing that the problem raised for common-sense morality is actually much more serious. For, as I have already pointed out, there are a lot of contentious moral issues, about which people who antecedently seem as likely as each other to get the answer right disagree. It seems that you should suspend judgement not just about the authority of morality but about any moral question that is—as so many are—controversial. You should no longer take a view on almost any interesting moral issue. And this is so even if common-sense morality is true, and your own views on all these moral issues would have been completely correct. It is no exaggeration to say that this is a devastating result for common-sense morality.

In the rest of this book I try to show where this argument goes wrong. In Part III, I will argue that, given common-sense morality, it is not always epistemically rational to suspend judgement in response to moral disagreements. I will defend arguments like HELP (moral reason) and use them to vindicate morality. At the same time, I will show that serious problems remain for egoism.

---

[29] It is possible that we should be equally concerned about our claims about the external world and our knowledge of it. It is plausible that, were you to find yourself in disagreement with an idealist or a sceptic who was your epistemic peer, you should suspend judgement about the nature of the external world and our knowledge of it. Of course, in philosophy there is a lot of disagreement about which theories are true, even amongst epistemic peers. This suggests that philosophical questions are hard, and so that when in disagreements with philosophers who are your epistemic peers you should suspend judgement (that is, it is epistemically rational for you to suspend judgement, or it is excusable to do so and not excusable to do otherwise). But, most philosophers do not suspend judgement about controversial questions of philosophy. Does it follow that we are all epistemically irrational? This raises extremely interesting questions about the standards of epistemic rationality in philosophy, which unfortunately I cannot pursue here (though I think that it may be rational (in some sense) for us not to suspend judgement about controversial matters of philosophy).

# III

# In Defence of Morality

# 8

# Epistemic Rationality

## 1. In Defence of Morality

At the start of Part II, I argued that ambitious vindications of morality are all likely to fail, and we will have to settle for a modest vindication. But by the end of Part II it seemed that even this modest hope was doomed. In Chapter 7, I showed that, given the most plausible accounts of how you should respond to disagreement, you must suspend judgement on the first premise of arguments like HELP (moral reason).

> HELP (moral reason)
> H1: I have moral reason to help those in need.
> H2: If H1, then egoism is false.
> H3: So, egoism is false.

But if you must suspend judgement on the first premise of this argument, clearly you cannot use it to defend morality. And it seems that any similar modest vindication of morality will fail in the same way.

In Part III, I defend modest vindications of morality. Ultimately, I will try to show that it can be epistemically rational for moral agents to accept the first premise of these arguments and they can be used against egoism. The argument for this conclusion is complex, and will take up all four chapters. On the way, I will defend some surprising claims: that even if there are moral facts, moral epistemology is not the same as the epistemology of non-moral matters of fact, where it is epistemically rational to form beliefs as if you are aiming for knowledge (or truth).[1] The aim of moral inquiry is something completely different: moral understanding. In

---

[1] Though I do not think that acquiring knowledge or truth is an explicit aim that we consciously pursue.

Chapter 9, I introduce the concept of moral understanding, distinguish it from moral knowledge, and explain why it is so important. I argue that it plays a vital role in good character and in morally worthy action. In Chapter 10, I draw out the implications of the role of moral understanding for the appropriate responses to moral disagreement. And, finally, Chapter 11 uses this new conception of moral epistemology to answer the egoist. In this chapter, however, I tackle a more basic question: how can we find out the right conception of epistemic rationality with regard to any particular subject area?

## 2. A Puzzle about Moral Epistemology

In the previous chapter, I argued that you should take people's opinions (expressed through what they say or otherwise) into account whether or not you have formed an opposing view, at least when you think that they are your epistemic peer:

Suppose that I have not witnessed the Olympic 100 metres swimming final and I have no evidence who won until you, who watched the race, tell me that swimmer B won (and I think that you are no more likely to make a mistake about this than I am). . . . I count your opinion that B won as evidence that B won, not as conclusive evidence of course, but evidence none the less. So what happens when I watch the race too . . . ? Does your opinion suddenly become less reliable? Does it somehow become irrelevant to the matter in hand, now that I am watching too? Surely if your opinion that B won is evidence when I miss the race, then it is still evidence when I watch it. Consider a case where, in a close race, I think that swimmer A won and you agree with me. Surely it would be rational for me to take your opinion as some confirmation that I was right. So is your opinion evidence when I am not an eyewitness, evidence when I am an eyewitness and you agree with me, but lesser evidence or not evidence at all when you disagree with me? It is hard to see a justification for this view.

So far we have found no reason to think that this argument does not apply to moral questions. If you find that other people (whom you reasonably think are your epistemic peers) disagree with you about moral matters—perhaps because they say so—you should take their opinions into account. If you find that others disagree with you on ordinary non-moral matters, it is sometimes appropriate to revise your own views to take account of the disagreement, and sometimes it is rational to suspend judgement. But few of us suspend judgement about moral matters, however controversial, despite being aware of fundamental disagreements with others. As Pettit remarks:

It would be objectionably self-abasing to revise your belief on matters like . . . the wrongness of abortion just in virtue of finding that others whom you respect take a different view. Or so most of us think. To migrate towards the views of others, even under the sorts of assumptions given, would seem to be an abdication of epistemic responsibility: a failure to take seriously the evidence as it presents itself to your own mind.[2]

Pettit hints in this passage that deferring to others on moral matters, changing your views in line with their judgements, is both a moral failing ('objectionably self-abasing') and an epistemological one ('an abdication of epistemic responsibility'). One might say that it is a failure of character not to listen to your own conscience on moral questions; and an epistemic failure not to make a judgement on the evidence that you have yourself.[3]

But if the argument of the last chapters is correct, this is extremely puzzling. For it is part of your evidence that others, whom you regard as epistemic peers, think differently. Since this is part of your evidence, it is hard to see why you should not take it into account. But if you do take it into account, you should suspend judgement on any contentious moral issue, including those concerning the authority of morality. But most of us do not. Moreover, many of us do not seem to think that we are in the wrong: on the contrary, like Pettit, we think that taking other people's opinions into account on moral matters is a moral and epistemological failing.

---

[2] Pettit 2006. Pettit argues that it is not moral beliefs as such that are immune from revision, but beliefs that are more embedded in your 'Quinean web of belief'. It is appropriate to revise only those beliefs that are less well embedded. I do not take a stand on this issue, but I think that many people would object to revising any moral belief in response to disagreement, even one that is not well entrenched. I argue that there is a relevant difference between moral and non-moral matters on exactly this issue.

[3] Kalderon argues (2005: chap. 1) that when faced with moral disagreement we do not take ourselves to be required to inquire further into who is correct and who is mistaken. He believes it is intelligible to be, as he says, unflinching, intransigent, and lacking a motivation to inquire further. This is a premise in his argument for non-cognitivism, for he believes that if moral conviction were cognitive, we would be required to inquire further. It is the latter claim that I take issue with in this and the following chapters.

So do we have any reason to think that it is a moral and epistemological *mistake* to suspend judgement on moral matters when others disagree?

Common-sense morality seems to be committed to there being truths about morality that are not dependent in any straightforward way on our beliefs or attitudes towards them. Lying, for example, is wrong, and we have reason not to lie, whether or not we disapprove of it or think it wrong. In that respect, at least, facts about morality and its practical authority seem to be similar to ordinary facts about the external world. We might expect, therefore, that moral epistemology would be similar to the epistemology of ordinary facts. On the other hand, however, there are interesting and potentially important differences between the way that we form moral beliefs and the way we form other beliefs with ordinary factual content.[4] For example, the status of *moral testimony* is complicated.[5] Consider the following example:

Eleanor has always enjoyed eating meat, but has recently realized that it raises some moral issues. Rather than thinking further about these, however, she asks a friend who tells her that eating meat is wrong. Eleanor knows that her friend is normally trustworthy and reliable, so she believes her and accepts that eating meat is wrong.

Many people believe that forming moral beliefs on the say-so of others, as Eleanor does, is wrong. Of course, no one thinks that moral testimony is entirely worthless. It is right for children to learn most of their moral beliefs through testimony. And adults may reasonably base some beliefs on testimony—for example, about relevant factual issues (who did what to whom) from which they can form their own moral views. Asking for other people's advice about moral matters and taking that advice seriously is

[4] These might be beliefs about what is morally right or wrong, for example, or they might be beliefs using 'thick' ethical terms, or they might be beliefs about our moral reasons for action. I will not try to explain what it is for a belief to have explicitly moral content. It may not be possible to draw a clear line between moral beliefs and other beliefs, or to give a proper account of the difference between the two. But I think that we can nevertheless distinguish between moral beliefs and non-moral beliefs sufficiently for my purposes here.

[5] By 'moral testimony' I mean testimony with *explicitly moral content*. Again, I will assume that we can, at least roughly, distinguish between moral propositions and others that have what I will call *ordinary factual content*. Of course, there is also a controversy about ordinary testimony—namely, whether testimony is a basic source of justification ('non-reductionism') or not ('reductionism'), discussed, for example, in Lackey and Sosa 2006. But this debate can be put to one side. If Eleanor was learning ordinary non-moral facts from her friend, both reductionists and non-reductionists would regard her as justified (for she knows that her friend is trustworthy and reliable). But, since she trusts moral testimony, pessimists think that there is something wrong with her forming beliefs on that basis.

clearly legitimate. But, once you have reached maturity as an adult and have the ability to think about moral questions by yourself—as Eleanor can—it seems to be important that you do so. When faced with a difficult moral question, simply doing what you were told to do is odd. Using testimony to find out ordinary matters of fact is utterly unobjectionable; using it to form your moral beliefs is much more dubious, or, more precisely, moral testimony has a more complex role than testimony about non-moral matters of fact: sometimes it is fine to trust testimony about explicitly moral matters, sometimes doing so is less acceptable.[6]

Everyone agrees that there are *experts* regarding non-moral matters of fact, people who are more experienced and more knowledgeable than the rest of us. Weather forecasters are much more experienced and knowledgeable than the rest of us at predicting the weather. Mathematicians are much more skilful at finding and assessing mathematical proofs. Travel writers know a lot about some foreign countries. We often *defer* to these experts: we form our beliefs on the basis of their judgements alone, without making our own assessment of their reasons for their judgements (perhaps without even being aware of those reasons). And we are often right to defer: this is a good way for us to acquire knowledge. According to some ethical traditions, there are experts regarding morality, just like any other subject, and the rest of us should defer to them. The experts may also be religious authorities—for example, priests or rabbis. These traditions value submission and obedience to the experts, rather than making up your own mind about morality.

By contrast, many people think that there are no moral experts, and perhaps even that there could be none. Of course, some people have thought for a long time about particular moral issues and are skilful at formulating moral arguments; some of these people are moral philosophers. People frequently ask for advice about moral questions, and they might prefer to consult people who had thought about the issues carefully. But many adults do not defer to the opinions of others in moral matters as they do in ordinary factual ones and they think that it is rarely, if ever, right to do so. Bernard Williams, for example, is briskly dismissive of the very idea of deferring to a moral expert:

---

[6] The epistemic status of moral testimony is disputed; see, for example, Jones 1999; Driver 2006; Fricker 2006; and Hopkins 2007. I will defend (what I take to be) common-sense morality: that there is a difference between deferring to experts and trusting testimony with regard to moral and non-moral matters.

There are, notoriously, no ethical experts . . . Anyone who is tempted to take up the idea of there being a theoretical science of ethics should be discouraged by reflecting on what would be involved in taking seriously the idea that there were experts in it. It would imply, for instance, that a student who had not followed the professor's reasoning but had understood his moral conclusion might have some reason, on the strength of his professorial authority, to accept it . . . These Platonic implications are presumably not accepted by anyone.[7]

A possibility so absurd, he claims, that only Plato believed it. According to Williams, this is a striking difference between the epistemology of morality and the epistemology of non-moral facts. There are no moral experts, or at least none to whom we should defer; but plenty of experts in other fields.

There are some obvious and uncontroversial reasons why we might not defer to moral experts or trust what they say. First, it may be more difficult to identify experts in ethics rather than other subjects. If we tried to establish the qualities essential to a moral expert, they would prove extremely contentious: is impartiality required? Or keen emotional engagement? Of course, a moral expert must be sensitive to morally important features, but what kind of sensitivity, to which features, is needed? The kind of people whom we might regard as moral experts—those who have spent much of their lives thinking about moral questions, for example—often disagree greatly amongst themselves about the right answers. Furthermore, moral experts, even if they have moral knowledge, may not transmit it reliably to others. And the stakes are often very high in situations where we face moral questions. The consequences may include doing something morally wrong, even if unwittingly. When your decision is so important, you may well prefer to trust your own judgement rather than defer to someone who may or may not be an expert.[8]

But, although it may be difficult to identify moral experts, this is not a particularly deep or in principle an insurmountable problem. Few people, if any, can properly be described as experts on all moral matters. But to discover someone who has better judgement or more experience than you in some particular area or about some single moral issue, and who seems

---

[7] Williams 1995: 205.

[8] However, as Hopkins points out, some moral truths are trivial, and some non-moral matters (will the rope hold my weight? will the bridge collapse if I stand on it?) are extremely important. So this cannot explain why, in general, deferring to experts and trusting testimony are more acceptable for ordinary factual matters than for moral questions (see Hopkins 2007: 621–3).

generally trustworthy, is not that difficult. Why not take her word on at least that moral question?[9]

Many people believe that the problem is much more serious. Williams does not think it is simply difficult to tell if your ethics professor is an expert or that she is trustworthy. It is absurd to defer to her, to put your trust in her testimony, he seems to imply, even if you know she is very likely to be right.

The treatment of testimony in ethics is interesting and important in its own right, but it is also extremely significant for the issue with which we are most concerned, the rational response to moral disagreements. In taking testimony seriously, you take as evidence what people say about p, in part because you are treating their belief that p as evidence that p.[10] In responding to disagreement, you have to decide to what extent you should treat other people's judgements about p as evidence that p when you have formed a different view yourself. In the next section, I consider how we might evaluate our practices of forming moral beliefs with regard to epistemic rationality.

## 3. Epistemic Rationality

I have suggested that there are differences between our treatment of experts, of testimony, and of disagreements in moral and non-moral contexts. What should we make of this? One possibility is that, with respect to moral questions, we are epistemically irrational. We fail to take into account all the evidence—we ignore significant and relevant evidence—and we are thereby making a mistake. It would be epistemically rational to trust moral testimony and to treat moral disagreements just the same as we treat disagreements over ordinary non-moral matters.

Another possibility is that moral epistemology is fundamentally different from the epistemology of non-moral matters of fact. We are not

---

[9] Hopkins makes this argument for gaining moral knowledge by testimony (2007: 623–6).

[10] This is not always quite true with regard to testimony. For someone can have unreliable beliefs about p but nevertheless make accurate assertions (in Lackey's example, a science teacher who is a Creationist may teach evolutionary theory accurately), and so it can be reasonable to trust her testimony (Lackey 2006). In addition, there may be extra reasons for trusting testimony: in asserting that p, or telling you that p, your interlocutor gives you an *assurance* that p, an assurance that you do not get when you discover in some other way that she believes that p (Moran 2006). But, often, at least part of the reason why her *telling you* that p is evidence that p is because her *belief* that p is evidence that p.

epistemically irrational in not trusting testimony and not suspending judgement in response to disagreements in moral matters. How can we determine whether the standards of epistemic rationality are the same for non-moral and moral matters, or not?

We are interested in finding out about the world, in forming mental representations of it. We can to some—if limited—extent choose what methods of inquiry to use, whose opinion to ask, where to seek information and so on, though the way in which we form representations of the world is obviously not wholly under our control. Nevertheless, we can still assess them with regard to epistemic rationality. What are the standards by which we should make these kinds of epistemic assessments? Are beliefs epistemically rational if they are true? If they are useful? Or are other standards relevant?[11]

One possibility is that epistemic rationality is really a kind of instrumental rationality; that is, standards of epistemic rationality are based on the cognitive goals that we have deliberately chosen to pursue.[12] We might choose truth, for example, and those methods of inquiry that lead to true beliefs would be epistemically rational. Or we might choose knowledge, in which case methods of inquiry that led to knowledge would be epistemically rational. Suppose that you had set yourself the aim of knowledge in non-moral factual cases but you had chosen a different cognitive goal when forming moral beliefs. It is possible that the standards of epistemic rationality would be different in the two cases, because the epistemic aims you had set for yourself in the two circumstances would be quite different.

Unfortunately, there are several problems with the idea that epistemic rationality is based on ends we have chosen for ourselves. First, the very idea suggests that it is possible to choose an epistemic goal and to choose your methods of pursuing that goal. But, as I have already mentioned,

---

[11] If we formed representations of the world that were not responsive to truth, it is possible that these representations would not count as beliefs (there is a considerable literature based on the idea that it is constitutive of beliefs to 'aim at the truth'; for example, Williams 1973; Velleman 2000: essay 11; Wedgwood 2002; Owens 2003). If this is right, then presumably truth will have to play an important role in the standards of epistemic rationality for any representation of the world that counts as a belief. But there may be different ways of forming beliefs that are responsive to the truth in slightly different ways, generating different standards of epistemic rationality; and we could form representations that were not beliefs (e.g., fantasies) and that were not responsive in any direct way to the truth. So we still have a question: what are the standards of epistemic rationality for the kind of representations of the world that we make, that will, for example, play a role in reasoning and in action.

[12] This suggestion is made by Kelly (2003) and he makes similar objections to it.

much of the formation of our beliefs is not under our control in this way. Whatever cognitive goal we chose to pursue, we would still form beliefs by perception. Nevertheless, even if forming beliefs in this way is not under our control, it still may be true that the epistemic assessment of those beliefs, in terms of epistemic rationality, is in terms of a cognitive goal that we have chosen to accept. If it turned out that those beliefs were epistemically irrational in terms of that goal, we might not be able to do anything to change them, or our methods of forming them (so there would be no interesting link between what is epistemically rational for us to do and what we can do). But in any case it is simply not plausible that a cognitive goal that we have chosen for ourselves grounds the standards of epistemic rationality.

Many people have quite clearly not set any epistemic aims at all for themselves. But it obviously does not follow that no standards of epistemic rationality apply to them. We can still assess their beliefs as epistemically rational or not. Even worse, it is conceivable that people might set idiosyncratic, bizarre epistemic goals. I might, for example, aim to form representations of the world that conform to the evidence that I discover on Tuesdays only, discounting all evidence that I find on other days. I would therefore have instrumental reasons to ignore evidence found on other days and to pay particular attention to what I saw on Tuesdays, and doing so would be epistemically rational for me. This would obviously be an absurd aim, and it is certainly not epistemically rational for me to comply with it. It is questionable whether representations of the world formed in this way would even count as beliefs, let alone as epistemically rational beliefs. So the standards of epistemic rationality are not determined by the epistemic aims that we choose for ourselves.

A second possibility is that epistemic rationality is basic. There is no further explanation for why these are the appropriate epistemic standards: they just are correct. This may well be right. But this leaves us with a significant problem. How do we determine what are the standards of epistemic rationality? When we have a common way of forming beliefs—such as our treatment of moral testimony and of moral disagreements—how can we tell whether or not it is epistemically rational?

Even if the standards of epistemic rationality are basic, however, there may be routes to finding out about epistemic rationality. We may, for example, be able to make some progress by looking at the function of belief—that is, the causal roles that beliefs play. For it is very plausible that the appropriate standards for assessing our formation of belief depend on the function those beliefs have: beliefs that meet the standards of epistemic rationality will tend to fulfil these functions well rather than badly.

Beliefs have many functions; but two are particularly important. First, beliefs are used in theoretical reasoning, to produce more beliefs. Can we find out about epistemic rationality from this function of belief, by working out what it is to reason well? Perhaps, but there is a problem with this approach. For what is it to reason well? Reasoning is a mental process of acquiring new beliefs, starting from your current beliefs. Successful reasoning clearly, then, is going to be reasoning where you perform the right kind of process. There are lots of ways of forming new beliefs—wishful thinking, using your imagination, taking wild guesses—that are not examples of good reasoning. But what is wrong with them?

Reasoning might be successful if you ended with beliefs that are true (or that would be true if your original beliefs were true). Or perhaps good reasoning is a mental process in which you finish up with knowledge, provided that you began with knowledge. Or perhaps it is a process through which you try to gain something else. How are we to decide? The problem is that the answer to this is clearly closely connected to the questions about the standards of epistemic rationality. The same standards of epistemic rationality that apply in the formation of our first beliefs presumably are at least relevant to and perhaps even apply in the same way to the formation of these later beliefs by reasoning. Of course, the relationship between these might turn out to be somewhat complicated (if you start with beliefs that are not epistemically rational, however well you reason, you will not end up with beliefs that it is epistemically rational to hold); nevertheless, to determine what a good piece of reasoning is, it is likely that we first need to know at least something about the appropriate standards to regulate the formation of beliefs. But that was exactly what we were trying to find out.

The second important function of belief is in action. Our representations of the world play a causal role in action, guiding what we do. This is more promising as a way of finding out the appropriate epistemic standards for belief. For if we can investigate the nature of action and find out how beliefs contribute to successful action, this should give us some indication of how it is appropriate for us to regulate the formation of our beliefs. Since the role of beliefs in successful action is unlikely to be determined by the standards of epistemic rationality, we seem to have an independent route to finding out about the standards of epistemic rationality.

Given this link between the standards of epistemic rationality for regulating the way that we form representations of the world and the role that those representations play in action, in the remainder of this chapter I will try to set out the standards of epistemic rationality for beliefs with non-moral content, based on their role in action.

## 4. Truth and Action

Actions are our attempts to change the world (or to make sure it stays as it was). Ordinary factual (non-moral) beliefs play an important role in action. To cook dinner, for example, you rely on a number of beliefs: the carrots will take fifteen minutes to steam, the pizza will be cooked in ten minutes, the oven needs to be hot but not at the highest temperature, and so on. To act successfully, you need to affect the world in just the way you envisaged: in other words, you need to achieve your aim.[13] Since often (but not always) your aim is to satisfy your desires, often this means getting what you want.

What is the connection between successful action and epistemic rationality? One of the major functions of belief is to play a causal role in directing our actions, to enable us successfully to achieve our aims. Yet, epistemic rationality is not a species of practical rationality. A belief is not epistemically rational simply because it leads you to achieve your aim in some particular circumstance. You might simply be lucky, or a belief might have good practical consequences on one occasion. It does not follow that the belief is epistemically rational.

The connection between epistemic rationality and success in action cannot be so direct. There must be two stages to any epistemic assessment.

---

[13] There are complications here, when you get what you were aiming at, but not by bringing it about yourself, or not by bringing it about in the right kind of way. This is for reasons familiar from Davidson's example of the climber who is caused by his desire to be rid of the extra weight to let the rope holding his companion slip from his grasp: the desire causes the desired outcome but not in the way appropriate for action (Davidson 1980: 79). If you are to act, executing your aim, your aim must cause you to move 'in the right way'. It is very difficult properly to characterize what 'the right way' is, but it involves your having control over what you do. Davidson's climber does not execute his aim because he does not control what he does; and so he does not act successfully, even though his aim was achieved.

Suppose that representations of a certain type T lead to successful action more reliably than those of any other type.[14] If all our beliefs were of type T, then we would tend to act successfully, and so our representations of the world would be fulfilling their function well. Therefore, type T beliefs are the *epistemic ideal* for our representations of the world. Of course it does not follow that, if you have type T beliefs, you will achieve your aims—you might not carry out your actions very well. Nevertheless, no other kind of representation of the world would more reliably contribute to your acting successfully.

We may not be able simply to form type T beliefs directly; instead we have to form beliefs in ways which may or may not be likely to lead to our acquiring beliefs of that type. Forming beliefs in ways that reliably lead to beliefs that are epistemically ideal is *epistemically rational*, and beliefs formed in those ways are epistemically rational (even if they fall short of the epistemic ideal, not in fact being type T beliefs).[15] By this I simply mean: forming beliefs on the basis of only some of your evidence; or forming your beliefs in response to all of your evidence.[16]

What type of representations of the world might reliably lead to successful action—that is, action in which you achieved your aim? It is not difficult to see why truth might be important. You are not going to get an edible

[14] I have in mind here classing beliefs in terms like: beliefs that are true, that are justified, that are knowledge; rather than, for example, classifying beliefs in terms of their contents.

[15] I do not intend to suggest by this that we *explicitly* have type T beliefs as our aim in inquiry—or that we should have. All that is intended is that it is in a properly conducted inquiry into ordinary matters of fact; it is epistemically rational to form beliefs as if you were aiming at having type T beliefs. This account of epistemic rationality may seem to support a very simple (and implausible) version of reliabilism—that beliefs are rational iff they have been formed by a reliable method—but I think that this is not necessarily so. Whether this simple form of reliabilism follows from this account of epistemic rationality depends on what the epistemic ideal turns out to be. As I explain later, I think that knowledge has a good claim to be the epistemic ideal, in which case beliefs are epistemically rational if they are formed in ways which are conducive to producing knowledge. This account of epistemic rationality will not, I think, be a form of simple reliabilism.

[16] There is a complication. Suppose that if you act on Type T beliefs, you are most likely to act successfully and achieve what you want. But it is extremely difficult to get Type T beliefs and if you aim to do so, you will almost certainly fail. By contrast, if you act on Type S beliefs, your act is less likely to be successful, but Type S beliefs are easier to obtain. Overall, if you aim at type S beliefs, you are more likely to act successfully than if you aim at Type T beliefs. In these circumstances, what is the epistemic ideal? Is it epistemically rational to form beliefs as if you were aiming for type T beliefs, or type S beliefs? Fortunately, I do not think that this circumstance arises for non-moral factual beliefs (there is no type S belief that is as easy to obtain as type T beliefs, i. e. that is a moderately successful rival to them). But I think that a somewhat similar possibility genuinely does arise in the case of action on the basis of moral beliefs, and I discuss what is epistemically rational in those circumstances in Chapter 10.

pizza if it will be ready in ten minutes but you think it will take two hours. We are much more likely to be able to achieve our aims with true beliefs rather than false ones.[17] Type T beliefs, then, must be true.

We cannot, of course, just decide to acquire true rather than false beliefs. And of course to a large extent belief-formation is not under our control. But, to some extent, we can decide which ways of forming beliefs to pursue (and if we form beliefs in other ways, we can try not to act on them and try to revise them); so we can try to form beliefs in such a way that the beliefs will be true.

What is a good way of forming true beliefs? Is it a good idea to ignore significant and relevant evidence? Obviously not. But other people's testimony is often significant and relevant evidence. If you want to find out how long to cook your pizza, you can ask your friends or consult with a cookbook. Of course, testimony can be misleading and you should not trust it when you have good reason to believe that the speaker is lying to you or that she has made an error. But if you think she is trustworthy then it is rational to give at least some weight to her testimony.

It may, however, seem more plausible that you should ignore the opinion of others when you disagree with them, since you have some relevant evidence yourself and you have made up your own mind on that basis. So, why listen to what anyone else thinks? After all, they may just lead you astray. But you should not ignore the opinions of others when you disagree with them, at least when they are your epistemic peer. It is possible that your opponent may have access to different evidence from you, in which case you certainly must take her opinion into account—for her beliefs may be your only access to what may be very important evidence. But, even if she has no extra evidence, she is potentially an important corrective to your own views; for you are not, after all, perfect at responding to your evidence. After all, you antecedently believed that she was as likely as you to get the answer right.[18] In general, you should

---

[17] Horwich (2006) defends (one aspect of) the value of true beliefs in this way. Craig (1990: 130–3) defends the importance of knowledge by a similar argument, focused on its significance in action.

[18] Could you not ignore disagreements precisely when your opponent is wrong and you are right? In doing so, you would retain true beliefs (and surely would act successfully), so this looks like a good strategy. This is not a problem specifically about disagreement, but potentially applies to any situation in which you have some evidence that is misleading: could you not always form your beliefs in response only to the non-misleading evidence? But ignoring only misleading evidence is clearly not a strategy

not ignore the judgement of your epistemic peer even when you disagree with her, and taking her opinions into account in hard cases is likely to mean that the balance of evidence supports (both of you) suspending judgement.

There is, of course, a difference between assuming that your opponent is making a mistake simply because she disagrees with you and having additional evidence that she is wrong (for example, you have evidence that she is not really your peer, or that something is interfering with her judgement in this case, and so on). When you do have additional evidence of this kind, you can give her opinion less weight. But, otherwise, the best strategy for you to form true beliefs is to take her opinion into account.[19]


## 5. Knowledge and Action

Is the epistemic ideal: true beliefs? If so, epistemic rationality would be a matter of forming beliefs in ways that are likely to produce true beliefs and, as we have seen, it follows that ignoring others' testimony or others' beliefs when they disagree with you is epistemically irrational. There is, however, another possibility: that the epistemic ideal is not truth but knowledge.[20] It

---

that you could realistically carry out, because you cannot always distinguish when your evidence is misleading—and ignoring evidence that you *think* is misleading is not a good strategy, because often you will be mistaken and end up with false beliefs. So, realistically, you can only choose to ignore certain kinds of evidence all the time (e.g., the judgement of your epistemic peers) or take it into account whenever you have no specific reason for discounting it (e.g., reasons for revising your view that your opponent is your peer) and clearly the latter strategy is likely to be better in terms of your acquiring true beliefs.

[19] I have suggested that in order to gain true beliefs your best strategy is not to ignore significant and relevant evidence, where this includes evidence from testimony and from the judgement of an epistemic peer even when they disagree with you (but also includes the original evidence on which you based your initial judgement, prior to your becoming aware of your peer's opinion). I think that this supports the Total Evidence view of the rational response to disagreements, where your original evidence, plus the evidence of your own and your opponent's judgements must be taken into account (rather than the Equal Weight view, according to which your own and your opponent's judgements are the only evidence that you consider). Even so, if your original evidence is not strong or it is hard to interpret, it is still rational to suspend judgement in response to a disagreement with an epistemic peer.

[20] Craig (1990: 132–3) argues that we should form beliefs by methods that will reliably result in true beliefs and that since we cannot be aware of all the details of our circumstances, we would prefer to form representations by methods that would still be reliable if minor features of our world changed. So the epistemic standard for beliefs will include truth and reliability, and these are usually considered to be marks of knowledge.

has been said that knowledge and action are the central relations between mind and world.[21] Through action we try to impose our will on the world. If we have knowledge, our mental representations fit the world, and it is no accident that they do. It would hardly be surprising if there were deep connections between the two. But, why think that knowledge is the epistemic ideal, rather than truth?

Consider the following situation: suppose that you truly believe that the shop you need is located on a particularly long road. You formed that belief because you overheard someone, who is usually very reliable, say that it was at the northern end. In fact, it is at the south end. As you start walking from the north, and fail to find the shop, you begin to lose confidence that you are in the right place at all, and give up.[22]

What has happened here is that you have a true belief, indeed a justified true belief, but it has not led you to act successfully. That in itself does not show that true beliefs are not the Type T belief that we have been searching for: however well you have formed your beliefs your actions still may not be successful. But, if there is a type of representation of the world that *more reliably* leads to successful action than true belief it is that type which is the epistemic ideal.

The example is an instance of a familiar type: a Gettier case in which your justification is inappropriately related to the truth of your belief: here you have based your belief on a witness who is usually correct, but in this case has a detail wrong. It is precisely because of this that you fail to have knowledge. And it is the connection between your justification and the truth of your belief that leads you astray in this case. You based your true belief that the shop was on the road on a premise that was false, that the shop was at the north end. And, as you gained more and more evidence that it was not on the north end you formed the (true) belief that it was not at the north end, and you wrongly concluded that it was not on that road. Of course, you ended up failing to do what you had set out to achieve.

Suppose, by contrast, that you had *known* that the shop was on the road because you had heard a reliable person correctly say that it was at the south end. This time you do not expect to come across the shop as you walk from the north. So you carry on until at last you arrive there.

---

[21] Williamson 2000: 1.

[22] Williamson uses a similar case to suggest that knowledge can play a role in causal explanations of action (ibid. 62).

Of course, people differ in how persistent they are prepared to be in pursuing their goals. Some people would carry on searching even if they had not found the shop where they were expecting it; others would give up straight away. But, the point is that given equal persistence you are still more likely to go wrong if you act on the basis of (justified) true beliefs than if you act on the basis of knowledge in Gettier-type situations. When your belief is true, but the connection between that belief and its justification is not of the right kind, you are more likely to be led astray by the false premise or inappropriate connection and to fail to get what you aimed at than if you had knowledge. Of course, Gettier situations may not be very common, so having true beliefs may usually lead you to act successfully, achieving your aims. But, it may nevertheless be true that knowledge rather than true belief, more reliably, more consistently, leads you to act successfully. If you have knowledge, you will act as successfully as you would do if you had true beliefs in non-Gettier situations, and you will tend to be more successful in Gettier cases. This suggests that it may be knowledge rather than true belief that is the epistemic ideal for ordinary factual beliefs.[23]

If there are close connections between action and knowledge there must also be an important relationship between knowledge and practical reasoning.[24] Much practical reasoning is reasoning about how to achieve our aims. If knowledge is the best representational state at achieving our ends, it follows that practical reasoning based on knowledge will be good practical reasoning.

A stronger thesis has recently been suggested: that knowledge is the norm of practical reasoning, in the sense that practical reasoning that is not based on knowledge is thereby defective.[25] This strong claim does not follow

---

[23] Could the epistemic ideal be something more than knowledge—for example, true beliefs justified in the right way, where the justification is stronger than is required for knowledge? There may or may not be an epistemic state that is more demanding than knowledge in the way suggested, and it may or may not lead to more successful actions (it may turn out that the extra justification does not make a significant difference). But, since the justification required for this state must at least be as great as for knowledge, it is reasonable to assume that if this state is the epistemic ideal, the standards of epistemic rationality relating to testimony and to disagreement will be at least as demanding as those that would hold if knowledge were the epistemic ideal. That is, it would not be epistemically rational to ignore significant and relevant evidence, including evidence based on testimony or on the opinions of epistemic peers, whether knowledge or some more demanding state is the epistemic ideal.

[24] Such a link is defended by Hawthorne and Stanley 2008; Hawthorne 2004; and Williamson 2000; amongst others.

[25] Though it may be excusable in the right circumstances, such as when you reasonably believe that you have knowledge. For example, Hawthorne tentatively endorses the following principle: 'One

from the argument given here linking knowledge and action (though it is, I think, compatible with it). According to my argument, practical reasoning based on knowledge will direct us to act in a way that makes it very likely that, provided we execute the action properly, we will achieve our aims. But we often, perhaps even typically, carry out practical reasoning in situations in which we are severely constrained by time and the availability of evidence. If you need to act straight away, you may not be able to spend time searching for sufficient evidence that you qualify as having knowledge. In these circumstances, it may be perfectly acceptable to reason on premises that you do not know, but which it is epistemically rational for you to believe. But, even so, knowledge will still play an important role. What makes it the case that certain beliefs or assumptions are epistemically rational and certain ones are not? Whether your beliefs are epistemically rational is determined by the epistemic ideal, that is, knowledge.

The connection between knowledge and practical reasoning is not important to my argument, so I will not try to settle in what way knowledge is a norm of practical reasoning. Instead, I want to consider the consequences if knowledge is the epistemic ideal for the epistemic rationality of responses to testimony and disagreement.

If you have knowledge, what you know must be true. So, anything that is not a good way of forming true beliefs will also not be a good way of gaining knowledge. Recall that ignoring testimony from and disagreements with your epistemic peers is not a good way of acquiring true beliefs. So, if knowledge is the epistemic ideal, ignoring testimony and ignoring the opinions of your epistemic peers is not rational.

There are additional considerations if knowledge is the epistemic ideal, however. To have knowledge, your representations of the world must not only be true, but they must also be justified (in some sense). Exactly what justification is, and in particular what kind of justification is needed for knowledge, is very controversial and I cannot even begin to deal with it adequately here. But, nevertheless, I think the following principle is very plausible. If you ignore some significant and relevant evidence that is available to you then your belief will not be properly justified, so that even if your belief is true it will not be knowledge.

ought only to use that which one knows as a premise in one's practical deliberations' (Hawthorne 2004: 29–30), though he makes some qualifications to this principle and claims that it holds only *ceteris paribus*.

Consider the following examples. Suppose that you choose (in so far as you can) to conform your beliefs to the evidence that you gather on Tuesdays, ignoring all other evidence. This is not a good way to get true beliefs. But, even if you happen to get true beliefs it is not a way of gaining knowledge. Why? Your beliefs will lack justification, for you will fail to take into account significant and relevant evidence available to you. Similarly, suppose that as a member of the jury you are confronted with a great deal of evidence that the defendant is guilty, but you choose to ignore this and continue to believe that he is innocent, not because you have some other evidence of his character or alibi to weigh against the courtroom case, just because you have a hunch. Even if it turned out that your belief that the defendant was innocent was true, you could not be said to know that he was innocent. Again, your belief would not be properly justified because you would have formed your view whilst ignoring significant and relevant evidence. So you cannot have knowledge.

Of course, taking into account all significant and relevant evidence that you have does not guarantee that you will have knowledge: your evidence may be incomplete, insufficient, or misleading.[26] But, if you wilfully choose to ignore some significant and relevant evidence when you form your beliefs you will not—you cannot—have knowledge. Consequently, it cannot be epistemically rational to ignore significant and relevant evidence if epistemic rationality is defined in terms of knowledge.

Provided that you have no good reason to think that a speaker is deceitful or in error (and perhaps some reason to think that she is reliable), her testimony that p is evidence that p. Ignoring her testimony, in those circumstances, would be to ignore some significant, relevant evidence that p, and this is not a good way of getting knowledge. Ignoring the opinions of epistemic peers is also a mistake if you are trying to gain knowledge, even when they disagree with you. For their opinions too are significant and relevant evidence that p. This is so, even if your original belief was

---

[26] Your taking into account the significant and relevant evidence that you have may be a necessary condition of your having knowledge or justified beliefs, but it is not sufficient, for the reasons mentioned, and perhaps because of other factors too. Whether or not you count as having knowledge, for example, may depend on factors unrelated to your evidence: pragmatic factors such as how much it matters whether you are correct (to yourself or to whoever is attributing knowledge to you). These additional factors are not relevant to my argument, however, since I am here interested only in the rational response to your evidence and the contribution that that makes to your acquiring knowledge or justified belief.

true. In general, this is not a good way to get knowledge; and were you to act on the resultant beliefs it would not in general be a good way of achieving your aims.

Is truth or knowledge the epistemic ideal? Knowledge has a good claim, I think, but fortunately I do not need to take a stand here. For, ultimately, the question does not matter for the issue with which I am really concerned: whether knowledge or truth is the epistemic ideal the same consequences follow for the standards of epistemic rationality with respect to trusting testimony and disagreements about non-moral matters of fact between epistemic peers. Ignoring significant evidence such as testimony or disagreement is not a good way to get true beliefs, and it is not a way to get knowledge at all. So, it is epistemically rational sometimes to trust testimony and to take account of your opponent's beliefs in disagreements about non-moral factual matters when she is your epistemic peer, whether truth or knowledge is the epistemic ideal. It follows that in disagreements with an epistemic peer about a non-moral matter of fact, at least when your original evidence is weak, it is epistemically rational for you to suspend judgement.

# 9

# Moral Understanding and Morally Worthy Action

## 1. The Puzzle Again

In the previous chapter, I argued that we can find out about epistemic rationality by looking at the role that beliefs play in action: it is epistemically rational to form beliefs in ways such that those beliefs are likely to perform their function well. I also argued that beliefs about non-moral factual matters that amounted to knowledge would perform their function of helping us to achieve whatever aim that we had set for ourselves best, and so it was epistemically rational to form beliefs as if we were aiming for knowledge.

Now take our moral beliefs, by which I mean our beliefs with an explicitly moral content. These might be beliefs about what is morally right or wrong, beliefs with a content of 'thick' ethical terms (e.g., what it is courageous or honest or cruel to do), or, most crucially for our purposes, beliefs about what we have moral reasons to do, and how those moral reasons stack up against our other reasons for action. In the last chapter, I noted that mature adults tend not to give the same weight to the testimony or the beliefs of others, even experts, about moral matters as we would for non-moral factual matters. Moreover, we do not regard this as a mistake that we should correct. Indeed, we regard people like Eleanor, who trusted the testimony of her friends regarding the moral status of vegetarianism, as making a mistake instead. This practice seems even more puzzling now. Why on earth should you refuse to give weight to evidence that is clearly relevant to a truth in which you are interested, indeed which you regard as very important. Surely this must be epistemically irrational. Is it any different from the plainly crazy practice of refusing to take into account evidence that you discover on a day other than Tuesday?

I do not think that it is crazy to ignore testimony, disagreement, and indeed expertise when we form our moral beliefs. In fact I will argue that it can be epistemically rational for us to do so. The argument for this will take up the next three chapters. In this chapter, I make a preliminary case that when we form moral beliefs in the ways that I have described, what we are doing makes sense. I concede right away that forming moral beliefs in these ways would not make sense if we were trying to attain moral knowledge. But, knowledge is not the only thing of epistemic interest. In this chapter I argue that understanding why p (where p is some moral claim) is different from both knowledge that p and knowledge why p. Section 2 introduces moral understanding. In section 3, I argue that moral understanding is very important in a variety of ways, but most crucially it has a significant role in morally worthy action.

## 2. What is Moral Understanding?

Consider some explicitly moral propositions:

It is morally right to help those in need.
I have moral reason not to lie.
Action X is morally wrong.

What is it to *understand why* any of these are the case?[1] Contrast the following cases.

---

[1] It is important to note that this conception of moral understanding—understanding why p (where p is some explicitly moral proposition)—differs from some other types of understanding. It is not the same as understanding the proposition itself; for example, understanding what 'it is morally right to help those in need' means. I assume that you need to understand the proposition itself to believe the proposition, let alone to know it or to understand why it is the case. My conception of understanding why p (where p is some moral proposition) should also not be confused with the idea of understanding morality as a whole. I do not have anything to say here about what it is to understand morality (considered as a whole subject area), though it may include having some moral knowledge or some moral understanding in my sense. My conception of moral understanding should also be distinguished from understanding that p (even where p is a moral proposition), a phrase that I think is often used as equivalent to believing that p (or perhaps knowing that p). It is also important to note that I am giving an account here specifically of moral understanding, not of understanding generally.

Sarah is five years old. Her parents have told her not to lie, that lying is naughty and wrong. She accepts what they say.

Peter is fifteen. He has heard many people say that helping those in need is morally right, but he does not agree. He thinks that the strong are entitled to trample on the weak and should not be distracted by talk of needs.

Mary believes that she has moral reason not to lie because lying to other people fails to respect them and in the long-run tends to make them unhappy. She can see that there are differences, sometimes important ones, between lying to people and not telling them the whole truth. She thinks that lying for your own benefit is normally wrong, but it is harder to say whether lying to someone in a way that makes her happy is ever acceptable, and this may depend on the exact circumstances of the case. She is able to apply these beliefs to new situations and make her own judgements about what it is morally right for her to do in them.

Let us suppose that Mary is approximately correct about why she has moral reason not to lie and about the other issues mentioned. She understands why she has moral reason not to lie. Peter, by contrast, has a false belief—that he has no moral reason to help those in need—so he cannot have moral understanding. In the sense in which I am interested here, moral understanding is 'factive': you cannot understand why p if p is false.[2] Since telling lies for your own benefit is morally wrong, you cannot possibly understand why it is right; since helping the needy is morally right, Peter cannot understand why it is wrong.[3]

Moral understanding, in this sense, is not transparent. You might *think* that you understand perfectly well that refusing to help the needy is morally

---

[2] Moral understanding as described here is compatible with a variety of metaethical theories, I believe. It is compatible with moral realism, but also with various forms of anti-realism (including sophisticated subjectivism, quasi-realism, and fictionalism), provided that they include a conception of truth in ethics.

[3] Other philosophers who have written about understanding in general (rather than moral understanding) have taken a different view. For example, Zagzebski (2001) develops a conception of understanding according to which understanding is transparent—if you understand that p, you understand that you understand that p—and which is not factive: you can understand that p even though p is false. This is completely different from the concept of moral understanding in which I am interested, and it is also, I think, rather different from our everyday use of the term. Kvanvig (2003) has a concept of understanding more similar to mine (though my account of moral understanding is developed in ways with which he might not agree, especially with regard to the importance of certain kinds of cognitive ability).

acceptable, but of course you do not: you cannot. It is fairly easy to see how you might fail to understand something that you thought you understood. Peter thought he understood why it was not right to help the needy but he was mistaken, he had no moral understanding. It is perhaps less clear that you can have more moral understanding than you think. But this is possible. Suppose that you are faced with a very difficult moral situation. You form a judgement about what to do based on what you take to be relevant. You are not at all sure that you have it right, and indeed you are quite concerned that you may have missed out some relevant factors or classed some of them wrongly. In fact, you have correctly identified all the factors and weighed them appropriately. It is quite possible that you understand why this action is right and alternatives are wrong, even though you do not realize that you do.

In order to have moral understanding in this sense, you do not have to deliberate extensively about each case and you may not need to deliberate at all. Peter may have thought about what is morally right and wrong much more than Mary has, but she has moral understanding and he does not. In more complex situations, careful and lengthy deliberation may be necessary.

Peter clearly cannot understand why helping the needy is not morally right, for he is mistaken about that. What about Sarah? She correctly believes that lying is morally wrong. But she does not understand why. In general, young children tend to lack moral understanding, even if they have been brought up with correct moral beliefs. Sarah, like other young children, is relying on her parents' moral opinions. Unlike Mary, she has not yet developed her own judgement. She does not yet grasp why lying is wrong, so she cannot understand why it is wrong.

Contrast Mary, too, with Eleanor. Suppose that Eleanor trusts her reliable friends, and thus knows that eating animals is wrong. But, whereas Mary was able to offer an explanation of why lying is wrong, Eleanor is not at all sure why eating meat is wrong. (Is it eating or killing that is wrong? Do animals have rights or is it a question of maximizing welfare?) In short, Eleanor may know that eating animals is wrong, but she does not understand why.

Understanding why p is clearly different from knowing that p. According to some accounts of understanding, there is nevertheless a close connection between understanding and a different type of knowledge: understanding why p is the same as knowing why p.[4]

Suppose that Eleanor's friend offered an explanation: eating animals is wrong because of the suffering of animals under modern farming methods. If this is correct and Eleanor believes her, she knows not just that eating animals is wrong but she knows why too. But she is still not in the same position as Mary. Eleanor cannot draw relevant distinctions, cannot come to correct conclusions about similar cases. (What about animals reared under better conditions? What about fish?) Eleanor has been told why eating meat is wrong, but she does not really *grasp* the reasons why it is wrong.[5]

This suggests that understanding why p differs both from knowledge that p and knowledge why p.[6] It is possible to have moral knowledge without moral understanding. But what exactly is the difference?

If you understand why X is morally right or wrong, you must have some appreciation of the reasons why it is wrong.[7] Appreciating the reasons why it is wrong is not the same as simply *believing that* they are the reasons why it is wrong, or even *knowing* that they are the reasons it is wrong. Moral understanding involves a *grasp* of the relation between moral propositions and the reasons why they are true; you have to have 'internalized' the relationship between a moral proposition p and these reasons so that you can, for instance, use that relationship to form new beliefs.[8]

---

[4] For example, Kitcher 2002; Woodward 2003: 179; and Lipton 2004: 30. Grimm (2006) defends a view of understanding according to which it is a 'species of knowledge', that involves a 'psychologically thick' notion of belief: if you understand that p, you must have 'grasped' that p. He does not discuss issues such as accepting that p on the basis of testimony, so it is not clear whether or not he would agree that understanding differs from knowledge in that regard.

[5] This testimony might be the trigger that Eleanor needs to think through the matter herself. She might as a result grasp why the welfare of animals is important, in such a way that she could make similar judgements about similar cases. If so, then she would understand why p.

[6] A very similar case is presented by Pritchard (forthcoming), and he draws the same conclusion, that understanding differs from knowledge and knowledge why.

[7] Note that moral understanding does not require a grasp of reasons 'all the way down': this would be far too demanding. Nor does it require a grasp of philosophically sophisticated justifications or of moral theory. It does not need any more than the kind of grasp of reasons that most of us have when we realize that we should help others, take care of our friends and family, and so on.

[8] Consider the different grounds that you might have for believing a moral proposition p; for example, 'Action X is wrong'. You might base your belief that action X is wrong on the claims that it is a lie told for your own benefit, and that it is wrong to deceive others because doing so fails to respect them, for example. These factors are reasons why it is wrong, that you could use to *explain* why that action is wrong. By contrast, you could base your belief on a completely different ground. You may have evidence that does *not* consist in the reasons that make the proposition true and that

Understanding is often associated with certain sorts of feeling: a flash of enlightenment, a light dawning. But these are not necessary: you need have no particular feelings at all when you finally come to understand why X is morally wrong. Nor are they sufficient. However much you feel the light dawning as you confidently turn aside from the needy, you do not understand—you cannot understand—that it is right to do so. Moral understanding is a matter of having thought through by yourself questions concerning that particular issue, so that you are able to draw conclusions or offer explanations without prompting, guidance, or assistance from other people. Once you have grasped the importance of not deceiving others and you can draw the conclusion that it is wrong to tell a lie simply for your own benefit, for example, you understand why it is wrong to lie. Your ability to draw the right conclusion or give the right explanation is not a matter of luck: it is explained by your appreciation of the reasons why p. Since you cannot understand why p unless p is true and you have the appropriate grasp of the reasons why p, understanding why p must be something that can be credited to you: understanding therefore is always a kind of achievement for you, though of course others can help you on the way.[9]

could *not* be used to explain why it is true. One obvious source of such evidence is testimony. If you learn that p by testimony, your reasons for believing that p are not usually reasons why p is true. If a reliable person tells you that p, or even if you discover that they believe that p, this is evidence for p; but it does not give you a clue why p is the case. You cannot offer as an explanation of why action A is wrong 'my friend told me it was'. We can call this type of evidence that does not consist in the reasons why p is true, *non-explanatory evidence*. When you understand why some moral proposition p is true, you can work out whether p on the basis of the reasons why p. It is a good question what kind of access we have to the reasons why moral propositions are true. I cannot give a proper account here, but I will make a couple of suggestions. You might consider moral arguments in favour and against the claim that lying is morally wrong when you are unlikely to be discovered. You may discover that, whilst recognizing that the arguments are not decisive, one side seems to you to have more forceful arguments in its favour. Your finding on reflection these arguments to be convincing is some evidence that they are sound. It is not decisive evidence, and it may be misleading. But it may none the less be reasonable to form your moral beliefs on the basis of your assessments of the strength of moral arguments. Alternatively, you might appeal to your emotional responses and morally relevant feelings, of guilt, shame, admiration, and so on. These feelings may be strong, and you may find that you are inclined on reflection to endorse at least some of them as appropriate or warranted. For example, you may notice that if someone lies to you you have feelings of resentment towards them. It is not just that you want them not to lie to you; you feel that they are treating you without respect and they have reason to respect you. On reflection, you regard these feelings as entirely warranted. This is some evidence that lying is morally wrong. Again, it is not decisive evidence, and your reflective judgements about your feelings can lead you astray. But it may be reasonable to base your moral beliefs partly on such judgements.

   [9] I do not mean to suggest here that moral thought has to take place in isolation. Thinking about moral questions with other people can be a way of coming to moral understanding. But if each

You cannot really understand why p is true if p and the reasons why p are the only things about the subject of which you are aware: it is not possible to understand why some isolated fact is true. To understand why p, you must have an ability to draw conclusions about similar cases, and to work out when a different conclusion would hold if the reasons why p were no longer the case. If you have this kind of appreciation of moral reasons you must have, at least to some extent, a systematic grasp of morality. This is not to say that you need to have a grasp of anything that could possibly be morally important. But if you understand why you have moral reason to help the needy, for instance, you must have some awareness that the needs of other people are morally important and some grasp of their relative importance compared to other moral and non-moral considerations (such as self-interest).[10] You must also be able to make appropriate judgements in similar cases—for example, that X' is morally wrong for the same reason, but Y is not. One sign that Eleanor and Sarah have no moral understanding is precisely that they are unable to draw conclusions about similar cases. If you do have the relevant abilities, you can generate new true moral beliefs (and perhaps new moral knowledge) without relying on help or advice from anyone else.

The grasp of the reasons why p that is essential to understanding involves a number of abilities: to understand why p, you need to be able to *treat* q as the reason why p, not merely *believe* or *know that* q is the reason why p.[11] If you understand why p (and q is why p), then in the right sort of circumstances you can successfully:

(i) follow an explanation of why p given by someone else;
(ii) explain why p in your own words;
(iii) draw the conclusion that p (or that probably p) from the information that q;

individual is to have moral understanding each must grasp the connections between p and the reasons why p, even if they have acquired that grasp through collective deliberation.

[10] This is perhaps one of the reasons why it seemed plausible to some that the virtues are unified in the sense that if you have one virtue you must have them all. It is not possible properly to understand one isolated moral reason. But, at the same time, you do not have to grasp the nature and significance of all moral reasons in order to understand one of them.

[11] The abilities listed below are, I think, individually necessary for moral understanding and I suspect that they may be jointly sufficient for it, provided that it is true that p and that q is why p (though I am open to the possibility that other abilities may be required in addition). I leave it open whether having moral understanding is identical with having these abilities, or whether they are connected in some other way that is not identity—but where having moral understanding requires that you have these abilities (to some extent at least).

   (iv)  draw the conclusion that p' (or that probably p') from the information that q' (where p' and q' are similar to but not identical to p
and q);

   (v)  given the information that p, give the right explanation q;

  (vi)  given the information that p', give the right explanation q'.

To understand why p, you have to have the abilities (i) to (vi), to at
least some extent. Of course, you can have these abilities to a greater or
lesser degree, which may make it tempting to say that moral understanding
comes in degrees. You have minimal moral understanding if you correctly
believe that q is why p and you can follow an explanation of why p.
You have greater understanding if you have (i) to (vi) to some extent and
you have full understanding if you have (i) to (vi) to the greatest extent.[12]
Alternatively, there might be a cut-off point before which you do not count
as having understanding, after which you do. This cut-off point might be
contextually determined—that is, in one context you might need (i) to
(vi) to only a minimal degree to count as having moral understanding; a
different context might have higher standards, so that you needed to have
(i) to (vi) to a greater extent to have moral understanding. I will not settle
this question here, as the differences between the two conceptions of moral
understanding will not much matter.

    You can know why p without having these abilities—that is one reason
why understanding why p is not the same as knowing why p. But it may
be tempting to think that having the abilities is simply to have extra pieces
of knowledge. For example, perhaps to understand why p, you need to
know why p (where q is why p) *and* to know that if q' rather than q were
true, then p' rather than p would be true. Moral understanding would not
be identical to knowing why p, but it would be the same as a combination
of knowing why p plus some other pieces of propositional knowledge.

    But I think that having these abilities is not the same as having extra
pieces of knowledge. Gaining this extra knowledge may help you acquire

---

[12] For example, Elizabeth Anscombe argued (1981) that dropping the atomic bomb on Hiroshima
was wrong because intentionally killing innocent civilians in war is absolutely wrong. Let us assume
that she was mistaken about that: intentionally killing innocent civilians in wartime can be permissible
provided that the benefits are sufficiently great. Let us also assume that in Hiroshima the benefits
were not sufficiently great. Given these (controversial) assumptions, Anscombe was right to condemn
dropping the bomb, and she partially understood why doing so was wrong: that it involved the killing
of civilians was certainly relevant. But she did not fully understand why it was wrong, though she
believed that she did.

the requisite abilities, but you might have the extra pieces of knowledge without having the kind of good judgement that enables you to generate new true moral beliefs yourself. Surely no extra piece or pieces of knowledge guarantee that you have these abilities. In order to have moral understanding you must have the internal grasp of the relationship between p and the reasons why p, and this does not seem to be a piece of propositional knowledge.

A second reason for doubting that understanding why p is simply knowledge why p plus some extra pieces of propositional knowledge is that moral understanding has a different relationship to epistemic luck than knowledge does.

Suppose that your school has been sent a set of extremely inaccurate textbooks, which have been handed out to your class. But you are very lucky because there is only one that is accurate, and by chance you have it. You read in your book that Stalin was responsible for the deaths of millions of people. You draw the obvious conclusion that he was an evil person. It is plausible that you do not know that Stalin killed millions of people, since you could so easily have got a different textbook which was wholly unreliable. As a consequence, you do not know why he was evil (that is, you do not know that he was evil because he killed millions of people, because you do not know that he killed millions of people). But I think that you can understand why he was. After all, you believe that he was evil because he killed millions of people, and that is correct, and you have—let us assume—the ability to draw the conclusion that he was evil from the reasons why he was evil and to do the same in similar cases. So it seems that you can have moral understanding why p without having knowledge why p.[13]

If this is right, moral understanding is distinct from propositional knowledge, but it has, I think, interesting similarities with knowing how: they

---

[13] This is the same sort of case as presented by Pritchard (forthcoming) for a similar conclusion. Pritchard concludes that understanding, but not knowledge, is compatible with 'environmental' epistemic luck, though he denies that it is compatible with all forms of epistemic luck. I am inclined to go further and to say that even if your own textbook was extremely inaccurate, but that you read in it the truth that Stalin killed millions, you could as a result understand why he was an evil person, though clearly you could not know that he was evil or know why on that basis (I think that Pritchard would deny this). I am inclined to think that you have moral understanding because your belief that Stalin killed millions is true and you formed it reasonably (assuming that you had no reason to think that your textbook was generally inaccurate) and you have grasped correctly he was evil because he killed millions—and this is all that is required for understanding why he was evil.

both have close connections to certain sorts of ability. Of course, the relationship between propositional knowledge and knowing how is itself a matter of dispute. Whilst, according to some accounts, knowing how and propositional knowledge are distinct, there are well-known arguments (e.g., Stanley and Williamson 2001) that knowing how is a species of propositional knowledge.[14] If these arguments apply to understanding why p as well as to knowledge how, one might conclude that moral understanding must be a species of propositional knowledge too.[15]

I am inclined to think that understanding why p is not a kind of propositional knowledge, for the two reasons that I have given here. But I do not intend to press this, since I do not think that ultimately it will matter whether moral understanding is classed as propositional knowledge or not. Suppose that Stanley and Williamson are right that knowing how is a species of propositional knowledge and their arguments also apply to understanding why p (as I conceive of it here). Nevertheless, they concede that there are some differences between the two. They make a distinction between knowing a proposition 'under a practical mode of presentation'—as you do when you have know-how—and knowing it under a different mode (say, a 'theoretical mode'). They say that it is difficult to characterize what it is to know a proposition 'under a practical mode of presentation' but it undoubtedly involves the possession of certain complex dispositions. Given this distinction, it seems that you might know propositions under one mode of presentation, but not the other (because you know it without having the relevant dispositions and so lack know-how; or because you have the relevant dispositions and so have know-how but do not have

---

[14] The best-known defender of the claim that know-how is not propositional knowledge is Gilbert Ryle (Ryle 1971); and that thesis is also endorsed by David Lewis (Lewis 1990). The argument given by Stanley and Williamson is complicated and I cannot do justice to it here. They claim that knowing how is a species of propositional knowledge, specifically that, for example, 'Hannah knows how to ride a bicycle' is true relative to a context c 'if and only if there is some contextually relevant way w such that Hannah stands in the knowledge-that relation to the Russellian proposition that w is a way for Hannah to ride a bicycle, and Hannah entertains this proposition under a practical mode of presentation' (Stanley and Williamson 2001: 430).

[15] Stanley and Williamson press the point that having knowledge how can involve having certain complex dispositions, and yet knowledge how may still be a species of propositional knowledge, so they would not find convincing the first reason I give for thinking that moral understanding and propositional knowledge are distinct. But, even if they are right about that, it is still true that moral understanding seems to be compatible with epistemic luck in a way that propositional knowledge is not, in which case understanding why p (where p is a moral proposition) cannot be a species of propositional knowledge.

knowledge in another form). In which case, moral understanding may include knowing propositions under a practical mode of presentation, but not necessarily under a theoretical mode of presentation—so moral understanding would be a form of propositional knowledge but very unlike ordinary propositional knowledge. As we shall see, the points that I want to make about moral understanding follow whether or not understanding why p is a form of propositional knowledge, provided it is propositional knowledge of a sufficiently special kind.

## 3. The Value of Moral Understanding

Why should we seek moral understanding? In this section, I will argue that moral understanding is valuable.[16] In the first place, it can be useful because if you have moral understanding you have at least to some extent a systematic grasp of the subject-matter and you therefore have the ability to make good judgements about similar cases: a route, perhaps the only route to reliably doing right.

### A. Reliably Doing Right

Moral understanding might be important because having yourself some systematic grasp of moral reasons might in practice be the only way that

---

[16] Adults are held morally responsible for what they do. Young children and animals are not, though it can be good that they do certain things, and they can 'do their duty'. Why are adults typically morally responsible when children are not? Moral responsibility is a very difficult subject and I will not attempt to give sufficient conditions for someone's being responsible. But I suggest one necessary condition, one feature that divides children from adults: the ability appropriately to orient yourself with regard to moral reasons, one component of which is the ability to understand why certain actions are wrong and why there are moral reasons not to perform them. Consider a child who is learning not to hit other children. Suppose that this child will reliably do the right thing, since she obeys parents who are themselves reliable; she may be able correctly to classify actions as morally right or wrong. At some stage, the child may have been told the reasons why some actions are right and others wrong and be able to state them if asked. But, until she can properly grasp those reasons (or until she acquires the sensitivity to respond to them under a non-moral description) it is not appropriate to hold her fully responsible for what she does. The child is likely to acquire this understanding gradually. At first she may have no idea why she ought not to do so: she is simply obeying adults, perhaps under threat of punishment. Then she may be told by these adults why she ought not to hit others: she may learn that doing so is morally wrong because it is wrong to hurt other people who have done nothing to you. Finally, she may be able to grasp fully why this is so, be able to extrapolate to similar situations, and use her own judgement in those, rather than relying on her parents. Once you are able to understand what is morally right and wrong you can be morally responsible for what you do. It would be extremely surprising if having this ability were of such great moral significance, when moral understanding itself was not.

you could reliably do the right thing. Whilst in principle your moral instincts might be infallible, so that you always instinctively choose the morally right action, or you might keep your moral guru by your side at all times to advise you, in practice these are obviously completely unfeasible. Moral decisions are often complicated. Moral reasons can be difficult to assess and interact in quite complex ways. Small differences in factual situations can make significant moral differences. You often have to make judgements of what to do quite quickly, so you do not have the time to find and consult with an expert. There is simply no one to ask; you have to make the decision on your own and you will make a good decision only if you have moral understanding—the ability to make accurate judgements in new circumstances—or luck.

So, moral understanding is worth having as a means to right action. Moreover, there is a second way in which moral understanding can be useful: in order to justify your actions to others.

## B. Justifying Yourself to Others

Suppose you have been injured in a car accident and, though you are my friend, I do not go to help you. You demand to know why. I reply that there are other people who are hurt more badly than you. You protest that you are my friend and that they are not. I reply that the injuries of the others are potentially fatal whereas yours is not, and I must look after them first.

A core ethical practice is the exchange of reasons. According to Scanlon's 'contractualist' theory, to be motivated morally precisely is to be motivated to find a justification for what we do that we could offer to anyone who might ask: I am motivated to help severely injured strangers rather than my friend because I am able to justify doing so to others, whereas I am not able to justify going to my friend first. Whilst I do not intend to defend contractualism generally, nor do I want to suggest that this is the only (or even the most important) kind of moral motivation, nevertheless, the practice of exchanging reasons and the motivation to find a justification that would be acceptable to others is clearly morally very important.

The requirement to be able to justify yourself involves at least being able to say what you take yourself to be doing and why you thought doing so was a good idea. You might say: I had to help those people who were strangers to me because they were very badly injured, whereas my friend's injuries were only minor. Giving a justification involves giving the reasons why what you did was right. If you do not understand why your action was right you are in a very awkward position.

Suppose your reliable friend has told you not to cheat your customers because doing so is unfair. You believe her, but on your own behalf you cannot really see anything wrong with enriching your shareholders at your customers' expense. There is a perfectly good sense in which you know why cheating your customers is wrong: you know that it is unfair. And yet you have not grasped the connection between the wrongness of the action and the reasons why it is wrong. So you say to your customers what you were told—citing the unfairness of giving the wrong change as a justification for your action—but you cannot give an explanation in your own words, and you cannot reassure customers that under slightly different circumstances you would treat them well (since you are not able to work out what you would have moral reason to do in those circumstances). Without moral understanding, your ability to participate in the exchange of reasons is necessarily limited.

So moral understanding is important in part because being in a position to justify yourself to others is morally important. On the other hand, there may be limits to how well you can justify yourself to others even if you understand why what you did was right. One of the abilities associated with moral understanding is the ability to give your own explanations, but you can have the other abilities and therefore qualify as having (some) moral understanding without being particularly articulate.

In any case, even if the exchange of reasons is genuinely morally important, this may not be the only, or the most basic reason why moral understanding is morally important. It may be very unlikely that anyone will ever ask you to justify what you do. You may know that no one will ask you: perhaps you acted in secret; maybe everyone is more concerned with their own affairs. Why should it be important that you can justify yourself to them if you know you will never have to? Perhaps you find yourself imagining other people watching you and you imagine trying to justify yourself to them. You might feel very uncomfortable if you found yourself unable to explain to them in your own words why what you were doing was right. But if you preferred not to exercise your imagination in this way it is difficult to see why you should care about justification to others at all, in situations where no one wants a justification.

I suggest that there is a more basic reason for the significance of moral understanding. I will argue that moral understanding is essential to good character and to morally worthy action—that is, to right actions performed for the right reasons. The argument will turn on some subtle but important aspects of what it is to respond to moral considerations in forming your moral beliefs and in action. I will begin with the role of moral understanding in having a good character.

## C. Virtue

What is it to have a good character, to have the virtues? Someone who is honest tends to tell the truth, to disapprove of lying and of breaking promises. Someone who is courageous is willing to stand up to danger when there is good reason to do so. In general, someone with a good character is disposed to feel, choose, and act rightly.

Being virtuous is obviously a complex matter consisting of a number of related dispositions. I want to separate out two aspects of good character: one cognitive and one non-cognitive. A virtuous person has *good motivations*: she wants to help others, to tell the truth, and so on. These motivations need not be explicitly moral but sometimes they may be: she may want to do what is just, for example, under that very description. Good motivation is essential to having a good character, but it is obviously not sufficient. To be virtuous, you have to care about helping others and telling the truth, but you cannot be fully virtuous if you consistently mistake what is just, honest, or kind. *Good judgement* is a second crucial component of virtue.[17]

If you do not have good judgement, it is likely that you will actually act wrongly quite often, however worthy your motivations. And if you do the right thing, it will be an accident, because by chance you happen to have hit on the right action. Similarly, someone with the wrong motivations—someone who is essentially selfish, for example—will often act wrongly, and if she does the right thing, it will be by accident. Of

---

[17] Compare Aristotle: 'the "product" is brought to completion by virtue of a person's having wisdom and excellence of character, for excellence makes the goal correct, while wisdom makes what leads to it correct' (*NE* 1144a6–9). I want, as far as possible, to leave open the connection between the two—for example, I do not intend to take a stand on whether, if you have good judgement, you need a separate motivation in order to act, or whether you must have a good motivation, if your judgement is good.

202 THE BELOVED SELF

So we might conclude that good motivations and good judgement are essential to virtue because with them you will *reliably* act rightly and without them you will not. But I do not think that this is the most fundamental explanation for their importance. After all, it is not impossible for you to be in circumstances in which selfishness will lead you reliably to do the right action. You might even know that you are in those circumstances, and so know that you will reliably do right. But you are not thereby virtuous. The real problem is that if you care only for yourself you are not really responding to moral reasons—even if you happen to be in circumstances in which reasons of self-interest are reliably aligned with moral reasons. A virtuous person's motivations must be *responsive to moral reasons*.

I think that the same is true for the cognitive aspects of virtue.[18] There are ways in which you might form beliefs about what is morally required of you, what would be just or kind in your circumstances that would reliably lead you to act rightly—and you might know that they would reliably lead you to act rightly—but you would still not be virtuous.[19] The most obvious

---

[18] McDowell defends a similar view, though he says that the virtuous have a 'reliable sensitivity to a certain sort of requirement which situations impose on behaviour' (1997: 142). He regards this sensitivity as delivering knowledge though, as I have explained, I think it is better characterized as moral understanding. There are other important features of McDowell's conception of virtue on which I do not want to take a stand (for example, his view that this 'knowledge' is sufficient for action).

[19] In order to have some virtues, you may not need to form explicitly moral beliefs. It may be sufficient to be generous, for example, that you simply judge that someone else is in need and that you could help them, and you go on to do so. But it is likely that you will have to make explicitly moral judgements some of the time and, with regard to some virtues (like justice, for example), you will almost certainly need to judge outcomes in moral terms (in this case, as just or unjust). There is in fact no sharp distinction between moral and non-moral motivations and moral and non-moral judgements. For example, one of the important ways that we recognize moral reasons is through emotional responses, some of which involve a distinctively moral attitude or a combination of non-moral response and moral judgement: we may feel anger at injustice or at cruelty; admiration at an example of courage and anxiety at whether we can live up to the same standards; respect for others can be a feeling which is not explicitly moral (which does not involve explicitly moral beliefs) or a distinctively moral attitude towards others that we deliberately take up. There is often continuity between our non-moral attitudes and emotions and those that involve explicitly moral descriptions and lead us to form explicitly moral beliefs. An honest person, for example, grasps why honest actions are important and why she ought to perform them. A courageous person is motivated to face danger, precisely when she grasps that it is worth doing so. Much (though not all) of the motivations and judgements associated with the virtues are explicitly moral.

is: you might ask someone else what to do. In the right circumstances, where you ask someone who is themselves virtuous and trustworthy, you will form true beliefs—indeed you will have knowledge—and if you have the right motivations you will reliably do the right thing. But you will not be virtuous. Consider the following case.

The Incompetent Judge

Claire has just been appointed as a judge and is very anxious to sentence people justly. But she finds it exceptionally difficult to work out the just punishment for various offences, though she listens to the evidence presented carefully and tries her best to get the right answer. Luckily she has a mentor, a more experienced judge, Judith, who has excellent judgement. Claire always consults with Judith and gives her decision in accordance with Judith's guidelines, offering Judith's explanation of why the sentence is just to the defendants.

Claire is not a good judge—she lacks important features of the virtue of judges, that is, of justice. This is not because she does what is just only occasionally and unreliably, or that it is only an accident when she acts rightly: she reliably gives the right sentence thanks to her good motivations and her knowledge. The problem is that she depends on someone else to tell her what to do: she is forming her beliefs in response to Judith, not in response to what is just.

Perhaps what is missing is extra knowledge: perhaps what she needs is knowledge *why* the sentence is just. But, suppose that Judith tells her that five years in jail is the just sentence because of the type of offence committed. Claire then knows why the sentence is just. But she herself is still not able to grasp that, given that type of offence, five years is the just punishment. That is, she lacks the capacity to derive the conclusion that that sentence is just from the reasons why it is just in this and similar cases. So she is simply unable to base her belief that a five-year term in prison is just on the reasons why it is just, she is still wholly relying on Judith's testimony. What Claire lacks, and what she needs in order to be just is *moral understanding*: the *capacity* to base her beliefs about what is just on the reasons why it is just. Moreover, the capacity itself—having moral understanding—is not sufficient either: she actually needs to form her beliefs about what is just *on the basis* of the reasons why it is just. She needs to *use* her moral understanding. Only then will she actually be forming her moral beliefs in response to moral reasons.

Why is responsiveness to moral reasons so important? Why is not reliably doing right sufficient? One answer is that a mark of a virtuous person is that she is an *authority* into what is right.[20] Claire is not an authority on what is just: no one should take Claire's advice or defer to Claire's judgement (though they might listen to Judith's advice, which Claire has passed on). Relying on the judgement of someone else—however dependable they are—is not a way for you to be an authority. It is, as it were, the difference between *being* a moral compass, and *having access to* a moral compass.

The second answer expands on this idea. Being a good person is not just about what you do. Reliably acting rightly is a part of having a good character, of course, but to focus too much on outward action is misleading. A good, virtuous person is someone whose *whole self*—her thoughts, decisions, feelings, and emotions as well as her actions—is structured by her sensitivity to morality. This does not mean, of course, that a virtuous person is so consumed by morality that she thinks of nothing else. But it does mean that she is responsive to moral considerations in all aspects of her character, whenever they are relevant.

I will call this responsiveness to moral reasons 'orientation'. Someone who is appropriately oriented is sensitive to the features of actions that determine whether those actions are right or not, and to whether she has reason (and what strength of reason) to perform those actions or not. You may be sensitive to those features of actions without conceiving of them in moral terms. But, when you form moral beliefs, appropriate orientation involves using your moral understanding. Knowledge, specifically knowledge from someone's testimony, is inadequate, because you are relying on *their* being appropriately oriented towards moral reasons, without being so yourself.

Suppose that action A is right because of reason R. If you have moral understanding then you can derive the conclusion (that A is right) from the reasons why it is true (that R), and if you use your moral understanding, you do derive the conclusion from the reasons why it is true, hence the structure of your moral beliefs, the way in which you base one belief on another, mirrors the structure of morality.

---

[20] As Aristotle says, the virtuous person has the ability to 'see what is true in every set of circumstances, being like a carpenter's rule or measure for them' (*NE* 1113a32–5).

Claire, by contrast, bases her belief that action A is right on the testimony of Judith. It follows that Claire's belief is not based on the reasons why it is true. Moreover, because she does not have moral understanding, she cannot derive the conclusion (that A is right) from the reasons why it is right, so even if she wanted them to, her moral beliefs could not mirror morality.

Might Claire reply that once Judith tells her why A is right she can base her belief that it is just on the reasons why it is right, so the structure of her moral beliefs can mirror morality after all? But I think that this is not sufficient for her to claim that she is correctly oriented. I said earlier that if you understand why p, you can *treat* q as the reason why p; Claire lacks the abilities characteristic of moral understanding, and she cannot treat R as the reason why A is right (though she believes that it is the reason). Consider the basis of Claire's belief that A is right. Since she has no moral understanding, Claire is not able to derive the conclusion that A is right from R without Judith telling her what to derive from what and helping her every step of the way, as shown by her inability to draw the conclusion in similar cases. Judith's testimony is the basis *both* of her belief that A is right *and* of her belief that R is why A is right. Claire's belief that A is right is explained by Judith's testimony and *there is no independent explanation for her belief*, as there would be if she had and used her moral understanding.[21] She is responding to testimony, not to moral reasons. Without moral understanding, you cannot be properly oriented with regard to your moral beliefs: moral understanding is the cognitive, intellectual aspect of correct orientation to moral reasons, and as such it is an essential part of good character.

---

[21] For example, Claire's belief that A is right is not counterfactually dependent on R or her belief that R, but on what Judith says. Of course, it will be difficult to distinguish these different dependences in practice, since in fact what Judith says about whether A is right will itself depend on R. But, though Judith is virtuous and trustworthy, she is not infallible, and Claire's belief depends on Judith's testimony, not on R (or her belief that R), when the two come apart. Counterfactual dependence is only a sign of the basis of one's belief though and it is not an infallible sign. If Claire gains and uses moral understanding, for instance, her belief that A is right may be based on *both* Judith's testimony *and* on her belief that R; both of these explain why she has that belief. I take it that it is sufficient for proper orientation that one explanation for your moral belief is your moral understanding. It may have other explanations too. When Claire does not have or does not use moral understanding, by contrast, her belief that A is right is explained by Judith's testimony, not by her belief that R.

I have drawn an analogy between two ways that you can fall short of virtue: cognitive and non-cognitive. But the analogy may seem like a mistake, and a very deep one. Surely a selfish person and the incompetent judge are actually very different, and in a morally significant way. The selfish person is blameworthy in a way that Claire is not, if she really is well-motivated and is doing her best.

It is true that having poor judgement is not blameworthy in exactly the same way as failing to have the right motivations, though we might well blame Claire if, having failed to get in touch with Judith, she is forced to make her own judgement and she makes a decision that is very badly mistaken. Nevertheless, it is certainly true that we would for the most part treat the selfish and the incompetent differently. But I do not think that this undermines my central claim that both motivation and judgement are required to be responsive to moral reasons and that this orientation is essential to virtue. We might not always blame the incompetent judge, but we would—and should–regard her as *less than fully admirable*. This is a negative evaluation of a different type than blame but it is still a negative evaluation—reflecting that lacking judgement is a different way of falling short of virtue than lacking right motivation, but that it is still a way of falling short.

## D. Morally Worthy Action

So far, I have argued that moral understanding is essential to good character. But I think that it also has a role to play in important kinds of moral action. There is a well-known distinction between doing the right action, and acting well or performing morally worthy actions. Your action is morally worthy only if it is a right action, performed for the right reasons, and I will argue that moral understanding is crucial to certain kinds of morally worthy action.

There is a connection between having a good character and performing morally worthy action: virtue can reasonably be regarded as a disposition to perform morally worthy actions. But you can perform morally worthy actions without being virtuous, because you do the right thing for the right reasons, though you do not habitually do so and you are not disposed to do so in other circumstances. And you can have the virtues without performing a morally worthy action on an occasion when you uncharacteristically fail to respond to moral reasons.

The best-known examples illustrating the difference between right action and morally worthy action involve different types of motivation. Kant famously drew a distinction between two shopkeepers. One gives the right change to his customers only for the sake of his reputation. He is not really acting well: he is doing what is morally right, but only because it is in his interests to do so. Whereas the shopkeeper who gives the right change because doing so is fair, in order to treat his customers with respect, is acting well and his action has *moral worth*.[22] But I will argue that your beliefs and the ground of those beliefs are also crucial to acting rightly for the right reasons. Just as virtue had motivational and cognitive components, morally worthy action does too.[23]

[22] What is it to act for the right reasons? Kant himself thought that morally worthy action was doing your duty *from duty*—though it is not exactly clear what that means. One possibility is that to do the morally right act for the right reasons you must choose it under an explicitly moral description 'the morally right action' or 'the action which I have overriding moral reason to perform' or 'my duty'. But that is a mistake. The use of the concept of a duty or of moral rightness—or indeed the use of any explicitly moral concept—is not essential to morally worthy action. What matters is that you respond to moral reasons, not that you do so under an explicitly moral description. In fact, as Williams emphasizes, we sometimes expect people to respond to moral reasons without thinking of them in explicitly moral terms, and responding to them under an explicitly moral description 'it's my wife; and in situations like this it is morally acceptable to save one's wife' seems to be 'one thought too many' (Williams 1981: 18). Williams's argument is compatible with moral beliefs playing an important background role; for example, your recognition that it is morally acceptable to save your wife might influence what you do even though it does not consciously cross your mind. But it is likely that you will form some moral beliefs and they should play an important role. Sometimes there is no clear distinction between explicitly moral and non-moral considerations. Sometimes non-moral motivations lead you astray and you need to form moral beliefs to correct them. Sometimes what is morally required is complicated and you need to deliberate and think in explicitly moral terms in order to work out what is morally right in your circumstances. It does not follow that our forming explicitly moral beliefs does actually help us to respond to moral reasons. Our moral beliefs can fail to fulfil this function in (at least) two ways: first, they may be false, and lead us astray; secondly, we may fail to act on them. And they can fail in both ways at once. Here is the story of Huckleberry Finn, as told by Nomy Arpaly (2003: 75–7). Huckleberry Finn has been brought up with deeply mistaken moral beliefs, which he still holds, that some people hold important property rights over other people. His natural sympathies for others are strong, however, and they are particularly so towards Jim when the two become friends. As a consequence, he does not act on his moral beliefs but, as Arpaly suggests, he may nevertheless be responding to moral reasons *de re* (moral reasons to treat Jim as a person and a friend and to help him escape). Finn's moral beliefs have failed to fulfil their function in both of the ways mentioned: they are false, so that if he acted on them, he would do wrong, and he ignores them anyway, so they do not actually play a role in his action. You can still act well—as Finn may do—if you do not act on your moral beliefs, or if your moral beliefs are false. But in that case your moral beliefs will not be fulfilling one of their most important functions, contributing to your performing morally worthy actions. And if you do act on your moral beliefs, I will argue, you need to have and to use moral understanding in order to act well.

[23] Arpaly's final account (2003: 84) of morally worthy action involves sensitivity to the right-making features of an action—plus deep moral concern—both of which are captured in my notion of orientation.

It is widely accepted that in order to act well it is not sufficient that you do the right thing because you (correctly) think it is morally right and you want to do the right thing, as an example from Nomy Arpaly illustrates.

The Extremist

Ron is an extremist, believing that killing a person is not generally immoral but that killing a fellow Jew is a grave sin. Ron would like to kill Tamara, but he refrains from doing so because he wants to do the right thing and he believes the right thing to do is to refrain from killing Jews. (Arpaly 2003: 74)

Ron does the right thing but not for the right reasons: it is right not to kill Tamara, but not because she is a Jew; instead, it is right not to kill her because she is a *person*. Notice that Ron is well motivated: he sincerely wants to do what is morally right. In that respect, Ron is very different from Kant's shopkeeper who does the right thing from selfishness. But in another regard his fault is similar: he is doing the right action but his action is not morally worthy.

Arpaly suggests two explanations of why Ron's action is not morally worthy. First, it is merely accidental that he did the right thing in this case: 'Just as in the prudent grocer case it is fortunate that the prudent action also happens to be the moral one, in Ron's case it is fortunate that favouring Jews in a certain way is moral.' (ibid.) Secondly, Ron's reasons for action have nothing to do with the right-making features of his action.

As we might expect, these two explanations are not equivalent. Consider a case in which it is not accidental that you act rightly, but you do not act for the right reasons. Suppose that Ron wanted to kill Tamara, asked his rabbi what to do and his rabbi, whom Ron knows to be a morally good person, and trustworthy, told him that it was morally right not to kill her. Ron now knows that it is morally right not to kill Tamara. Suppose Ron then wonders why it is right, and not being very good at moral reasoning decides that it is because she is a fellow Jew. Ron's mistaken explanation for why not killing Tamara is right does not, I think, undermine his knowledge that not killing her is right.[24] So we can restate the example.

[24] If he believed that killing Tamara was wrong on the basis of a false belief, he would not have knowledge. But he does not believe it on that basis, he believes it because he was told it by a source he knows to be trustworthy, and it is hard to see that his justification for that belief is undermined because he has independently come up with a mistaken explanation for it. Compare: you have a lot of knowledge from perception, and sometimes you come up with mistaken explanations for it; for

The Knowledgeable Extremist

Ron is an extremist, believing that killing a person is not generally immoral but that killing a fellow Jew is a grave sin. Ron would like to kill Tamara, but he refrains from doing so because he wants to do the right thing and he *knows* (on the basis of his rabbi's testimony) that the right thing to do is to refrain from killing her.

Ron does the right thing, on the basis of his desire to do what is right and his knowledge that his action is morally right. It is not accidental, then, that he does the right thing. But he does not act well: he does not do the right thing for the relevant moral reasons, namely, that Tamara is a person.

Suppose, however, that Ron's rabbi tells him why it is right not to kill Tamara. Ron believes him and so knows that it is right not to kill Tamara and he knows why, though he does not understand why. Nevertheless, Ron does the right thing, and, if asked, will say that he did it because it was right and that it was right because Tamara is a person. Surely he must now count as doing the right thing for the right reasons?

I will argue that Ron cannot, in fact, be doing the right thing for the right reasons, even when he knows why it is right not to kill Tamara. This turns on exactly what it is to act for a reason. There are two ways in which Tamara being a person could be Ron's reason for action. First, he might respond to it directly—that is, he might choose not to kill her because she is a person, without explicitly forming any moral beliefs at all.[25] But clearly Ron did not make that choice: left to himself without the intervention of his rabbi he would have killed Tamara, and even after the intervention he would not have responded to her being a person without being told that that fact was morally significant.

Secondly, Tamara being a person might be Ron's reason for action in the sense that he chose the action because he thought it was right, and he thought that it was right because Tamara is a person. But Ron formed the belief that it was right not to kill Tamara on the basis of the rabbi's testimony, not on the basis of his belief that she was a person. Even when he was told by the rabbi that this was the explanation of why it was right not to kill her he was unable to draw the conclusion himself from the

example, you know that the sun rises in the morning because you see it, even though you mistakenly believe that it does because the sun orbits the Earth. The mistaken explanation does not undermine your perceptual knowledge.

[25] He would then be responding to moral reasons *de re* (rather than under an explicitly moral description).

reasons why it was right. He *cannot* have formed the belief that it was right not to kill in response to the reasons why it was right—he is responding to testimony, not to moral reasons, just as Claire the incompetent judge was doing.[26]

If p is your reason for action, your belief that p must be among the causes of your action.[27] Ron's belief that Tamara is a person is *not* among the causes of his action. So Tamara's being a person is not—cannot be—his reason for action. Though Ron does the right thing, and if asked would correctly explain why it is right, he is not responding to those reasons when he acts. Once again, there is a difference between your believing (or knowing) that p is the reason why q, and your being able to *treat* p as a reason why q, the latter requiring the kind of abilities characteristic of moral understanding, not moral knowledge.[28]

---

[26] Ron's action is therefore counterfactually dependent on the rabbi's testimony (specifically, his testimony that the action is right) together with his belief that the rabbi is reliable and trustworthy, but not counterfactually dependent on his belief that Tamara is a person. Of course, this is complicated by the fact that the rabbi also testifies that Tamara is a person and that this fact is morally relevant, but if the rabbi had given a different explanation of the rightness of the action, Ron would still have done what the rabbi told him was right, whatever he believed about Tamara's being a person. This is, I think, grounds for claiming that Ron's belief that Tamara is a person is not among the causes of his action.

[27] This is a part of what is sometimes called the 'standard model' of acting for reasons, defended, for example, by Davidson (1980: 3–19, esp. p. 9), according to which acting for the reason R is being motivated to act by the belief that R. The standard model has recently come under attack on the grounds that your action can be caused by a belief and a desire without your acting for reasons (Velleman 2000: 2–9). I am sympathetic to these concerns, but I think that a causal connection between your belief that R and your action is going to be part of any plausible account of acting for the reason R, even if it is not sufficient: in order for a reason for an action to be *your* reason for action, it must *cause* your action. Setiya (2007: 28–48), however, suggests that though this is true in the 'overwhelmingly typical' case it may not be true in unusual cases, such as in self-deceptive action. He suggests a different connection: 'In what we may think of as the paradigm case of acting for a reason, an agent takes it that he is hereby doing φ because he believes that p, where this is the "because" of motivation' (Setiya 2007: 45). In other words, to act for the reason p, you must believe that your belief that p caused you to act (even if in fact it did not). Circumstances in which the belief that p did not in fact cause you to act (though you think that it did) Setiya describes as 'marginal' cases of acting for a reason. But I think a better description of this kind of case is: you thought that you acted for the reason that p but in fact you did not—since your belief that p did not in fact cause you to act. In any case, Ron has no reason to think that his belief that Tamara is a person caused him to act (either directly or indirectly, via a belief that it is right not to kill her). So, even if Setiya's account of acting for reasons is correct, Ron has no grounds for claiming that he is acting for the right reasons (and if my interpretation of what Setiya calls the 'marginal' case is correct he does not act for the right reasons).

[28] Ron might object to this characterization of him. He might say that initially he did not base his belief that it was right for him not to kill Tamara on his belief that she is a person. But now that he has talked with his rabbi, he believes that that is why it is right for him not to kill her. So now he can derive the conclusion that it is right not to kill her from the reasons why it is right: because she is a person. But it does not follow that he is responding to moral reasons. Like Claire, Ron's belief that his action is right, and why it is right, is *solely* explained by testimony; in particular, his belief that the action is

Ron might concede that Tamara's being a person was not among his reasons for action, but nevertheless insist that he chose his action because it was right. Is this not sufficient for his action to be morally worthy? Ron has good motivations: he wants to do what is morally right and chooses in accordance with those desires; and he has moral knowledge, too. But more is required for morally worthy action: you need to act for the reasons that *make* your action right. Morally worthy actions are sensitive to moral considerations and for that you need to be oriented properly, not just in your outward actions but in your motivations, your choices, and your beliefs, too.

Of course, the contribution that your beliefs make to morally worthy action is not the same as the contribution of your motivations: failing to be properly oriented with regard to beliefs is very different from failing to be oriented with regard to motivations; and different negative evaluations are appropriate of agents who are not well-motivated compared with those whose moral beliefs are not well-based. It might not be appropriate to blame Ron, but it would be appropriate to regard him, like Claire, as not fully admirable.

Does orientation matter? It might be objected that we do not (or ought not to) mind whether other people have moral understanding. What matters is how they treat us, in terms of their outward actions towards us.

From the first-person perspective, from which I morally evaluate my own actions and myself, it is not at all plausible that outward action is all that matters to us or that it is all that should matter. How one thinks about things, whether one has grasped what is morally right and wrong, how one makes decisions about what to do, and how one judges actions; these are important, too. And these are combined in the idea of acting well. It is perfectly reasonable to be morally concerned with moral understanding, as well as doing the right thing.

This could make it appear that it is rather self-regarding or morally self-indulgent to concentrate on morally worthy action: morally worthy

---

right has no independent explanation, as it would do if he had moral understanding and he had drawn the right conclusion from the reasons why it was right independently of the testimony of others. What is required for Ron to do the right action for the right reasons is that in acting he is responsive to the reasons why it is right, and that will only happen if he responds directly to those reasons (choosing not to kill Tamara because she is a person) or if he does what he thinks is right; and his belief that the action is right is responsive to the reasons why it is right: that is, he has and uses moral understanding. Since he does neither of these things, he does not act for the right reasons.

action is essentially about yourself and your own mind, rather than how you treat other people: to take an interest in the moral worth of one's actions, rather than whether they are morally right or wrong, is to focus inappropriately on oneself.[29]

There are circumstances in which outward action is particularly salient. If I am in desperate need, the reasons why someone chose to give me help simply may not matter at all to me. Suppose that through a series of terrible misfortunes I end up homeless, ill, and starving. You buy me lunch and find me a doctor and a place to stay. Obviously, I am very grateful to you, and I have no inclination to inquire too closely into your reasons: do you genuinely intend to help me because of my needs or because someone told you to do so? I am just glad of some food and a place to sleep; nothing else matters to me. But this does not mean that it is not in fact important whether or not you understand why you have reason to help, even if my circumstances are so grave that I no longer care. This is a reflection of my own dire straits and does not imply that acting well is not really significant: it is quite reasonable, for example, for other people to be interested in whether you acted on the basis of moral understanding. It is important to us that other people grasp, for example, that when we are in need, this itself is a reason for them to help us. The reason is not that we may be able to reciprocate for them some time, or because someone told them to help, even though people acting for those reasons might be reliable assistants. We quite reasonably value not simply being treated rightly; but being treated well—that is, being treated rightly for the right reasons.

We do tend to evaluate differently those who do the same outward action. But, it may be objected, perhaps this does not show that morality is primarily concerned with acting well, rather than doing the right thing. When we make these judgements, it is possible that we are not really

---

[29] Arpaly argues (2003: 69) that the moral worth of an action corresponds to the moral praiseworthiness or blameworthiness of the agent—that is, the extent to which she deserves praise or blame for performing those actions. If this is right, there is another way in which focusing on morally worthy action could be self-indulgent: the agent could primarily be motivated to be praised. It would not be particularly admirable to aim to perform morally worthy actions because you want praise (though Arpaly does not suggest that it is). But, according to my conception of acting well, morally worthy actions are right actions performed for the right reasons. Since *to get praise* is not usually the right reason for action, someone who was motivated primarily by praise would not be performing morally worthy actions. Instead, they would choose the right because there were forceful moral reasons to do so. Acting for these moral reasons is not self-serving or self-indulgent.

focusing on actions at all. Considerations about understanding may be relevant to an evaluation of the agent's *character* but not her *actions*.

I have argued that moral understanding (and, more broadly, orientation) is essential to good character, and that there are close links between good character and morally worthy action. I suggest that we can conceive of actions in two ways: as 'outward' actions, or as 'actions-for-reasons'. With regard to outward actions, the honest and the selfish shopkeeper do the same thing when they both give the right change, as do Claire and Judith when they pass the same sentence, and Ron and the rabbi when they refrain from killing Tamara. But, with regard to action more broadly conceived, 'acting-for-a-reason', their actions are not the same. There is a perfectly good sense in which action that is based on moral reasons is different from action that is not. Each of Claire and Judith and the honest and selfish shopkeepers can and should be evaluated negatively or positively *for what she did*, not just for the kind of person that she is.

The moral evaluation of an action understood in this broad sense cannot be separated from an assessment of the agent's reasons for action. You can respond to morality through your choices and your moral beliefs as well as your motivations and your outward actions. You can be—you should be—properly oriented with regard to your whole self and you can express this orientation in morally worthy action. Moral understanding is important not just because it is a means to acting rightly or reliably acting rightly, though it is. Nor is it important only because it is relevant to the evaluations of an agent's character. It is essential to acting well.[30]

## 4. Conclusion

I have argued that moral understanding, understanding why p, is different from moral knowledge, both knowledge that p, and knowledge why p. It is possible to have knowledge when you do not have understanding, and it is possible to have understanding when you do not have knowledge.

I have also argued that moral understanding is very important, both in having a good character and in morally worthy action. In both cases, moral

---

[30] This is, I think, similar to Aristotle's view that the end of *phronesis* is not the production of something distinct from the productive process but 'doing well itself serves as end' (*NE* 1140b7–8).

understanding is the cognitive aspect of orientation towards moral reasons. I have already indicated some tensions between trusting moral testimony and forming beliefs on the basis of moral understanding, and in the next chapter I consider the implications of aiming for moral understanding rather than moral knowledge for moral testimony and moral disagreement, and I draw some conclusions about epistemic rationality for moral beliefs.

# 10

# Moral Testimony and Moral Disagreement

## 1. Moral Testimony

In the last chapter, I argued that it is essential to virtue and to morally worthy action that you base your moral beliefs on your moral understanding. Ultimately I want to draw out the significance of this for the rational response to disagreements between moral agents and egoists (I will discuss this in Sections 3–4). But I will start by looking at a less controversial matter: what is the best way to respond to moral disagreements and to moral testimony if you want to have and to use your moral understanding to form your moral beliefs? I will begin with moral testimony.

To understand why p, you need the abilities to:

   (i)  follow an explanation of why p given by someone else;
  (ii)  explain why p in your own words;
 (iii)  draw the conclusion that p (or that probably p) from the information that q;
 (iv)  draw the conclusion that p' (or that probably p') from the information that q' (where p' and q' are similar to, but not identical to, p and q);
  (v)  given the information that p, give the right explanation q;
 (vi)  given the information that p', give the right explanation q'.

If someone tells you that p, that q, and that q is why p, under the right circumstances you will know why p. It is possible that you will thereby acquire the abilities (i) to (vi). Having been told that lies that make people happy are not always right, for instance, you will immediately see why this is so, and how to apply your grasp of these considerations to other similar cases (where, for example, you do not lie but fail to tell the whole truth, or where a lie is the only way to avoid a really terrible outcome). But, as with many abilities, you will not always or even typically acquire these abilities through testimony. Most people cannot learn to ride a bike, to perform brain surgery, or to type at 100 words a minute by listening to someone describe how to do so, or reading even an exceptionally good textbook. Still less can they learn to do so by having someone merely describe the outcome at which they are aiming. These are difficult skills to master, and most people need to *practise* them.

Moral understanding involves intellectual rather than practical abilities, but the skills in question are difficult. Moral questions are often hard. Which actions are morally right and wrong is not always obvious, nor is it obvious why they are right or wrong, nor is it straightforward to make moral judgements in new and unfamiliar circumstances.

Most people cannot learn to make correct moral judgements by listening to those who are good at making judgements describe what they do, and they certainly cannot learn to do so simply by hearing what the correct moral judgements are. To get started making moral judgements yourself, of course, you may need a stock of true moral beliefs on which to draw while making further judgements, and so it is very plausible that, to begin with, you will need to form some moral beliefs by trusting what others tell you. Recall Sarah.

Sarah is five years old. Her parents have told her not to lie, that lying is naughty and wrong. She accepts what they say.

It is obviously right for Sarah to accept what her parents say. Most young children are immature moral agents, which is why it is perfectly in order for them to trust moral testimony and defer to the judgements of the adults around them. In fact, it is likely to be impossible—or at least exceptionally difficult—for them to gain moral understanding unless they begin by forming beliefs in this way. The same is true for any immature moral agent—anyone who does not have the requisite stock of true moral beliefs—so it may be acceptable for some adults to defer to moral testimony too, if they come to judge that their starting-points are too far off the mark.[1] But most people cannot acquire the ability to make moral

---

[1] Children may acquire moral understanding by learning the habit of doing what is right and not what is wrong, and eventually coming to grasp the reasons why some actions are morally right and

judgements themselves whilst deferring all the time to others. They need to practise drawing moral conclusions (this action is morally right, I have moral reason not to perform that action . . . ) and offering explanations for those conclusions (the action is right because it is helping someone in need; I have moral reason not to do that because it will make people unhappy . . . ). Only by 'screening-off' what others have said and trying to make up their own mind about difficult moral questions will they develop the ability to make their own moral judgements, without wholly relying on the help and advice of others.

This marks a key difference between knowledge (including knowledge why p) and understanding. If you are attempting to gain knowledge, testimony can serve as the justification for your own belief, but it is not usually a good way of acquiring moral understanding. Understanding why p will not—cannot—have the same relationship to testimony as knowing why p. In the last chapter, I drew an analogy between moral understanding and know-how and it is also true that knowing how is often not successfully transmitted by testimony—most people need to practise riding a bike: they cannot successfully do so on the basis of a verbal description—in Stanley and Williamson terms, they may know a way to ride a bike, but they do not know it 'under the practical mode of presentation'. This practical mode is often not transmissible by testimony. Often we do not even try to give someone else the abilities to put the explanation of p into her own words, or to draw the conclusion that p from q, for example, by testimony. But, despite this, further testimony of any kind will not usually help you acquire understanding why p. Therefore, *even if moral understanding is a species of propositional knowledge after all* it need not have the same relationship to testimony as other forms of propositional knowledge.

Suppose that you are a mature moral agent and you have no reason to think that moral understanding is out of your reach. Should you never trust testimony about moral matters? You are in a situation in which practising drawing conclusions from the reasons why they are true, and devising

others wrong (this is a simplified version of Aristotle's conception of moral education). At the first stage of this acquisition, they learn from the testimony and example of those around them what they have moral reason to do (and not to do)—so moral testimony plays a crucial initial role—then they habitually do the right thing and testimony plays less of a role. The final stage of acquiring moral understanding, however, where they come to grasp why it is right to do what they already habitually do, requires them to exercise their own judgement. It is this stage that needs practice, and moral testimony can play at most a guiding role.

your own moral explanations, are worthwhile. But testimony can still be important in a number of ways.

In the first place, understanding why an action is morally right or wrong often involves knowing a combination of both moral and factual matters. Understanding why you should give money to X, for example, involves both truly believing that X is in need and understanding why you should help those in need. It is perfectly acceptable to trust the testimony of someone on the factual matter—that X is in need—and use this in forming your moral judgement. So testimony can play a very significant role. What is more, often it is difficult to disentangle the factual and the moral matters and in practice there may be no clear division between the two. Consider the following example, from Julia Driver.

It might make perfect sense, for example, for someone to delegate a decision to an expert. Suppose that Stanley must decide whether or not to authorize keeping his ailing father alive using 'extraordinary' means. Suppose that Stanley has good reason to trust another person—someone with experience, perhaps the family's physician. Then, when the physician says 'Trust me, Stanley, you ought not to do it—it will cause unnecessary pain', doesn't it make sense to say that Stanley knows it (given it is true and he believes it)?[2]

What exactly does Stanley learn from the family doctor? The physician is clearly a medical expert, and can speak confidently about the probable outcomes of various surgical procedures. He may be able to tell Stanley that his father would be suffering unnecessarily, in the sense that without medical intervention he would die peacefully and without pain. Stanley would obviously be well advised to pay attention, given the doctor's expertise and experience. But the doctor may be giving advice of another kind. He may be saying to Stanley that the suffering his patient would undergo would be unnecessary in the sense that his life is no longer worth living, and it ought not to be prolonged any further. Since the doctor is so experienced, Stanley would be wise to listen to his advice about the value of his father's life, think the question through himself, and see if he agrees with the doctor. But it is much less obvious that Stanley has a strong reason to simply place his trust in what the doctor says on this moral question and defer to his judgement. At the same time, it is clearly difficult to separate

[2] Driver 2006: 639.

completely the factual and moral issues. It may be unclear to both whether Stanley is asking for and accepting guidance about factual matters, about the pain that his father would suffer, or moral issues, such as the value of his father's life. Does Stanley lack a grasp of the value of human life when he defers to the doctor's moral expertise? Or does he understand all the relevant moral issues but lack relevant medical knowledge? It may be difficult, if not impossible, to say. So it may simply be unclear in a case like this whether it is right to trust someone else's testimony.

Testimony can also play a role—sometimes a vital role—in helping you grasp the reasons why p. For example, if someone who is an expert, tells you that p is true, it is reasonable for you to bear this in mind when you survey the reasons why p yourself. You are probably expecting this to support p. You can use testimony to guide you through the reasons why p and to form beliefs in response to those reasons appropriately. Most importantly, you can ask people who already have beliefs about p about their basis for those beliefs. Testimony therefore can have a very important indirect use: it can point you to relevant reasons why p that either you are not aware of or whose significance you have failed to appreciate.

Testimony can have only a limited role in the acquisition of moral understanding. But, suppose that you have moral understanding already and you could use it to form your moral beliefs, but you prefer not to.

Recall Eleanor, who was perfectly capable of working out for herself whether it was wrong to eat meat, but chose to trust her friend's testimony instead. If Eleanor fails to use her moral understanding she is not properly oriented and she cannot act well. To act well on the basis of moral beliefs it is not sufficient that you have moral understanding: you need to *use it* to form your moral beliefs, too, so that your belief that your action is right, for example, is explained by the reasons why it is right.[3] Trusting testimony

---

[3] As before, this need not be the only explanation of your moral belief, but it must be one explanation of it. For example, suppose that you are struck very strongly that an action—for example, experimentation on a human—is wrong (let us assume that your belief is true), but you are not sure why. You may be able to offer some sort of explanation—that human life is sacred—but not one that stands up to much scrutiny. It is rare, though it may sometimes happen, that you are struck that an action is right or wrong with absolutely no idea why. But, even if you have some minimal grasp of the reasons why p, this may not be sufficient for you to understand why p—you may need a more secure and detailed grasp of the reasons why p. To find the right explanation, you may need to do some investigation, to discover more about the action and its consequences and you need to think about which of its features is morally significant, in such a way that you acquire the abilities (i) to (vi). In this case, you have not formed your belief that p by conforming your belief to the reasons why p—in

is a *rival* basis for your belief. At best it is worthless, since you need to base your belief on another ground anyway, and at worst it is harmful, since it could make it less likely that your belief is grounded in the right way, hence make it less likely that you act well.

I said earlier that taking moral advice was perfectly acceptable even though trusting testimony is not, and we are now in a position to see why, by distinguishing between two responses to testimony. First, you may *trust* or *defer* to moral testimony, where you simply believe what is said to you. You make no attempt to gather the reasons why p and draw conclusions yourself, or to devise explanations for moral propositions that you have accepted. You simply believe what you are told.

It does not follow that you suspend use of your critical faculties entirely. You may not simply believe any moral proposition that is said to you by anyone. You may take into account how expert and trustworthy the speaker is. Nevertheless, once you have decided that she is reliable (or at least not wholly unreliable) you simply trust what she says without exercising your own judgement on that particular matter. In this case, you are relying on the judgement of other people, not your own judgement.

Secondly, you may treat the testimony as *moral advice*, which you subject to critical scrutiny and you decide whether or not to accept *on its own merits*. Here you are exercising your own moral judgement. You take into account what others have said to you as a guide to your own reflections. Even though you are paying attention to moral testimony, you are not putting your trust in it or deferring to it, you are essentially using your own judgement about the matter at issue. If Eleanor took advice from her friends, and used it as a guide to her own reflections on whether she should become a vegetarian, she would be orienting herself properly with regard to moral reasons.

Of course, in practice it may be difficult to distinguish these two ways of treating moral testimony, but nevertheless in principle the difference is clear. If you are trying to develop and use your moral understanding, it is perfectly in order to take testimony on explicitly moral matters as moral advice to guide your own reflections. But what you cannot do is to treat

---

fact you formed your belief that p before you were aware of the reasons why p. But, nevertheless, you have understanding only if you have a sufficient grasp of the reasons why p (expressed by the abilities (i) to (vi)) that you would be able to form your belief on the basis of the reasons why p. In order to act well, it is important that you do base your belief that p on the reasons why p, even if there is some other explanation of the belief too.

testimonial evidence as having authority independently of the reasons why p
that you are aware of or to which you can gain access. If proper orientation
is your aim, the only purpose to which you can put testimonial evidence
is to help you with your grasp of the reasons why p, and what follows
from them. There are significant limits to the possibility of a 'division of
epistemic labour' with regard to moral understanding: there are no benefits
to the theft of other people's conclusions over honest toil on your own.

So far I have assumed that you can base your moral beliefs on your moral
understanding and I have argued that you should. But, suppose that you
cannot. If your moral judgement about a particular matter is bad and does
not improve when you reflect, you may never have moral understanding.
However long you thought, you might get to the right answer only
by accident. You also have a serious problem, however excellent your
judgement, if you do not have any idea of the reasons why p. If you are in
this position, it is simply not possible for you to gain moral understanding.
I shall discuss what you should do in this difficult situation in section 3. But
first I turn to what you should do if you are faced with disagreement.


## 2. Moral Disagreement

So far I have been considering the role of moral testimony in your acquiring
and using moral understanding to form your moral beliefs. Now I need to
discuss how you should respond to moral disagreements, if you have the
same aim.

Noting the disagreement, you might reconsider your own arguments
and reflect on your evidence and see if you reach the same judgement as
before. You should listen to the arguments of your opponents and their
objections to your views. Perhaps they can share with you some compelling
argument or insight that you missed the first time around, or give you some
new reasons to consider. If so, then you may have to rethink the whole
question and perhaps change your mind.

If you do not find any reason to change your mind about your original
evidence, however, what should you do? Suppose that you were to give
some weight to the opinions of your opponents (whatever epistemic
standing you think they have compared with you); that is, once you have
taken into account the reasons why not-p that they cite, you give some

extra weight to the fact that they believe that not-p. Their beliefs are not reasons why not-p is true. If you changed your mind on the basis of their opinions that not-p, you would have done so on the basis of *non-explanatory evidence* (that is, evidence that could not be used to explain why not-p is true) not on the basis of reasons why not-p is true (that is, *explanatory evidence*, that could be used to explain why not-p is true). To be oriented properly, you need to base your moral beliefs on the reasons why they are true, rather than to give weight to non-explanatory evidence. Listening to the views of others, and sometimes taking their advice, is very sensible. But if you give weight to their conclusions, independently of the force of the reasons that they cite for those conclusions, you are not forming your moral belief for the right reasons. The structure of your moral beliefs is not mirroring morality, and when you act you cannot act for the right reasons, even if you do the right action. You cannot act well.

In other words, if you want to acquire and to use your moral understanding to form your moral beliefs *it is not rational for you to suspend judgement in response to any disagreement, whatever your opponent's epistemic standing, and however strong the original evidence.*

Suppose that you are wondering whether eating meat is wrong and in your opinion the strongest arguments favour vegetarianism. But, you have other evidence—namely, your friends' beliefs that eating meat is morally acceptable. If you form your moral beliefs on the basis of your moral understanding you must 'screen off' and give no weight to the judgements of your friends—for their judgements are not reasons why vegetarianism is right or wrong. Of course, if vegetarianism is not morally right then you cannot possibly understand why vegetarianism is right; but provided that it is right and you have correctly grasped why, then you understand why vegetarianism is right, in spite of your disagreement with your friends, and you can form moral beliefs on the basis of that understanding.

This feature of moral understanding marks an important difference, I believe, with moral knowledge. If you have based your judgement that vegetarianism is right on reasons why it is right, you have at the end of this process understood why it is right and the opinions of your peers are irrelevant to you. But, to gain knowledge, you cannot ignore any significant and relevant evidence; so if you ignore the views of your epistemic peers you cannot know that p (even if you are right about it and they are wrong).

Suppose that you aim for knowledge. According to the Total Evidence view, what you should believe depends on the strength of each kind of evidence. If your explanatory evidence that p is weaker or is difficult to interpret (the question that you are considering is hard, as are moral questions and questions about reasons for action) then you should suspend judgement and you cannot know that p. According to the Equal Weight view, it is rational to suspend judgement in response to all peer disagreements. So, whichever view is correct, if you are aiming for knowledge you are rationally required to suspend judgement in response to any disagreement with a peer. In your situation you cannot know that vegetarianism is right.

You can therefore be in the somewhat surprising situation of understanding why vegetarianism is right without being in a position to know that it is right.[4] As we shall see in the following chapters, this type of situation is extremely important for a defender of common-sense morality who is trying to respond to an egoist.

## 3. Epistemic Rationality Again

I have argued that if you want to acquire and to use moral understanding you have excellent reasons not to defer to moral testimony and not to give weight to your opponent's judgement in a moral disagreement.

But, what kind of reasons are these? It seems that they are grounded in your wanting moral understanding, and in moral understanding being valuable. In other words, they are *practical* reasons not *epistemic* ones. It does not follow that it is epistemically rational to treat moral testimony and moral disagreements in this way. Of course, these are unusual practical reasons, because they are based on a goal—moral understanding—which is (arguably) *epistemically* valuable. But, epistemic rationality cannot be closely connected to the goals you set for yourself—even when those

---

[4] This is another reason, I think, for distinguishing moral understanding and moral knowledge. But, if one were to insist that moral understanding was a species of propositional knowledge one might put the point in terms of the distinction between the types of propositional knowledge set out by Stanley and Williamson (2001), where moral understanding is a type of propositional knowledge 'under a practical mode of presentation'. In this sort of situation, you may know that p under a practical mode of presentation without being in a position to know it under a different (theoretical) mode of presentation.

goals are epistemically valuable—for reasons I have already laid out in Chapter 9.

What are the standards of epistemic rationality for moral beliefs? In Chapter 9, I suggested that we could discover the standards of epistemic rationality by looking at the function of belief in action, and I argued that, with regard to ordinary non-moral beliefs, knowledge (or perhaps truth) will result in successful action most often. So the standards of epistemic rationality for non-moral beliefs are set by knowledge (or, if not knowledge, truth). But, if the function of moral beliefs in action is the same as non-moral beliefs (by acting on those beliefs you will act successfully, achieving your aims) then the standards of epistemic rationality will be the same too, and it will be epistemically rational to give weight to moral testimony and to moral disagreements.[5] You might have decided that moral understanding is worth having and have chosen to pursue it, in which case you would have excellent instrumental reasons not to take non-explanatory evidence directly into account. So you could be in the awkward situation in which it is *pragmatically rational* but *epistemically irrational* for you to insist on making up your own mind on moral matters.[6]

---

[5] Suppose you want moral understanding. Then your aim is to gain moral understanding. And your action is successful if you do gain moral understanding—that is, if you do achieve your aim. So it seems that moral understanding is the epistemic standard most likely to lead you to act successfully. And surely it follows that epistemic rationality should be related to moral understanding, not knowledge. But this is to mistake the connection between success in action and epistemic standards. The appropriate epistemic standard is not necessarily the one which will lead you to succeed in some particular action here and now: after all, all sorts of false beliefs might lead you to succeed in your action here and now, but it does not follow that it is epistemically rational to acquire false beliefs (even if you were able to do so). Instead, the standards of epistemic rationality are based on trying to acquire the type of mental representation that is most likely to lead you to achieve success in actions generally. In ordinary circumstances, the standard of success of these actions is: achieving your aim. And the mental representation most likely to lead you successfully to achieve your aim is knowledge (or perhaps true belief).

[6] If epistemic and pragmatic rationality were to conflict, what overall would it be rational for you to believe? It might be argued that practical rationality is never relevant to beliefs: taking into account the practical consequences of having some belief is always inappropriate. It is only epistemic rationality that matters. Recall that it would be clearly epistemically irrational for you to ignore all the evidence that you gained on every day except for Tuesdays, even if you had set this end for yourself. But, on the other hand, it is not obvious why epistemic rationality but not practical rationality should count in every circumstance when it comes to the formation of belief. Perhaps in the above case it is not rational for you to ignore evidence on non-Tuesdays, because the goal of conforming your beliefs to evidence found on a Tuesday is not a worthwhile aim. If you had a valuable goal—to achieve moral understanding, for example—perhaps it could be rational for you to form your beliefs in response to instrumental reasons relating to that goal. Perhaps there simply is no answer, at least at such a high level of generality, over whether practical rationality should or should not influence our beliefs. Though

However, in the last chapter, I argued that moral beliefs played a very important role in a distinctive kind of action: morally worthy action (that is, in right actions performed for the right reasons). I argued that action that is based on moral beliefs can only be morally worthy if you act on the basis of your understanding why you have moral reason to act (or why doing so is morally right, and so on). It is impossible to act well on the basis of explicitly moral beliefs, therefore, unless you have moral understanding.[7]

One possibility is that this is the *only* significant function of moral beliefs in action. Call this the *strong claim*: contributing to your acting well is the *only* role that is important for moral beliefs.

*Strong claim: the function of moral beliefs.* The only significant function of moral beliefs in action is to contribute to morally worthy actions. Moral worth is the only thing of practical significance: if you cannot perform morally worthy actions, it does not matter what you do.

If the strong claim is correct, then the only important function for moral beliefs in action is in contributing to your morally worthy actions. So, if your moral beliefs are to perform their function well, contributing to your performing morally worthy actions, you must form those beliefs on the basis of moral understanding. It follows that moral understanding is the epistemic ideal for moral beliefs, and that it sets the standards of epistemic rationality for moral beliefs, and this is so no matter whether or not you can actually obtain moral understanding.

*Strong claim. Epistemic rationality of moral beliefs is set by moral understanding.* The epistemic ideal for moral beliefs is moral understanding. Moral understanding sets the standards of epistemic rationality for moral beliefs under all circumstances.

Since to acquire and to use moral understanding requires you not to defer to the opinions or the testimony of others, if moral understanding is the

---

this question is interesting, however, fortunately I do not have to answer it here as I will argue that ultimately epistemic rationality for moral beliefs is based on moral understanding after all.

[7] I have *not* claimed that it is possible to perform morally worthy action only on the basis of explicitly moral beliefs. I do think that you can do the right thing for the right reasons without conceiving of your action or reasons for action in moral terms. But in some circumstances it will be difficult or impossible to do the right thing without moral beliefs (and therefore without moral understanding). For example, in some situations, it may be difficult to work out what is the right action or the action you have most reason to do without thinking of it in moral terms. Sometimes it may be essential that you do a just act, for example, because it is just—you must regard it in explicitly moral terms. So the function of moral beliefs (and therefore moral understanding) may be to play an important role in morally worthy action, even though morally worthy action is possible without moral beliefs.

epistemic ideal, *it is epistemically rational for you not to defer to the testimony or beliefs of others, whatever their epistemic standing.*

Recall Bernard Williams's scorn at the very idea of ethical experts:

> There are, notoriously, no ethical experts . . . Anyone who is tempted to take up the idea of there being a theoretical science of ethics should be discouraged by reflecting on what would be involved in taking seriously the idea that there were experts in it. It would imply, for instance, that a student who had not followed the professor's reasoning but had understood his moral conclusion might have some reason, on the strength of his professorial authority, to accept it.[8]

Suppose that the Professor says that scientific experimentation on humans is usually wrong, but on animals it is (sometimes) acceptable. The student understands what he said but has little or no idea why it might be true. If she simply defers to him on the strength of his 'professorial authority' she may gain a true moral belief, perhaps even moral knowledge (if he is right). But she will not thereby gain moral understanding, and if she acts on the basis of that belief she will not be acting for the right reasons. Since moral understanding is the epistemic ideal for moral beliefs, setting the standards for epistemic rationality, it is not epistemically rational for her to defer to his professorial authority. So Williams is right that there are no ethical experts, if ethical experts are people to whose judgement it is epistemically rational to defer.[9]

Similarly, suppose that you and an egoist who is your epistemic peer disagree about whether you have some reason for action. Because moral understanding sets the epistemic standards for moral beliefs, and for you to acquire moral understanding and use it appropriately you need to form the belief that some action is right (for instance) on the basis of the reasons why it is right, it is not epistemically rational for you to give any weight to the opinion of the egoist independently of your assessment of the reasons he gives for his judgement. If the strong view is correct it is epistemically rational for you not to suspend judgement in response to a disagreement about moral reasons for action with an epistemic peer.

---

[8] Williams 1995: 205.

[9] I do not think that the lack of ethical experts to whom we should always defer necessarily has any implications for a 'theoretical science' of ethics, however.

## 4.   Other Functions of Moral Beliefs

It is not very plausible that the strong claim is true, however. Moral beliefs have important functions in action other than contributing to morally worthy action. It matters not only whether your actions are morally worthy, but also whether they are morally right. Consider the original two shopkeepers together with a third.

> Grocer 1: gives the right change because doing so is honest and fair.
> Grocer 2: gives the right change because he wants a good reputation.
> Grocer 3: gives the wrong change when he can get away with it and increase his profits.

Of course, there is a difference between Grocer 2, who does the right thing, and Grocer 3, who does not. But, if morally worthy action is all that matters, the difference is not morally weighty: there is nothing to be said in favour of Grocer 2 over Grocer 3.

But, even though Grocer 1's action is the best, the difference between Grocers 2 and 3 is obviously morally significant. It is morally better to give the right change than not to do so, whatever your motivation. Selfish Grocer 2 may not be acting well, but he is not acting as badly as cheating Grocer 3. One of the functions of moral beliefs is to ensure that, even if we do not act well, at least we avoid doing what is morally wrong.[10]

*Moderate claim: the function of moral beliefs.* The most significant function of moral beliefs is to contribute to morally worthy actions. A secondary function is to ensure that you do what is morally right, and avoid what is morally wrong (at least when there are powerful moral reasons to do so).

According to the moderate claim, the role that moral belief can play in right action is an important secondary function, after the role that it can play in morally worthy action. What type of representation is best suited to fulfilling this function, of contributing to your reliably doing the right thing? In the last chapter, I argued that, in practice, having moral understanding might be the best way for you to perform right actions

---

[10]   Again, it is important to note that you can do the right action without conceiving of it in moral terms, and so without forming any explicitly moral beliefs. But forming moral beliefs will often be helpful in identifying the right action, and it is very plausible that this is part of the function of moral beliefs in action.

reliably. Moral decisions are often complicated and you often have to make judgements of what to do quite quickly in a situation which is not exactly like any you have faced before. You do not have time to find and consult an expert. It is characteristic of moral understanding that you have the ability to make accurate judgements in circumstances that you have not yet faced. So there is a reasonable argument that, even given the secondary function of moral beliefs in contributing to right action, moral understanding is still the epistemic ideal and it alone sets the standards of epistemic rationality for moral beliefs.

*Moderate claim 1. Epistemic rationality of moral beliefs is set by moral understanding.*

The epistemic ideal for moral beliefs is moral understanding. Moral understanding sets the standards of epistemic rationality for moral beliefs.

Again, it follows from this that it is epistemically rational to try to gain moral understanding, even if moral understanding is unavailable to you (and you know that it is). But, on the other hand, though you cannot act well without moral understanding, it is not as clear that you really need moral understanding in order to do what is right and avoid what is wrong: you can do that just as well if you *know* what is morally right and wrong and what you have moral reason to do. So, moral knowledge has a good claim to be the ideal with regard to the secondary function of moral beliefs, this function of contributing to right action and avoiding doing wrong.

If this is right, then moral beliefs could have a primary epistemic ideal—moral understanding—which is likely to fulfil their primary function best, and a secondary epistemic ideal—moral knowledge—which can fulfil their secondary function just as well. What would follow for the standards of epistemic rationality for moral beliefs? There are a number of options, and I will sketch two of them (which I think are the most plausible) here.

The first option is that moral understanding sets the standards of epistemic rationality for moral beliefs; unless it is clearly unavailable, in which case moral knowledge sets the standard.

*Moderate claim 2. Epistemic rationality of moral beliefs is set by moral understanding, then moral knowledge.*

The epistemic ideal for moral beliefs is moral understanding. Moral understanding sets the standards of epistemic rationality for moral beliefs. But, when moral understanding is clearly unavailable there is a secondary ideal: moral knowledge. This sets the standards of epistemic rationality for moral beliefs when moral understanding is clearly unavailable.

According to Moderate Claim 2, how is it epistemically rational for you to form moral beliefs? Since moral understanding is the epistemic ideal, it sets the standards for epistemic rationality. If there is a possibility that you might gain moral understanding, even if that possibility is rather remote, you should form beliefs as if you were aiming for understanding. Only if it is *clearly impossible* for you to have moral understanding—which is not usually the case—should you form your beliefs as if you were aiming for knowledge.

Alternatively, it could be epistemically rational to form beliefs on the basis of a weighted sum of your chances of gaining understanding compared with your chances of knowledge or true belief relying on the judgements of others (weighted by their relative importance in action, that is, the relative importance of performing morally worthy action, rather than simply avoiding what is morally wrong).

*Moderate claim 3. Epistemic rationality of moral beliefs is set by a weighted combination of moral understanding and moral knowledge.*

There is no single epistemic ideal for moral beliefs. The standards of epistemic rationality are set by a weighted combination of moral understanding and moral knowledge, based on the probability that you will attain moral understanding, the probability that you will attain moral knowledge, and the relative importance of each.

According to this view, how should you respond to disagreements with an egoist who is your epistemic peer? Whether it is right to trust testimony and to defer to the judgements of others in these circumstances depends on a number of factors that will be different in different situations, in particular: (1) how likely you are to acquire moral understanding if you try; (2) how likely you are to gain moral knowledge if you trust the testimony or judgements of the people around you; (3) the relative importance of morally worthy action and, more generally, proper orientation, compared to doing the right thing but not for the right reasons.

It is difficult to assess the probability that you will acquire moral understanding, if you tried, and the probability that you would gain moral knowledge, if you trusted the people around you. As we saw earlier, it is a matter of controversy who are the moral experts (and even if there are any) and there is a lot of disagreement about many moral questions. So it is far from obvious whom to trust about moral matters. There will be situations in which you are more likely to gain moral understanding by thinking things through yourself than you are to gain moral knowledge by trusting others. Moreover, I have argued that it is reasonable to regard morally worthy action as more valuable than simply right action (that is not done for the right reasons). It is not always worthwhile trying to develop moral understanding; sometimes it may be better to trust the judgement of others.[11] But, on the other hand, in many circumstances it is reasonable for you to take advice and use your own judgement in order to leave open the possibility at least of your acquiring and using your moral understanding, orienting yourself properly, and acting well.

So it is likely that it is acceptable to give considerable weight to using your own judgement when you are in disagreement with an epistemic peer. And, though it may be rational for you to reduce your confidence in your initial view, it is, I think, unlikely that it is epistemically rational for you to suspend judgement, unless you have good reason to think that there is very little chance that you can attain and use your own moral understanding.

---

[11] This is the best interpretation, I think, of a well-known example from Karen Jones, of a situation in which Peter and his housemates are trying to choose someone else to share their house: 'White women and women of color had advocated rejecting three white men on the basis of their perceived sexism, and in one case, racism. Peter had a settled and serious commitment to the elimination of racism and sexism, but he was not very good at picking out instances of sexism and racism. Thus, his commitment often remained theoretical and he saw fewer occasions as calling for antisexist and antiracist responses than he might have seen. Such blindness can sometimes indicate insincerity but in Peter's case it did not. He genuinely did want to understand the perspective of the women and he wanted to be able to share it, if indeed it turned out to be correct. He could pick out egregious instances of sexism and racism, and could sometimes see that "sexist" or "racist" applied to more subtle instances when the reasons for their application was explained to him, but he seemed bad at working out how to go on to apply the word to non-egregious new cases. Problems arose for Peter when he could not see the reasons why the women were calling someone sexist, and could not see, or could not see as evidence, the considerations that the women thought supported viewing the would-be members as sexist . . . I think that in this case, Peter should have been willing to accept the women's testimony that these men were sexist. But for him to have done so would have been to accept and act on a moral judgement on someone else's say-so. It would have been to borrow moral knowledge' (Jones 1999: 59–60). Peter has evidence that he has poor judgement in this area and that despite his best efforts he has been unable to acquire moral understanding. He also has evidence that in trusting the women's testimony he would acquire moral knowledge. In this situation it may be right for him to do so.

## 5. Conclusion

I have set out a number of different accounts of epistemic rationality for moral beliefs. Which of these is correct? It does not really matter for our purposes, because what is most important is the epistemically rational response to disagreements with an epistemic peer. According to each of the accounts of epistemic rationality, moral understanding is (or is a primary component of) the epistemic ideal, and, according to each, it is not epistemically rational for you to suspend judgement when you are in dispute with an egoist who is your epistemic peer, unless it is impossible or unlikely that you will be able to attain and use moral understanding. It is epistemically rational for you to continue to believe (though perhaps with less confidence than before) that, say, you have moral reason to help others, or you have moral reason not to lie.

The accounts given here of the appropriate response to moral disagreement have some of the features described by Robert Adams as 'moral faith'.[12] A key component of moral faith is that a moral person will hold on to certain of her moral convictions even though she cannot provide an argument for them 'beyond reasonable doubt'—that is, she cannot provide an argument that will convince any reasonable person of them. Adams thinks that the moral person's beliefs in certain moral convictions are stronger than is reasonable: as Adams puts it, morality supports these convictions more strongly than reason does. Is faith really an essential part of common-sense morality?

If the argument of this part of the book is right, in at least one respect morality and reason are not as far apart as Adams supposes. It can be epistemically rational to hold on to your moral convictions even though others may not be persuaded by the arguments that you find convincing. Suspending judgement or even changing your views simply in response to moral disagreements with anyone whom you regard as your epistemic peer is not usually appropriate. If moral understanding is epistemically important in the way I have suggested, then Adams is right that a moral person may continue to be committed to her moral convictions even if she cannot

---

[12] Adams 1995. Adams's account of 'moral faith' is rich and multifaceted, and I cannot fully do justice to it here, but one of his most important arguments is that morality 'outruns' reason and requires faith in response to egoists and moral sceptics. It is this contention that I dispute.

convince others of them (even when they are her epistemic peers—or even her epistemic superiors). But, this is *not* a matter of faith, in the sense of a conviction that goes beyond what is called for or permitted by the standards of epistemic rationality. If moral understanding is the epistemic ideal for moral beliefs, then it is typically epistemically *rational* to retain your moral beliefs in the face of disagreement. There may of course be other aspects of our ordinary moral practice that better deserve the term 'faith' and that require a moral person not to form her moral beliefs in an epistemically rational fashion. But it is usually epistemically rational for a moral agent to retain her moral convictions, even when she thinks they are not 'beyond reasonable doubt'.[13]

---

[13] Of course, it does not follow that moral agents really do have moral understanding. If they really do have a grasp of moral reasons and they are responding appropriately to the evidence that they have, then they will have moral understanding. But they may be wrong. Their beliefs may be false; they may have no grasp of moral truth at all. Even so, their moral beliefs may be, in their own terms, epistemically rational, because they are responding appropriately to the evidence that they have.

# 11

# Against Egoism

## 1. A Reply to the Egoist

My goal in this book is to defend common-sense morality, and in particular
its claims about the practical authority of morality. I argued that an ambitious
vindication, an argument from premises that an egoist would accept, was
unlikely to succeed. Instead, I tried to provide a modest vindication, an
argument against egoism that a moral agent (but not an egoist) would
accept.

> HELP (moral reason)
> H1: I have moral reason to help those in need.
> H2: If H1, then egoism is false.
> H3: So, egoism is false.
>
> THE LIE (moral reason)
> L1: I have moral reason not to lie.
> L2: If L1, then egoism is false.
> L3: So, egoism is false.

But, there seemed to be a significant problem with these arguments.
Given that you have epistemic peers who deny the first premises of these
arguments, and you have no specific grounds for thinking that they rather
than you are mistaken, it seems that you must suspend judgement on H1
and L1. So you cannot use these arguments against egoism.

However, Part III has shown that that is not so. *If you accept common-sense
morality, and you judge that you do have moral reason not to lie and you do have
moral reason to help others, you can use the HELP (moral reasons) argument and
THE LIE (moral reasons) argument against egoism.*

234 THE BELOVED SELF

The argument has been quite complicated, and it may be helpful to recap its stages here. First, I argued that the standards of epistemic rationality for a type of belief can be understood as related to an epistemic ideal, which in turn can be discovered by looking at the function of those beliefs in action. Moral beliefs and non-moral beliefs play a different role in action. Knowledge is the epistemic ideal for ordinary non-moral beliefs since actions based on knowledge most reliably achieve your aims; moral understanding is the epistemic ideal for moral beliefs (or is the primary component of that ideal), since only actions based on moral understanding can be morally worthy. It follows that it is epistemically rational for you not to give (much) weight to the moral beliefs of others, whatever their epistemic standing, and however hard the question. So it is epistemically rational for you to retain your belief about controversial moral questions, in spite of disagreements with your peers, including your belief that morality has practical authority. You can use these arguments against egoism.

Of course, the argument of the last few chapters depends on a number of claims about the distinctive function of moral beliefs. These claims are, I think, a part of common-sense morality. The argument therefore relies on common-sense morality being correct about the nature and importance of morally worthy action. The part of common-sense morality that is crucial here is not the same as the one initially in dispute between the moral agent and the egoist, regarding the practical authority of morality. But, nevertheless, an egoist is not going to accept it. So it is worth emphasizing that this defence of morality is *modest*: it will satisfy a moral agent but not an egoist.

Nevertheless, it is clear that common-sense morality is in a much stronger position than it seemed at the end of Part II, where it appeared not to be rational to believe that common-sense morality was true, even if it was. I have shown that if common-sense morality is true it is epistemically rational to retain your beliefs about contentious moral questions, including about the practical authority of morality (if perhaps with less confidence than you would otherwise have in the absence of disagreement). If you want to give an argument that proves to your own satisfaction, as a defender of common-sense morality, that it is epistemically rational for you to believe that egoism is false, HELP (moral reason) and THE LIE (moral reason), together with the argument of the last few chapters will do the job. *We can modestly vindicate morality after all.*

## 2.  Can a Standard Egoist Respond?

Can egoists respond to HELP (moral reason) or THE LIE (moral reason) with a modest vindication of their own?

> SELF-HELP
> SH1: I have reason to help those in need only when doing so will benefit me.
> SH2: If SH1, then common-sense morality is false.
> SH3: So, common-sense morality is false.

This argument is valid, though (if common-sense morality is true) it is not sound. But, in the remainder of this chapter I will argue that *most* egoists will not be able to use this argument. Most egoists should suspend judgement on the first premise SH1, so they cannot employ SELF-HELP to defend egoism against common-sense morality. And this is so even if egoism is true.

  Is it epistemically rational for an egoist to accept that she has reason to help those in need only when doing so will benefit her? I have argued that we can discover the standards of epistemic rationality by looking at the function of beliefs in action. According to egoism, what is the function in action of beliefs about reasons for action?

  The most common form of egoism, the kind that a moral agent is most likely to meet in real life, I have called standard egoism. According to this version of the theory, everyone has reason to maximize her own happiness, and no other reasons for action. The role of beliefs, including beliefs about reasons for action, is to contribute to your maximizing your happiness.

  As we have already seen, you are more likely to achieve whatever it is that you set out to do if you have true beliefs or perhaps knowledge, and achieving what you aimed to do usually helps to make you happy (though, of course, the success of some aims will contribute more to your happiness).[1]

---

[1] According to standard egoism, it can be better for you to have false beliefs (to believe, for example, that it is worth cultivating relationships with your friends and family for their own sake,

This suggests that knowledge (or true belief) is probably the epistemic ideal, according to standard egoism, and so it is epistemically rational to form beliefs as if aiming for knowledge (or truth). It follows that it is epistemically rational to trust testimony and to give weight to other people's opinions when you reasonably believe that they are your epistemic peer.

What about beliefs specifically about reasons for action or the importance of self-interest? Do they have a special role, according to standard egoism, as moral beliefs do according to common-sense morality?

The answer, I think, is no. Suppose that you are a standard egoist and you have a guru who always tells you what you have reason to do. If you trusted what he told you, you would know what you had most reason to do and, if acted on accordingly, you would be happy. In fact, doing so would be an excellent way of ensuring that you did become happy. Knowledge about reasons for action is most likely to contribute to successful action—that is, action which results in your happiness. So beliefs about reasons have the same epistemic ideal as beliefs about ordinary factual matters, according to standard egoism, and so standard egoists should form their beliefs about reasons for action as if they were aiming at knowledge.

We could define a notion of 'egoist understanding'—that is, under-standing why you have reason to act when all reasons for action are in your self-interest. Egoist understanding would include not just truly believing that you have a reason for action and why, but also involves a set of abilities, including the ability to:

   (i)  follow an explanation of why you have a reason for action given by someone else;

   (ii)  explain why you have a reason for action in your own words;

when really you have reason to do so only for the sake of your own happiness). But in fact it is unlikely to be best for you to have no idea that your happiness grounds your reasons for action. This is because, whilst pursuing those goals can make you happy, pursuing them in the wrong way (becoming too obsessed with them, pursuing some at the expense of others) can make you unhappy. Knowing that these aims are ultimately worthwhile because of their contribution to happiness should help you avoid these problems. So even if your happiness is not always at the forefront of your mind, it is likely to be better if it is somewhere in the background, able to play a role if necessary in regulating the pursuit of your other goals. Successful standard egoists are most likely to have adopted a 'two-level' version of standard egoism, whereby they pursue other goals, occasionally checking that those are contributing to their happiness rather than believing that standard egoism is actually false.

(iii) draw the conclusion that you have a reason for action from the information that q (e.g., this action would make you happy, or contribute to your interests in some way);

(iv) draw the conclusion that you have a reason for action (perhaps of a different strength than in (iii)) from the information that q' (e.g., this action would make you happy or contribute to your interests in some different respect than if q were the case);

 (v) given the information that you have a reason for action, give the right explanation, q;

(vi) given the information that you have a reason for action (perhaps of a different strength than in (v)), give the right explanation, q'.

Egoist understanding requires an agent to grasp the relationship between her having a reason for action and the reasons why she has a reason for action. To acquire the abilities essential to egoist understanding you need to practise making your own judgement; and the best way to do so will not be to defer to what others say or what they think. If it is important to have egoist understanding, and to form your beliefs about your reasons for action on the basis of your understanding of them, you should not defer to testimony about reasons for action, and you should not give weight to the opinions of others about reasons for action, even if they are your epistemic peers.

I have argued that the epistemic ideal for beliefs about reasons for action, according to standard egoism, is not egoist understanding but knowledge. But, could a standard egoist make the case that acting on the basis of egoist understanding—understanding why he has reasons for action—makes him happy? If so, he does have a reason to aim for understanding with regard to those beliefs after all. But, I think that it is quite implausible that understanding your reasons for action is an important component of happiness. Most people are not happier just because they have the ability to put into their own words why they have a reason to help themselves, or because they can draw conclusions about what they have reason to do by themselves, or because they have done these things and acted on that basis. Whilst it may be better for a standard egoist to know that their reasons for action were ultimately based on happiness, so that happiness can play a role in regulating their pursuit of any other goals, there are no grounds to think that they need to understand why they have those reasons for action.[2]

Knowledge, not egoist understanding, is the epistemic ideal if standard egoism is true. Consequently, a standard egoist, when faced with an apparently rational moral agent whom she reasonably regards as her epistemic peer, is obliged to take her opinion into account. This egoist has no reason (or, at least, no non-question-begging reason) to think that she is more likely to be correct than the moral agent. She should suspend judgement about reasons for action in response to this disagreement.[3] Recall the 'modest vindication' of standard egoism, SELF-HELP.

> SELF-HELP
> SH1: I have reason to help those in need only when doing so will benefit me.
> SH2: If SH1, then common-sense morality is false.
> SH3: So, common-sense morality is false.

Standard egoists, given their own theory, should not believe SH1. It follows that standard egoists cannot use SELF-HELP to argue against

---

[2] Consider the three most familiar conceptions of happiness: pleasure, desire-satisfaction, and 'objective goods'. Understanding why you have reason to act does not normally give you pleasure, and since most people do not care about this sort of understanding it does not contribute to desire-satisfaction either. So, on the first two conceptions, egoist understanding does not make you any happier. Typical 'objective goods' that are thought to contribute to happiness include: pleasure, having good relationships with your friends and family, having a good career, having good health, and so on. Understanding why you have reason to act does not seem to contribute to these, and so will not make you happy according to this conception either. Of course, one could simply stipulate that egoist understanding was among the objective goods that contributed to happiness, but this would not, I think, be a particularly compelling conception of happiness.

[3] I suggested previously that the Total Evidence view is the best account of the rational response to disagreement if knowledge is the epistemic ideal, as it is according to standard egoism. It follows that it is epistemically rational to suspend judgement when you are faced with a disagreement with an epistemic peer, if the evidence for your view is weak. It is excusable for you to suspend judgement (and not excusable to do otherwise) when you disagree with an epistemic peer in the sort of hard case in which your evidence is difficult to interpret. Clearly, given the many intransigent disagreements about reasons for action, questions about reasons for action must be hard. So in a disagreement with an epistemic peer about reasons for action it is either epistemically rational for you to suspend judgement, or it is excusable for you to do so and inexcusable for you to do otherwise—but, either way, it is not epistemically rational for you to retain your original belief. If, on the other hand, the Equal Weight view is correct, it is epistemically rational to suspend judgement in response to any disagreement with an epistemic peer—so the egoist would still have to suspend judgement regarding SH1.

common-sense morality and they cannot give even a modest vindication of their theory.

Standard egoists might not be too worried. It is a well-known consequence of their theory, they might say, that it can be better, in standard egoism's own terms, not to believe standard egoism, but to believe and act as if you have good reasons to develop hobbies and friendships, for example, for their own sake.[4] So they are already perfectly happy to concede that it might not be best, in practical terms, to believe egoism. This is not a new issue for egoism—and really it is not a problem at all.

But, standard egoism cannot escape so easily. There is a very important difference between egoism being practically self-effacing and its not being epistemically rational to believe it. It is not that unusual for us to have practical reasons not to believe X despite the evidence in favour of it. It might be too distressing for a mother to believe that her son committed some serious crime despite the very strong evidence that he is guilty: she has practical reasons not to believe in his guilt. There might be very good consequences for me if I believe that I am practically skilful in spite of the evidence otherwise. It need not be a major problem for egoists that they have good *practical* reasons not to believe that egoism is true.

But, I have argued that, given the function of beliefs about reasons for action and the corresponding epistemic ideal for those beliefs, according to standard egoism, it is *epistemically* rational for a standard egoist to suspend judgement about reasons for action.[5] This is an entirely separate problem for egoism. It is also much more damaging.

When standard egoism is self-effacing, egoists no longer accept the theory and choose what to do on that basis. But, there is a perfectly good sense in which standard egoism nevertheless has a highly significant practical role. When they have practical reasons not to believe egoism, egoists are not supposed randomly to select and act upon any old theory of reasons for action instead. The theory that they ought actually to believe and act upon is itself *set by standard egoism*: an egoist should believe whichever theory of reasons for action that will result in her maximizing her happiness.

---

[4] Though as I have suggested, it will in fact rarely be better even in practical terms for standard egoists not to believe their own theory.

[5] Or—if the evidence favouring egoism is strong but hard to interpret—in epistemic terms it is excusable to suspend judgement and inexcusable to do otherwise.

Even when it is completely self-effacing, standard egoism plays a crucial practical role.

But, if it is simply not epistemically rational to believe egoism, the egoist should suspend judgement on what she has reason to do. She should not believe any particular theory of reasons for action—neither standard egoism nor any other theory either. Standard egoism is not now playing a role 'behind the scenes' guiding her at one remove by setting which theory of reasons she should accept and act upon. When she considers what to do, standard egoism can offer nothing. *In an epistemically rational agent, it should play no practical role whatsoever.*

There is an asymmetry between standard egoism and common-sense morality. When an egoist and a moral agent who are epistemic peers disagree, the standard egoist, in her own terms, should suspend judgement, but the moral agent, according to her own view, should not.[6] Nor can standard egoists insist that this is just an example of egoism being self-effacing. It is not: it is much more serious. It entails that, for anyone who is epistemically rational, standard egoism is *completely useless.*

Of course, egoists will not be very impressed by the asymmetry with morality. They think that moral agents are wrong about everything, not only about the authority of morality but also about the importance of moral understanding. But, from the point of view of a moral agent, the epistemic ideal is related to the role of moral beliefs in action, which is itself an integral part of common-sense morality. The moral agent must be prepared to listen to the egoist's arguments, but if she does not find them convincing she need not suspend judgement on whether she or the egoist is correct. One of the things that she does not have to suspend judgement about is the importance of moral understanding. In their own terms, moral agents are perfectly entitled to ignore the opinions of standard egoists. But not vice versa.

---

[6] It is important to note that the asymmetry is not that it is epistemically rational for the egoist to suspend judgement and the moral agent not to do so. If the moral agent is right about the distinctive function of moral belief, moral understanding is the epistemic ideal and it can be epistemically rational for her not to suspend judgement. But, if common-sense morality is false, and there simply is no distinctive function for moral beliefs, it is in fact not epistemically rational for her to ignore the egoist. It is nevertheless true that, *assuming* common-sense morality and its conception of morally worthy action, it is epistemically rational to do so.

## 3.  Other Versions of Egoism

It is simply not plausible that egoist understanding rather than knowledge is the epistemic ideal, according to standard egoism, because it plays no important role in maximizing your happiness. But, though standard egoism is probably the most common kind of egoism and the kind that the moral agent is most likely to come across in real life, it is not the only version. It is possible that other versions of egoism may support standards of epistemic rationality for beliefs about reasons for action that are similar to the standards of epistemic rationality for moral beliefs according to common-sense morality. What is the function of beliefs about reasons for action in action, according to other egoist theories? It might seem to be impossible to answer this question without looking individually at each of them. But, there are some general points that should apply to any egoist theory.

First, achieving your aims is likely to be a crucial part of any plausible account of self-interest. And knowledge (or true beliefs) is sufficient for you to do that. Consider your guru, who always tells you the action you have most reason to do. Provided that you do as she says, you will promote your self-interest. It seems that any plausible egoist theory will have to concede that you are not missing out on anything because you do not understand why you have reason to act. So, according to most egoist theories, the epistemic ideal for all beliefs, including beliefs about reasons for action, is likely to be knowledge (or true belief). It follows that, like any standard egoist, each of these egoists should suspend judgement on whether egoism is true when she is confronted with a disagreement with a moral agent whom she reasonably believes to be her epistemic peer. In their own terms, it is not epistemically rational for these egoists to believe their own theory.

Is there any way for an egoist to avoid this requirement to suspend judgement? There seem to be two possibilities. First, egoists could argue that it is in your interests to understand why you have reason to act and to act on this understanding. If this were true, understanding why you have reason to act would be the epistemic ideal (since only then could you act successfully on the basis of your beliefs). And, as a consequence, it would *not* be epistemically rational to suspend judgement when you disagree with a moral agent who is your epistemic peer.

Could it in fact be in your interests to understand why you have reasons to act? I have argued that it does not usually make you happier to act on the basis of your understanding why happiness is important. Hence, standard egoism is unlikely to include understanding your reasons for action as part of your self-interest.

Could understanding be part of self-interest as the virtue egoist conceives of it—that is, could it be part of what it is to flourish in a non-moralized sense that you understand why you have reasons to act of that kind? Perhaps, but this is not very plausible. Flourishing in a non-moralized sense is likely to include living a long, healthy, and happy life. Is it really an essential part of having this kind of life that when you act in ways characteristic of the virtuous egoist you understand why you have reason to do so? Why should it? Why is it not sufficient that you do in fact do things like help people when it is in your interests to do so, avoid danger, keep promises when others are watching and may return the favour later. Provided you do these things successfully, you will have a good life. The fact that you may not fully grasp on every occasion why you have reason to do them does not seem to make that life substantially worse. The virtue egoist can simply *insist* that understanding the importance of flourishing is a part of flourishing, as he conceives of it: appreciating your reasons for action does benefit you. But, then he would have to base his theory around a conception of flourishing that is not very appealing.

In Chapter 9, I argued that it is part of being a morally virtuous agent that you are an authority on what to do, and that having moral understanding is an essential part of that. Could an egoist similarly claim that it is part of being egoistically virtuous that you are an authority on egoist reasons? He could. But, it is much easier to see why being an authority is part of moral virtue than egoist virtue. It is plausible that being an authority is essential to moral virtue, because it is part of the role of a moral agent to be the source rather than the recipient of moral advice. A morally virtuous person is someone whose advice—based on their own judgement—you should take seriously. But, it is much harder to see why this should be part of egoist virtue, since virtue egoists have no interest in and no reason to advise anyone (except in so far as doing so in their own interests). There is no reason why being an authority should be essential to egoist virtue.

Could it be part of your interests as a Kantian egoist to act from Kantian egoist reasons, rather than in accordance with them? This is perhaps more plausible than that understanding might be part of self-interest according to standard egoism or virtue egoism, since self-interest, according to Kantian egoism, is a matter of respect for your own rational nature, and may have something to do with the way in which you relate to reasons for action. On the other hand, why should it be part of treating yourself as an end that you grasp the significance of your rational nature rather than simply doing what is required to respect it? The Kantian egoist would have to show that understanding genuinely does contribute to respect for rational nature; but there is no reason to think that it contributes any more than knowledge of one's reasons for action and their ground. The idea of respect for one's rational nature was set out in Chapter 3 without reference to understanding, and it is not obvious that understanding is a component of such respect.

A Kantian egoist might suggest that in order to act autonomously, in the Kantian sense of acting for considerations that are not independent of the will, you must understand why you have reasons for action. There are two issues here: first, does acting autonomously require that you understand why you have reason to act?[7] Secondly, is acting autonomously part of your self-interest (according to any plausible account of self-interest)?[8] In neither

---

[7] Kantian autonomy is often associated with the rejection of moral testimony, but it is unclear that not giving weight to what others say or think about morality or reasons for action is an essential part of autonomy. According to one conception of Kantian autonomy, to be autonomous you must accept a law of practical reason that is not based on anything outside of the rational will. But the moral law and Kantian egoism meet this requirement by being based on the importance of rational nature (and you can accept either one on these grounds). Nothing need follow about your own grasp of why you have those reasons: knowing that you have them may be sufficient. It need not follow that you understand why you have reasons for action. This is the account of Kantian autonomy that I favour, but there is a different conception, according to which the will must 'give itself' the law of practical reason in order for that law to have authority. According to this conception of autonomy, if you accept a principle of practical reason on other grounds—on the basis of testimony or the opinion of others, for example—it cannot be authoritative for you. It follows that you must use your own judgement when forming beliefs about reasons for action. I do not find this second conception of autonomy compelling, because it seems to me that reasons for action can be forceful—and you can recognize their force—even if you have not 'given the law to yourself'. So I am not convinced that a plausible account of Kantian autonomy does require you to use your own judgement about reasons for action.

[8] As I mentioned in Chapter 6, it is open to a Kantian egoist to reject the importance of autonomy altogether. But, if they do accept the significance of autonomy, it is not clear that they can do so on the

case is the answer obviously yes. Of the three egoist theories considered in Part I, Kantian egoism is the theory whose conception of self-interest is most likely to include understanding why you have reason to act, but it seems to me that the most plausible version of the theory will not necessarily encourage you to acquire and act upon egoist understanding.

But, one of the themes of Part I of the book is that there are very many egoist theories. We could simply construct one according to which understanding why you have reasons to act is in your self-interest.

*'Understanding reasons' egoism.* Each agent has reason to benefit herself and no other reasons for action. The grounds for this reason are the agent's own interests (or that the agent's own interests are good). One of the most important ways of benefiting yourself is to understand why you have reason to act.

According to this egoist theory, understanding why you have reason to act is very important. Indeed, it follows from this theory that understanding must be the epistemic ideal for your beliefs about reasons for action. So, anyone who accepts this theory may claim that it is epistemically rational for her to use her own judgement rather than to suspend judgement when in disagreement with a moral agent who is her epistemic peer. But, 'understanding reasons' egoism is not an attractive form of egoism. Its conception of self-interest is highly intellectual. It lacks the appeal of any of the other forms of egoism we have so far considered (not surprisingly, since it was devised simply in response to the problem of disagreement) and it could not be described as a very plausible form of the theory.

Egoists can make room for understanding by including it as part of their conception of self-interest. But they may decide that doing so strains the notion of self-interest too far. So they might consider another strategy. They might endorse a form of 'egoistically worthy' action that is somewhat similar to morally worthy action. Egoistically worthy action is 'right' action (doing that which you have most egoist reason to do), done for the 'right' reasons, *understanding why* you have reason to do this.[9]

---

basis of its contribution to self-interest—except by simply stipulating that it is in your self-interest to be autonomous.

[9] I have simplified the idea of egoistically worthy action. Strictly, it should be possible to do the 'right' thing for the 'right' reasons without egoist understanding, since you might respond appropriately to the reasons in favour of action without conceiving of them in egoist terms at all (just as one might perform morally worthy actions without any explicitly moral beliefs). I have ignored this possibility for the sake of simplicity; it makes no difference to the overall argument.

We can call egoist theories that include claims about egoistically worthy action, *impure egoism*.

*Impure egoism*. All reasons for action are based on self-interest. But it is important not just that you act in accordance with these reasons but also that you understand why you have reason to act, even though this understanding does not contribute to your self-interest. The function of beliefs about reasons for action is to contribute to 'egoistically worthy' action: doing what you have egoist reason to do on the basis of your understanding why you have reason to do it.

Why, according to impure egoist theories, is egoistically worthy action important? It cannot be because it is in your interests to perform egoistically worthy action. That would be a version of the first strategy, an argument that it is in your interests to understand why you have reason to act, and we have already seen that the resulting conceptions of self-interest are not very plausible. An impure egoist will have to argue that all substantive reasons for action are derived from self-interest, but there are other requirements on you—to understand why you had reason to act in certain ways—that are important independently of your self-interest. Though it is reasonable to continue to class these theories as forms of egoism, since they retain the core egoist claim that all substantive reasons for action are derived from self-interest, they are *impure*, as they include other independent requirements on action in addition.

Consider the reasons why moral understanding was important for the moral agent. It was morally important not just that you did what happened to be the right action, but that you oriented yourself the right way with respect to reasons for action. But, this is not typically a consideration that an egoist cares about. Orienting yourself with regard to reasons is not significant for its own sake, according to egoism: what matters fundamentally is that your life goes well.

There is no natural connection between egoism and egoist understanding as there was between common-sense morality and moral understanding. But, nevertheless, egoist theories can add the relevant claim about egoistically worthy action and the importance of understanding. Egoists who accept these impure theories agree with moral agents about the importance of understanding the reasons why you ought to act in certain ways, even though, of course, they disagree about which are the right reasons. As a consequence, they will accept the same epistemic standards as the moral agent. They should form beliefs as if aiming for understanding rather than knowledge. When in a disagreement with a moral agent, it may well be epistemically rational for them not to suspend judgement. But, without a proper justification of their 'impurity', though these egoist theories are not inconsistent or incoherent, they are ad hoc and unmotivated. They are awkward hybrids of egoist and non-egoist considerations. If egoists claim, for example, that responding to reasons by acknowledging their force rather than merely acting in accordance with them simply is worth doing for its own sake, independently of its impact on self-interest, the rest of us will immediately ask: why is this consideration important independently of self-interest, but no others? Egoists seem to have no response.

So the egoist's dilemma is this. Either they accept an impure egoist theory and deny that self-interest is the only important thing or they accept a pure egoist theory and find that in their own terms (in most cases) it is not epistemically rational for them to believe their chosen theory.[10] Either self-interest is not the only thing of practical importance or, on epistemic grounds, no plausible conception of self-interest should have any practical significance whatsoever.

## 4. What Kind of Criticism of Egoism?

I have argued that it is epistemically rational in her own terms for a moral agent not to suspend judgement about what she has reason to do. As a consequence, it is possible to give a modest vindication of morality. Recall the modest arguments:

> HELP (moral reason)
> H1: I have moral reason to help those in need.
> H2: If H1, then egoism is false.
> H3: So, egoism is false.
> THE LIE (moral reason)
> L1: I have moral reason not to lie.

---

[10] A pure egoist theory is one according to which all reasons for action are based on self-interest and there are no requirements on action that are not based in self-interest.

L2: If L1, then egoism is false.
L3: So, egoism is false.

Anyone who accepts common-sense morality can use these arguments against egoism. In her own terms, it is epistemically rational for her to accept the first premises of those arguments, and therefore to accept their conclusions. These arguments are only modest vindications of morality. Their conclusion is that egoism is false, but their premises are not ones that egoists must accept. It might be epistemically rational in her own terms for a moral agent to believe that she has a moral reason to help others, but egoists are not compelled to agree. Nevertheless, the moral agent is not in such a weak position as it has sometimes seemed: she can, after all, defend her own views on morality. We can vindicate morality—albeit modestly. The same is not true of most forms of egoism. Most egoists cannot use arguments like SELF-HELP against common-sense morality. For it is epistemically rational for most egoists to suspend judgement about reasons for action.[11] In their own terms, most egoists should not accept their own theory.

I have argued that this is a serious problem for egoists, that it follows that no plausible egoist theory can play any practical role whatsoever in an epistemically rational agent. But this might seem a very peculiar objection to egoism. Surely what is really wrong with egoists is that they are—as Harry Flashman describes himself—scoundrels, liars, cheats, thieves, and cowards. Egoists are morally bad people who are prepared to, and sometimes do, perform morally wrong actions. To criticize egoists on *epistemic* grounds is surely missing the point.

Of course, it is true that egoists typically have all the flaws and vices mentioned and probably more besides. That is indeed what is wrong with their character and with their actions, and from the point of view of common-sense morality that is what really matters; it is why egoism is really pernicious. The epistemic argument given here is not supposed to be a substitute for moral criticisms of egoists. Nevertheless, it is true that egoists are selfish, unjust, and so on, *and* that in their own terms most of them are not epistemically rational.

---

[11] Or it is excusable for them to suspend judgement and inexcusable to do otherwise.

But, why spend so long establishing an epistemic flaw in egoists if the real problem is elsewhere? The attractive feature of the epistemic argument against egoism is that it results in a criticism of egoism that even the egoist will have to acknowledge. No one could think that it was anything other than a problem for a theory if that theory itself implied that it was not epistemically rational to believe it. Moreover, this is not a problem for anyone who accepts common-sense morality. So egoists will have to concede that in at least that one respect common-sense morality is the more appealing theory. By contrast, criticizing the egoist in moral terms, though in some ways much more to the point, does not leave a mark on the egoist that he must recognize as such. He might even accept that he is selfish, cowardly, unjust, and so on, and simply say that he has no reason to be any different. He certainly will not be reduced by that kind of censure to admitting that common-sense morality is any better than his own preferred theory of reasons for action. Whilst there is nothing to be lost for moral agents in pressing the moral case against egoism, in the absence of the egoist undergoing a conversion and suddenly seeing the light, there is not much to be gained either. At least the epistemic argument wrings a genuine concession from him.

An ambitious vindication of morality is an argument from premises that the egoist must accept that his theory is false. The argument given here does not prove that egoism is false. So this is not an ambitious vindication of morality.[12] Nevertheless, the argument does have some attractive features in common with an ambitious vindication. The point of an ambitious vindication is to attack the egoist from premises that she accepts; to defeat the egoist in her own terms. Any egoist will have to admit that it is not

---

[12] Notice how different this argument is from the ambitious attempts from Nagel, Korsgaard, and others in Chapter 6. They argued that there was something wrong with the egoist's conception of practical reasons (or, in the case of Parfit, with the egoist's conception of the importance of personal identity), and so egoism must be false. I am not arguing here that, for example, the fact that no plausible theory of egoism can include understanding proves that egoism must be false. Rather, this fact, together with the fact of widespread disagreement about reasons for action, means that it is not epistemically rational for most egoists to believe that egoism is true. This argument is not ambitious in a different sense too: it is directed at pure theories of egoism only (that is, theories according to which all requirements on action are based on self-interest). I have conceded that impure theories which include a conception of egoistically worthy action can avoid the problem. Even pure theories could do so, if they could specify a conception of self-interest that required egoist understanding. But, as I have indicated, I am sceptical that any such account of self-interest or of egoistically worthy action will be plausible.

an appealing feature of a theory of practical reason that it is epistemically irrational to believe it. So, most egoists will have to acknowledge that their own theory is flawed. The flaw may not be fatal—for the fact that it is not epistemically rational to accept a theory does not prove that the theory is false—but it is none the less extremely serious.

# 12

# Conclusion

The Holy Grail of moral philosophy is an ambitious argument that egoism is false: a vindication of the authority of morality that even an egoist can accept. Some valiant attempts have been made at ambitious vindications, trying to show that egoist reasons are not real reasons, or that egoists cannot act freely and autonomously, or that egoism conflicts with metaphysical facts about the nature of a person. But, none of these arguments achieved its aim, nor is there any realistic prospect of success in the future. More modest arguments against egoism begin with a premise that moral agents, but not egoists, will accept, such as the first premise of HELP (moral reason): I have moral reason to help those in need. It follows from this premise that egoism is false. But, even these exceptionally modest arguments turned out to be problematic, because a moral agent might have to suspend judgement on the first premise, and therefore on the conclusion that egoism is false. If there is no ambitious vindication of the authority of morality, and no modest one either, then there seems to be no vindication at all. It is epistemically rational for us all to suspend judgement about the authority of morality, and indeed on any ethical question about which equally reasonable people disagree.

The last part of this book, however, establishes a different conclusion. Anyone who accepts common-sense morality should form moral beliefs as if she were aiming for moral understanding. It follows that, in our own terms, it is epistemically rational for us to accept the authority of morality. Egoists, by contrast, face a dilemma. Either they accept that self-interest is not the only thing of practical importance, or that (in most cases) it is not epistemically rational for them to accept egoism. They should suspend judgement about their reasons for action instead.

It follows that we can modestly vindicate morality after all. It is epistemically rational for moral agents to accept the first premise of HELP (moral reason) and similar claims, and so they are entitled to use arguments like HELP (moral reason) to conclude that egoism is false. Moreover, most egoists cannot make parallel arguments like SELF-HELP, for it is not epistemically rational for them to believe that they have no moral reason to help people, nor that egoism is true. In their own terms, it is epistemically rational for moral agents to accept their own theory and for most egoists to give up their own theory and suspend judgement. It is those egoists who are relying on faith—faith in the practical importance of self-interest—rather than reason. This obviously leaves defenders of morality in a much more satisfactory position than most egoists.

The arguments of the last few chapters also have implications for those interested in morality, and in particular they raise fundamental questions about moral philosophy. What is the role of moral philosophy, if we should be trying to achieve moral understanding? Experts in moral philosophy can be highly skilled at producing arguments and analogies, developing moral theories, and criticizing them. But, though an expert may pass on to others their own views about which courses of action are morally right and their judgements may be completely correct, they cannot thereby help someone perform a morally worthy action, unless the person can as a consequence understand why it is right.

Once we recognize that moral understanding is important in ethics, we also see that the role of moral experts is necessarily limited. There is no point merely deferring to an expert if you disagree with their judgement when you are trying for understanding rather than knowledge. Simply taking on their view without thinking it through for yourself will not help you to gain understanding. But, this is not to say that there is no room for experts at all. Some people may be better informed than others about moral matters, have more experience and have better judgement. Experts can still play an important role in helping others achieve moral understanding, by explaining as far as possible what kinds of considerations are important, how important they are, and in what way.

Can moral philosophy help us acquire moral understanding? I think that this is clearly one of the aims of moral philosophy, and is reflected in its practice. We do not typically defer to others, even those who have studied certain moral problems for longer than ourselves. And we do not regard disagreement with others as such, even those we regard as epistemic peers, as a reason for us to suspend judgement. There is a lot of disagreement amongst moral philosophers about the content and the authority of morality that is considered reasonable.

Through moral philosophy, we can acquire expertise of a kind. We become very good at devising moral theories, arguments for and against those theories, and so on. But, one can be very skilled at arguments and constructing moral theories without having good judgement about what genuinely is of moral significance and what is not. Does moral philosophy improve moral judgement? Or could it make one's judgement worse?

Moral philosophy is characterized by sustained reflection on questions of the content and authority of morality. It involves taking rival views seriously, thinking about unusual examples and thought experiments. This sort of reflection could improve your moral judgement. It might bring to your attention considerations that you had ignored or undervalued. You could correct casual or biased first impressions. Could this kind of reflection be corrupting? Could it actually make your judgement worse? It is possible for instant judgements to be better than reflective ones. Reflection can introduce bias, mistakes of reasoning, the influence of others can lead you astray, and so on. Reasoning about ethics can turn into a rationalization of whatever it is most convenient for you to think.

These questions about moral philosophy are genuine and should concern us. But, on the other hand, they do not give us reason to think that reflection of the kind characteristic of moral philosophy—designed to counteract bias and mistakes—typically introduces more of these than it corrects. So, in the absence of further reasons to doubt the outcomes of philosophical reflection, we are not compelled to conclude that moral philosophy decreases our moral understanding. And we have some grounds for the hope that it may increase it, at least to some, if limited, extent.

Much further work is still needed on these and similar topics. The account of moral understanding I have given here is compatible with a variety of metaethical theories about moral properties—including sophisticated versions of anti-realism, as well as realism—but we need to know more about these properties and especially about the evidence for them, if indeed there is any. Is there any reason why we should take our moral intuitions seriously, whether they are based on emotion, feelings of resentment and other attitudes, or arguments of the kind with which moral philosophy is concerned? I have not shown here that we actually can have moral understanding, or that any of us do have it, or that we can acquire it through moral philosophy. We are not at the conclusion of a theory of moral epistemology. But, we may be at the end of the beginning, having made a start by recognizing what the subject-matter of the theory ought to be.

# Bibliography

Adams, R. M. (1995) 'Moral Faith', *Journal of Philosophy*, 92: 75–95.

Allison, H. E. (1990) *Kant's Theory of Freedom*. Cambridge: Cambridge University Press.

——(1996) 'On the Presumed Gap in the Derivation of the Categorical Imperative'. In H. E. Allison, *Idealism and Freedom*. Cambridge: Cambridge University Press.

Anscombe, G. E. M. (1981) 'Mr Truman's Degree', *The Collected Philosophical Papers of G. E. M. Anscombe*, iii. *Ethics, Religion, and Politics*. Oxford: Blackwell.

Aristotle (2002) *Nicomachean Ethics*, trans. S. Broadie and C. Rowe. Oxford: Oxford University Press.

Arpaly, N. (2003) *Unprincipled Virtue*. Oxford: Oxford University Press.

Audi, R. (1996) 'Intuitionism, Pluralism and the Foundations of Ethics'. In W. Sinnott-Armstrong and M. Timmons (eds), *Moral Knowledge?: New Readings in Moral Epistemology*. New York: Oxford University Press.

——(1997) *Moral Knowledge and Ethical Character*. New York: Oxford University Press.

Baron, M. W. (1995) *Kantian Ethics Almost Without Apology*. Ithaca, NY and London: Cornell University Press.

Benacerraf, P. (1973) 'Mathematical Truth', *Journal of Philosophy*, 70: 661–79. Repr. P. Benacerraf and H. Putnam, *Philosophy of Mathematics: Selected Readings*. 2nd edn. Cambridge: Cambridge University Press. 1983.

Brink, D. O. (1988) 'Sidgwick's Dualism of Practical Reason', *Australasian Journal of Philosophy*, 66: 291–307.

——(1992) 'Sidgwick and the Rationale for Rational Egoism'. In B. Schultz (ed.), *Essays on Henry Sidgwick*. Cambridge: Cambridge University Press.

——(1997a) 'Kantian Rationalism: Inescapability, Authority, and Supremacy'. In G. Cullity and B. Gaut (eds), *Ethics and Practical Reason*. Oxford: Oxford University Press.

——(1997b) 'Rational Egoism and the Separateness of Persons'. In J. Dancy (ed.), *Reading Parfit*. Oxford: Blackwell.

Christensen, D. (2007) 'Epistemology of Disagreement: The Good News', *Philosophical Review*, 116: 187–217.

Cohon, R. (1986) 'Are External Reasons Impossible?' *Ethics*, 96: 545–56.

Copp, D. (1992) 'The "Possibility" of a Categorical Imperative: Kant's *Groundwork* Part III', *Philosophical Perspectives*, 6: 261–84.

—— and D. Sobel (2004) 'Morality and Virtue: An Assessment of Some Recent Work in Virtue Ethics', *Ethics*, 114: 514–54.

Craig, E. (1990) *Knowledge and the State of Nature*. Oxford: Oxford University Press.

Crisp, R. (1996) 'The Dualism of Practical Reason', *Proceedings of the Aristotelian Society*, 96: 53–73.

—— (2002) 'Sidgwick and the Boundaries of Intuitionism'. In P. Stratton-Lake (ed.), *Ethical Intuitionism: Re-evaluations*. Oxford: Oxford University Press.

Cummiskey, D. (1996) *Kantian Consequentialism*. Oxford: Oxford University Press.

Dancy, J. (2000) *Practical Reality*. Oxford: Oxford University Press.

Darwall. S. L. (1983) *Impartial Reason*. Ithaca, NY and London: Cornell University Press.

Davidson, D. (1980) *Essays on Action and Events*. Oxford: Oxford University Press.

Denis, L. (1997) 'Kant's Ethics and Duties to Oneself', *Pacific Philosophical Quarterly*, 78: 321–48.

Driver, J. (2006) 'Autonomy and the Asymmetry Problem for Moral Expertise', *Philosophical Studies*, 128: 619–44.

Elga, A. (2007) 'Reflection and Disagreement', *Noûs*, 41: 478–502.

—— (forthcoming) 'How to Disagree about How to Disagree'. In R. Feldman and T. Warfield (eds), *Disagreement*. Oxford: Oxford University Press.

Feldman, R. (2003) *Epistemology*. Upper Saddle River, NJ: Prentice Hall.

—— (2006) 'Epistemological Puzzles about Disagreement'. In Stephen Hetherington (ed.), *Epistemology Futures*. Oxford University Press, Oxford.

Foot, P. (1978) *Virtues and Vices*. Oxford: Oxford University Press.

—— (2001) *Natural Goodness*. Oxford: Oxford University Press.

—— (2002) *Moral Dilemmas*. Oxford: Oxford University Press.

Frances, B. (forthcoming) 'The Reflective Epistemic Renegade', *Philosophy and Phenomenological Research*.

Frankena, W. (1974) 'Sidgwick and the Dualism of Practical Reason', *Monist*, 58: 449–67.

Fraser, G. M. (2005) *Flashman*. London: HarperCollins.

—— (2006) *Flashman at the Charge*. London: HarperCollins.

Fricker, E. (2006) 'Testimony and Epistemic Autonomy'. In J. Lackey and E. Sosa (eds), *The Epistemology of Testimony*. Oxford: Oxford University Press.

Gert, J. (2002) 'Korsgaard's Private-Reasons Argument', *Philosophy and Phenomenological Research*, 64: 303–24.

Gibbard, A. (1999) 'Morality as Consistency in Living: Korsgaard's Kantian Lectures', *Ethics*, 110: 140–64.

Grenberg, J. M. (2001) 'Feeling, Desire and Interest in Kant's Theory of Action', *Kant–Studien*, 92: 153–79.

Griffin, J. (1986) *Well-being: Its Meaning, Measurement, and Moral Importance*. Oxford: Clarendon Press.

Grimm, S. R. (2006) 'Is Understanding a Species of Knowledge', *British Journal for the Philosophy of Science*, 57: 515–35.

Guyer, P. (1996) 'The Value of Agency', *Ethics*, 106: 404–23.

—— (1998) 'The Value of Reason and the Value of Freedom', *Ethics*, 109: 22–35.

—— (2000) *Kant on Freedom, Law and Happiness*. Cambridge: Cambridge University Press.

Harman, G. (1977) *The Nature of Morality: An Introduction to Ethics*. New York: Oxford University Press.

Hawthorne, J. (2004) *Knowledge and Lotteries*. Oxford: Oxford University Press.

—— and J. Stanley (2008) 'Knowledge and Action', *Journal of Philosophy*, 105: 571–90.

Herman, B. (1993) *The Practice of Moral Judgment*. Cambridge, Mass.: Harvard University Press.

Hill, T. E. (1991) 'Promises to Oneself'. In T. E. Hill, *Autonomy and Self-Respect*. Cambridge: Cambridge University Press.

—— (1992) 'Kant's Argument for the Rationality of Moral Conduct'. In T. E. Hill, *Dignity and Practical Reason in Kant's Moral Theory*. Ithaca, NY and London: Cornell University Press.

Hills, Alison E. (2003) 'Duties and Duties to the Self', *American Philosophical Quarterly*, 40: 131–42.

—— (2008) 'Kantian Value Realism', *Ratio*, 21: 182–200.

Hooker, B., and B. Streumer (2004) 'Procedural and Substantive Practical Rationality'. In A. R. Mele and P. Rawling (eds), *The Oxford Handbook of Rationality*. Oxford: Oxford University Press.

Hopkins, R. (2007) 'What is Wrong with Moral Testimony', *Philosophy and Phenomenological Research*, 74: 611–34.

Horwich, P. (2006) 'The Value of Truth', *Noûs*, 40: 347–60.

Hume, D. (1975) *An Enquiry Concerning the Principles of Morals*. In L. A. Selby-Bigge (ed.), *Enquiries Concerning Human Understanding and Concerning the Principles of Morals*. 3rd edn. rev. P. H. Nidditch. Oxford: Clarendon Press.

Hurka, T. (1993) *Perfectionism*. Oxford: Oxford University Press.

Hursthouse, R. (1999) *On Virtue Ethics*. Oxford: Oxford University Press.

Johnson, R. (2002) 'Happiness as a Natural End'. In M. Timmons (ed.), *Kant's Metaphysics of Morals: Interpretative Essays*. Oxford: Oxford University Press.

Johnston, M. (1992) 'Reasons and Reductionism', *Philosophical Review*, 101: 589–618.

—— (1997) 'Human Concerns without Superlative Selves'. In J. Dancy (ed.), *Reading Parfit*. Oxford: Blackwell.

Jones, K. (1999) 'Second-hand Moral Knowledge', *Journal of Philosophy*, 96: 55–78.

Kalderon, M. E. (2005) *Moral Fictionalism*. Oxford: Oxford University Press.

Kant, Immanuel (1974) *Anthropology from a Pragmatic Point of View*, trans. M. J. Gregor. The Hague: Martinus Nijhoff.

—— (1991a) *Groundwork of a Metaphysic of Morals*, trans. H. J. Paton. London: Routledge.

—— (1991b) *Metaphysics of Morals*, trans. M. Gregor. Cambridge: Cambridge University Press.

—— (1997) *Critique of Practical Reason*, trans. M. J. Gregor. Cambridge: Cambridge University Press.

—— (1997) *Lectures on Ethics*, trans. P. Heath; ed. P. Heath and J. B. Schneewind. Cambridge: Cambridge University Press.

—— (1998) *Religion within the Boundaries of Mere Reason*, trans. A. Wood and G. di Giovanni. Cambridge: Cambridge University Press.

—— (2000) *Critique of the Power of Judgment*, trans. P. Guyer and E. Mathews. Cambridge: Cambridge University Press.

Kelly, T. (2003) 'Epistemic Rationality as Instrumental Rationality: A Critique', *Philosophy and Phenomenological Research*, 66: 612–40.

—— (2005) 'The Epistemic Significance of Disagreement'. In Tamar Szabó Gendler and John Hawthorne (eds), *Oxford Studies in Epistemology*, i. Oxford: Oxford University Press: 167–96.

—— (forthcoming) 'Peer Disagreement and Higher Order Evidence'. In R. Feldman and T. Warfield (eds), *Disagreement*. Oxford: Oxford University Press.

Kerstein, S. J. (2001) 'Korsgaard's Kantian Arguments for the Value of Humanity', *Canadian Journal of Philosophy*, 31: 23–52.

Kitcher, P. (2002) 'Scientific Knowledge'. In P. Moser (ed.), *Oxford Handbook of Epistemology*. Oxford: Oxford University Press.

Korsgaard, C. M. (1996a). *Creating the Kingdom of Ends*. Cambridge: Cambridge University Press.

—— (1996b). *The Sources of Normativity*. Cambridge: Cambridge University Press.

—— (1997) 'The Normativity of Instrumental Reason'. In G. Cullity and B. Gaut (eds), *Ethics and Practical Reason*. Oxford: Clarendon Press. Repr. C. M. Korsgaard, *The Constitution of Agency*. Oxford: Oxford University Press. 2008.

Korsgaard, C. M. (1998) 'Motivation, Metaphysics, and the Value of the Self:
Reply to Ginsborg, Schneewind and Guyer', *Ethics*, 109: 49–66.
——(1999a) 'The Myth of Egoism'. University of Kansas Lindley Lecture. Repr.
C. M. Korsgaard, *The Constitution of Agency*. Oxford: Oxford University Press.
2008.
——(1999b) 'Self-constitution in the Ethics of Plato and Kant', *Journal of Ethics*,
3: 1–29. Repr. C. M. Korsgaard, *The Constitution of Agency*. Oxford: Oxford
University Press. 2008.
——(2009) *Self-constitution: Agency, Identity, and Integrity*. Oxford: Oxford Uni-
versity Press.
Kvanvig, J. (2003) *The Value of Knowledge and the Pursuit of Understanding*. Cambridge: Cambridge University Press.
Lackey, J. (2006) 'Learning from Words', *Philosophy and Phenomenological Research*,
73: 77–101.
——and E. Sosa (eds) (2006) *The Epistemology of Testimony*. Oxford: Oxford
University Press.
Lawrence, G. (1995) 'The Rationality of Morality'. In R. Hursthouse,
G. Lawrence, and W. Quinn (eds), *Virtues and Reasons*. Oxford: Clarendon
Press.
Lewis, D. (1976) 'Survival and Identity'. In A. O. Rorty (ed.), *The Identities
of Persons*. Berkeley, Calif.: University of California Press. Repr. D. Lewis,
*Philosophical Papers*, i. Oxford: Oxford University Press. 1983.
——(1990) 'What Experience Teaches'. In W. G. Lycan (ed.), *Mind and Cognition:
A Reader*. Oxford: Blackwell: 499–519.
Lillehammer, H. (2000) 'The Doctrine of Internal Reasons', *Journal of Value Inquiry*,
34: 507–16.
Lipton, P. (2004) *Inference to the Best Explanation*. 2nd edn. London: Routledge.
McDowell, J. (1995) 'Might There be External Reasons?' In J. E. J. Altham and
Ross Harrison (eds), *World, Mind, and Ethics: Essays on the Ethical Philosophy of
Bernard Williams*. Cambridge University Press, Cambridge. 1995: 68–85.
——(1997) 'Virtue and Reason'. In R. Crisp and M. Slote (eds), *Virtue Ethics*.
Oxford: Oxford University Press. First pub. *Monist*, 62 (1979): 331–50.
McGrath, S. (2004) 'Moral Knowledge By Perception', *Philosophical Perspectives*,
18: 209–28.
Mackie, J. L. (1977) *Ethics: Inventing Right and Wrong*. Harmondsworth: Penguin.
McNaughton, D., and P. Rawling (1993) 'Deontology and Agency', *Monist*, 76:
81–100.
————(1995) 'Value and Agent-Relative Reasons', *Utilitas*, 7: 31–47.
Marras, A. (2003) 'Audi on Substantive vs Instrumental Rationality', *Philosophy
and Phenomenological Research*, 67: 194–201.

Monk, R. (1991) *Ludwig Wittgenstein: The Duty of Genius*. London: Vintage.

Moore, G. E. (1903) *Principia Ethica*. Cambridge: Cambridge University Press.

—— (1959) 'A Defence of Common Sense'. In G. E. Moore, *Philosophical Papers*. London: George, Allen and Unwin. First pub. *Contemporary British Philosophy*. 2nd ser., ed. J. H. Muirhead. London: Allen and Unwin. 1925: 193–223.

Moran, R. (2006) 'Getting Told and Being Believed'. In J. Lackey and E. Sosa (eds) *The Epistemology of Testimony*. Oxford: Oxford University Press.

Nagel, T. (1978) *The Possibility of Altruism*. Princeton, NJ: Princeton University Press. First Published 1970 by Oxford University Press.

—— (1986) *The View from Nowhere*. Oxford: Oxford University Press.

O'Neill, O. (1989) *Constructions of Reason*. Cambridge: Cambridge University Press.

Owens, D. J. (2003) 'Does Belief Have an Aim?' *Philosophical Studies*, 115: 283–305.

Parfit, D. (1984) *Reasons and Persons*. Oxford: Oxford University Press.

—— (1997) 'Reasons and Motivation', *Proceedings of the Aristotelian Society*, suppl. vol. 71: 99–130.

Paton, H. J. (1963) *The Categorical Imperative*. 4th edn. London: Hutchinson.

Paton, M. (1990) 'A Reconsideration of Kant's Treatment of Duties to Oneself', *Philosophical Quarterly*, 40: 222–33.

Pettit, P. (2006) 'When to Defer to Majority Testimony—And When Not', *Analysis*, 66: 179–87.

Plato, *Republic*. Trans G. M. A. Grube; rev. C. D. C. Reeve. Indianapolis, Ind.: Hackett. 1992.

Pritchard, D. (forthcoming) 'Knowledge, Understanding and Epistemic Value'. In A. O'Hear (ed.), *Epistemology*. Cambridge: Cambridge University Press.

Pryor, J. (2000) 'The Skeptic and the Dogmatist', *Noûs*, 34: 517–49.

—— (2004) 'What's Wrong with Moore's Argument?' *Philosophical Issues*, 14: 349–78.

Reath, A. (1993) 'Intelligible Character and the Reciprocity Thesis', *Inquiry*, 36: 419–30.

—— (1997) 'Self-Legislation and Duties to Oneself', *Southern Journal of Philosophy*, 36 suppl.: 103–24.

Regan, D. H. (2002) 'The Value of Rational Nature', *Ethics*, 112: 267–91.

Russell, Bertrand (1969) *The Autobiography of Bertrand Russell, vol. 3*. London: Allen and Unwin.

Ryle, G. (1971) 'Knowing How and Knowing That'. In *Gilbert Ryle: Collected Papers*, ii. New York: Barnes and Nobles: 212–25.

Scanlon, T. M. (1998) *What We Owe to Each Other*. Cambridge, Mass.: Harvard University Press.

Scheffler, S. (1994) *The Rejection of Consequentialism.* rev. edn. Oxford: Oxford University Press.

Setiya, K. (2007) *Reasons without Rationalism.* Princeton, NJ: Princeton University Press.

Shafer-Landau, R. (1994) 'Ethical Disagreement, Ethical Objectivity and Moral Indeterminacy', *Philosophy and Phenomenological Research,* 54: 331–44.

—— (1995) 'Vagueness, Borderline Cases and Moral Realism', *American Philosophical Quarterly,* 32: 83–96.

—— (2003) *Moral Realism: A Defence.* Oxford: Oxford University Press.

Sider, T. (1996) 'All the World's a Stage', *Australasian Journal of Philosophy,* 74: 433–53.

Sidgwick, H. (1907) *The Methods of Ethics.* 7th edn. London: Macmillan.

Singer, M. G. (1959) 'On Duties to Oneself', *Ethics,* 69: 202–5.

—— (1963) 'Duties and Duties to Oneself', *Ethics,* 73: 133–42.

Skorupski, J. (1995) 'Agent-Neutrality, Consequentialism, Utilitarianism . . . A Terminological Note', *Utilitas,* 7: 49–54.

—— (1998) 'Rescuing Moral Obligation', *European Journal of Philosophy,* 6: 335–55.

Smith, M. (1994) *The Moral Problem.* Oxford: Basil Blackwell.

—— (1995) 'Internal Reasons', *Philosophy and Phenomenological Research,* 55: 109–31.

Sosa, E. (1990) 'Surviving Matters', *Noûs,* 24: 297–322.

Stanley, J., and T. Williamson (2001) 'Knowing How', *Journal of Philosophy,* 98: 411–44.

Stratton-Lake, P. (2002) *Ethical Intuitionism: Re-evaluations.* Oxford: Oxford University Press.

Street, S. (2006) 'A Darwinian Dilemma for Realist Theories of Value', *Philosophical Studies,* 127: 109–66.

Sturgeon, N. (1974) 'Altruism, Solipsism and the Objectivity of Reasons', *Philosophical Review,* 83: 374–402.

Sullivan, R. (1989) *Immanuel Kant's Moral Theory.* Cambridge: Cambridge University Press.

Sussman, D. (2003) 'The Authority of Humanity', *Ethics,* 113: 350–66.

Szabó Gendler, Tamar, and John Hawthorne (eds) (2005) *Oxford Studies in Epistemology,* i. Oxford: Oxford University Press.

Thompson, M. (1995) 'The Representation of Life'. In R. Hursthouse, G. Lawrence, and W. Quinn (eds), *Virtues and Reasons.* Oxford: Clarendon Press.

Väyrynen, P. (2008) 'Some Good and Bad News for Ethical Intuitionism', *Philosophical Quarterly,* 58: 489–511.

Velleman, J. D. (2000) *The Possibility of Practical Reason.* Oxford: Clarendon Press.

Wallace, R. J. (1990) 'How to Argue about Practical Reason', *Mind*, 99: 355–85.

Wedgwood, R. (2002) 'The Aim of Belief', *Philosophical Perspectives*, 16: 267–97.

—— (2007) *The Nature of Normativity*. Oxford: Clarendon Press.

Wick, W. (1960) 'More About Duties to Oneself', *Ethics*, 70: 158–63.

Williams, B. A. O. (1972) *Morality: An Introduction to Ethics*. Cambridge: Cambridge University Press.

—— (1973) 'Deciding to Believe'. In B. A. O. Williams, *Problems of the Self*. Cambridge: Cambridge University Press.

—— (1981) *Moral Luck*. Cambridge: Cambridge University Press.

—— (1993) *Ethics and the Limits of Philosophy*. London: Fontana Press. Third impression with amendments.

—— (1995) *Making Sense of Humanity*. Cambridge: Cambridge University Press.

Williamson, T. (2000) *Knowledge and its Limits*. Oxford: Oxford University Press.

Wood, A. W. (1999) *Kant's Ethical Thought*. Cambridge: Cambridge University Press.

Woodward, J. B. (2003) *Making Things Happen: A Theory of Causal Explanation*. Oxford: Oxford University Press.

Wright, C. (1985) 'Facts and Certainty', *Proceedings of the British Academy*, 71: 429–72.

—— (2002) '(Anti-)sceptics Simple and Subtle: G. E. Moore and John McDowell', *Philosophy and Phenomenological Research*, 65: 330–48.

—— (2004) 'Warrant for Nothing (and Foundations for Free)?' *Aristotelian Society Supplementary Volume*, 78: 167–212.

Zagzebski, L. (2001) 'Recovering Understanding'. In M. Steup (ed.), *Knowledge, Truth and Duty: Essays on Epistemic Justification, Responsibility and Virtue*. Oxford: Oxford University Press.

# Index